George Baden-Powell

Protection and Bad Times

With special reference to the political economy of English colonization

George Baden-Powell

Protection and Bad Times
With special reference to the political economy of English colonization

ISBN/EAN: 9783337411695

Printed in Europe, USA, Canada, Australia, Japan

Cover: Foto ©Suzi / pixelio.de

More available books at **www.hansebooks.com**

PROTECTION AND BAD TIMES

WITH SPECIAL REFERENCE TO THE

POLITICAL ECONOMY OF ENGLISH
COLONIZATION

BY

GEORGE BADEN-POWELL, M.A.

F.R.A.S., F.S.S.

AUTHOR OF "NEW HOMES FOR THE OLD COUNTRY,"
ETC. ETC.

LONDON

TRÜBNER AND CO., LUDGATE HILL

1879

(All rights reserved)

PREFACE.

THE following pages essay to contain a comprehensive
and yet succinct investigation of three main problems.
The *first* of these includes the nature and effects of protection. The *second* is concerned with the diagnosis of
commercial depressions ; including a sufficient account
of effective and non-effective remedies, together with
the presently important question of the possibilities
of free-trade. The *third* deals with the England of
to-day as an example of these things : an examination of her economic course is entered upon, and a
wider attention is invited to the new prospects
afforded by the presence of an extending empire.

Professor Bonamy Price has well remarked that
we cannot satisfactorily boast of our advance in
economical knowledge, and so in industrial and commercial power, in the face of that widespread distress
and depression which now broods over those very
nations which we deem to be the most advanced
in civilization. Nor have we more reason for confidence when we are brought to acknowledge that
we cannot as yet look for the definite abandonment
of economical theories that are conclusively proved
to be wrong and hurtful both by experience and by

b

reason. We find protection, for instance, dominating the United States and Germany, two of the most "advanced" communities of the present day.

To account for these inconsistencies is to hold that we are in an intermediate stage half-way between barefaced ignorance and full-fledged knowledge. It may be suggested, indeed, that political economy itself has not advanced far since the days of Aristotle. The claims of this Nineteenth Century rest on the wider dissemination rather than on the actual advance of knowledge. The Greek masses may have known nothing of economical truths. But then at best the modern English masses only know in part. Even in the House of Commons it has recently been asserted that "the consumers are not more probably than one-tenth of the human race." The epoch has yet to dawn when all men shall know in full. And it may well be doubted whether this intermediate stage is not worse than the first. It is certainly more liable to lead men dangerously astray. Thus, there needs more than ever a perpetual witness to the best knowledge of the day ; or counterfeit knowledge will assert a sway to which pure ignorance never aspired.

False ideas unfortunately blossom into policies with no less frequency than true ideas. And it is the special mission of political economy to expose the economical fallacy of any ideas that are put forward from time to time as the bases of possible policies. By this means alone is statesmanship secured against the adoption, through ignorance or through this more specious semi-knowledge, of courses that can only lead to economical disaster.

There is the essential difficulty for the political economist himself to come by true ideas. The first chapter of this book is devoted to the task of establishing an efficient method for this purpose. Many authorities on political economy tell us this science is served by induction, deduction, verification or observation, but that it lacks the important aid of experiment, the great ally of the physical investigator. But it may be advanced that the criticism of the contentions of other thinkers is to the political economist a very fair substitute for the material proper to the activity of experiment. As a critic he is enabled to dissect and experiment upon any body of opinions that has been consistently set up as a true explanation of facts.

Thus, if in the following pages theorists find doubts implied in their theories, may these doubts act as the dull steel, and strike from their sharp flints sparks of greater enlightenment for us all.

G. B. P.

8, St. George's Place, S.W.

CONTENTS.

PART I.

INTRODUCTORY.

PART II.

PROTECTION.

PART III.

COMMERCIAL DEPRESSIONS.

Contents.

PART IV.

ENGLAND AS AN EXAMPLE.

CHAPTER XIV.—ENGLAND IN GENERAL.

CHAPTER XV.—ENGLAND IN PARTICULAR.

CHAPTER XVI.—ENGLAND IN HER EMPIRE.

ERRATA.

Page 20, line 24, *for* "will show," *read* "well shows."
  „ 33, „ 2, *for* "its destruction," *read* "this obstruction."
  „ 65, „ 10, *insert* (in Contents of Chapter XV.) "§ 4. Free-trade in Land."
  „ 80, „ 10, *for* "manner," *read* "measure."
  „ 297, „ 1, *for* "with," *read* "for the."

PROTECTION AND BAD TIMES.

PART I.—INTRODUCTORY.

CHAPTER I.

POLITICAL ECONOMY.

§ 1. Scientific Method—§ 2. Human Reasoning—§ 3. Political Economy is a Human Science and must be Provisional; § 4. and Comprehensive; § 5. and is a Particular Science for a Particular Purpose—§ 6. The scope of Political Economy.

§ 1. *Scientific Method.*—When it is intended to explain phenomena; when the mind sets about forming a judgment which is to shape a course of action, a certain method of investigation is entered upon. It is necessary to premise that in the various branches of human inquiry, this method, a mere incidental instrument or tool, has a strange tendency to concentrate on itself the intellectual efforts it was originally intended to assist. And, though much salutary and necessary information is to be obtained through a due consideration of the nature and varieties of method, to allow this ancillary investigation to

usurp the place of its principle is to mistake with an
essentially human perverseness, the manner for the
matter, the form for the thing. Yet is it specially
desirable to insure correct method where the ground
to be explored is indefinite in extent and uncertain
in character. It is no wonder, then, that method
has usurped a too prominent position in the investigations of political economists. Pure deduction
seduces the allegiance of the students of one school,
just as pure induction glamours the intellects of
those of other schools:—these so-called methods
draw their devotees away to exclusive worship of
themselves; and we find many of the disciples and
even the high priests of these schools so abiding
in their methods as to merge the probable advantages of borrowing from their opponents in the proud
retention of an exclusive creed. The evil result
of thus allowing the method to usurp the place of
the subject-matter is seen in the unreal " simpli-
fications," which are the particular boast of each
type of such scientific rigour. When political economy
is set out in the terms of mathematical formulas
or exclusive legal phraseology, it loses its hold on
a public that works by the common sense of a less
confined view. Political economy thus loses credit
with the multitude for whose benefit it was instituted.

That deduction and induction on mere phases or poles of the one essential form of reasoning which is "natural" to the human mind, is perhaps nowhere more clearly demonstrated than in the comparison of the various "systems" of political economy. It is a study of these comparisons which proves with admirable distinctness that the one form of reasoning is an impossibility without the other. When we speak of verifying by Induction the suggestions of Deduction, what is this but to say some facts we have already noticed seem to apply or be connected in our reasoning with other facts we now notice. And even in the arguments of the strictly deductive and strictly inductive schools, we notice that the distinction is merely the predominance of what may be termed the present over the past, or the past over the present.

Disciples of a purely deductive school would have us set down as the sole basis of a science of political economy the " human desire for wealth at the least possible sacrifice." And next, inductively they find themselves forced to admit the active presence of various "disturbing or modifying causes," which, it is allowed, do influence human action in production, but are antagonistic to, or distinct from, this one essential motive. They consequently find themselves saddled with the task of attempting the elimination of these causes. The disciples of a purely inductive school say, " Let us not imagine causes, let us turn to facts; and, if we group together a sufficient number of these, the causes will appear of themselves." This second school does certainly leave the door open for those "subordinate causes, whether physical or mental, political or social," on which Professor Cairnes lays such proper stress. But this school soon finds itself bound up in the self-restricted view of inevitable deduction. Bagehot explained political economy as "the science of business, as business is in large production and trading communities." But he is led to base such a science on the theory of "man's preference of a greater gain to a less." And then this inductive view of political economy is confined once more by a most deductive definition of this "greater gain." We are told these gains are essentially homogeneous ; always alike in quality ; always representing success in this world as measured in money : this is the end set out as inspiring the motive. Yet, if induction were not thus bound to deduction ; if facts could be viewed with even a momentary absence of this particular theory, men might assert that there are other "gains" inspiring human action ; rank, present ease, and even the very waste of this particular species of gain will appear as frequent factors in human action.

It may be asserted that a man will squander as soon as save : that indeed in the majority of cases he does, as a fact, prefer present gratification even though he know the balance of future good to be on the wrong side. In Mr. Lowe's words, " Labour and thought create wealth ; and idleness and waste poverty." We shall presently come to regard wealth and poverty as the positive and negative matter of political economy ; induction shows their existence ; deduction necessarily interposing, has a tendency to cut out this negative and leave us alone with the positive.

We are often sent to physical science to admire the success of a pure induction ; yet in this, its asserted stronghold, we find deduction presiding. We are told to " collect facts, so shall we find laws developing of themselves." But to collect implies a previous notion or principle of colligation and comparison. We cannot face the present to any profit without appealing to the past. Buckle would solve psychological problems solely by means of statistics. It is indeed true of such pure induction that it can tell *what* man does. But to attempt to explain psychology on such evidence alone is to make out that records, without any mental effort on our part, have some subtle and unknown means of informing us *why* men do so. Statistics are, in the first place, themselves the inductive product of the application of deduction. And, in the second place, they are mere dead matter till breathed into by some mind ; till treated collectively ; till compared or analysed ; till brought under the vivifying influence of fresh deductive effort.

Again, we find deduction an acknowledged instrument of great value to the inductive sciences. It is by looking for expected manifestations that the investigator can proceed most expeditiously. It is in working experiments on the lines of some theory that advance is most rapid. The theory may indeed succumb in the operation ; the expected manifestations may prove other and unexpected causes to be in operation, but it is by this *à priori* aid that *à posteriori* results are hastened. There is more in the nominal signification of these terms than is ordinarily conceived. It is from what we have learned that we can proceed to learn more. The former enables us to judge the better of the latter ; the past of the present. The Athenian dialectician argued there could be no beginning to such a process of knowledge, and thence he could predicate its impossibility. We hold, with the support of comparative anatomy, that we, men, are born into this world inheriting or at all events possessing many instincts, many embryo forms of knowledge, which at once and immediately have the power of adding to themselves and developing themselves towards more perfect growth. The theories we work with are the mere impressions of facts; the facts are the mere points on which theories are arrested.

In a word, when we enter upon the explanation of the actual we bring a mind to bear upon matter, but a mind already cognisant of matter. So far as human experience goes, the universe, all that we know, revolves as it were round an axis at one end of which is mind, the capacity for judging; and at the other is matter, the material for judging. Between these two poles, mere vanishing points "without parts or magnitude" to the present form of human intelligence, revolving round this axis, bulges out the human world of to-day. As we leave one pole so do we leave the negative realms of a wilderness of unexplored and as yet unexplorable mind, for increasingly known and used fields of mental effort. But we journey over these until we approach the other pole, and become arrested in the waste of unexplored and as yet unexplorable matter. At the present we can conjecture and conceive, but we know nothing concerning either of these poles. The ground we do know is none the less essentially and necessarily a mixture of the two, of judged and judging, of matter and mind. These we cannot separate; we

live in the zones where mind and matter are mixed ;
and until we leave these zones it is apparently hopeless to attempt to separate the two; and, consequently,
useless to work as though fact and theory were
possibly separable.

The recent history of the physical sciences
presents to us a suggestive analogy.   There are men
so pleased with the victories of "science" they begin
to assert—now theoretic must yield the ground to
applied science.   The final cause of science is the
promulgation of practicable arts.   We must get as near
as we can to the principles of mechanics if we
would make the best use of our pulleys.   We must
take the indications of history, the suggestions of
what is recorded for us, and we must take them as
influenced by and as influencing minds ; we must
add the explanations of these that from time to time
are given by other minds; the result will be the best
present knowledge of the subject.   But there is no
line of demarcation between this knowledge and its
bases. It *is* them. Pasteur well deprecates the popular
tendency towards such a mischievous demarcation.
He writes, "Non, mille fois non, il n'existe pas une
catégorie des sciences auxquelles on puisse donner le
nom de science appliquées.   Il y a la science et les
applications de la science, liées entre elles comme le
fruit à l'arbre qui l'a porté."   If we would grow fruit

we must study the tree ; and we must know more than mere botanists ; we must know more than its "local habitat," its "scientific name," or even the motions of its sap and the type of its flower and its leaf. We must refer to chemists and agriculturists, and foresters and meteorologists ; must, in short, focus upon this question of fruit all the light of knowledge that will apply. The fruit will come of all this. But when we eat this fruit we shall remember we are but enjoying the tree ; and that without the tree we cannot have the fruit. Without the science we cannot have the art ; without the knowledge we cannot reap the harvest of the knowledge. There is the deductive theory and there is the inductive application : the one is barren and profitless without the other ; and this latter is impossible without the former.

Thus, if we are not led astray to prefer the manner to the matter, the method to the subject, we shall regard political economy as falling to the care of that method which Mill emphasised, and which Aristotle suggested ; that " conciliance of induction and deduction," which gives the two classes of methods their right place as inseparable phases of the one real process of human reasoning. Bacon himself had to concede, for human purposes, an " inquisitio activa"—a practical application to particular instances of the results of his heaven-seeking induction : protesting the while, for consistency's sake, that this divergence " per scalam descensoriam," was in direct opposition to the profitable inductive ascent from the " nobis notius" to the " simplicitur notius :" from human imperfection to divine perfection.

§ 2. *Human Reasoning.*—The ordinary human reasoning proceeds from reality to thought, but fails to return to reality. We can trace to Aristotle this distinction between the reality (αἴτιον γενέσεως) and the knowability (αἴτιον γνώσεως) of any object. These two abstractions of attributes or appearances of any one thing have long been mistaken for separate things. And this prostitution of an invaluable mental instrument it seems impossible to guard against with the majority of human intellects. Knowledge progresses indeed from " there is," to " it is," but seldom has patience to think out the subject sufficiently to arrive at "this is ;" thus it becomes as a rule stranded in a world of unreality, created by itself, for itself, and in which it nevertheless imagines it has discovered that " ordo ad universum," which it considers so far higher, truer and more absolute than that " ordo ad nos," which it began by recognising, but omits to explain.

These errors cannot accrue if we can bear in mind the method of human reasoning as a whole. The bases (τὰ πρῶτα) of deduction are given by that ἐπαγωγή which leads us from the " nobis notius" of Bacon, to the "simplicitur notius;" from the facts of experience to their explanations. But this ἐπαγωγή proceeds, we must remember, δία πόλλων and not δία πάντων; it is colligation of as many as possible, not of all, instances. This may make us hesitate to ascribe to these τὰ τρῶτα universal or absolute validity; and it is this salutary hesitation must bring us to recollect that deduction is bound up with a supporting induction. And then again we find that this ἐπαγωγή, this supporting induction, this colligation of experiences, implies the previous presence of experience (ἐμπείρια) and so of remembrance (μνήμη), and so, in the first instance, of appreciation of instances (αἴσθησις). But to discriminate and to notice implies colligation and justaposing. Thus is made evident the circle of complete reasoning.

Scientific method is the process by which the world becomes to us what it is in itself. But it is a process; and this implies the too often forgotten fact that the steps are, in their very essence, provisional, and not final. Remembering this, can we alone view rightly the essentially provisional distinction between the judgments of synthesis and the judgments of analysis. This then becomes a mere distinction of degree to our growing intelligences. Our intelligences are in process from noticing the actual to explaining the actual. Each human judgment presupposes synthesis, or the putting together of experiences. But each judgment is in itself an analysis ; or a finding, in this synthesis, of common points ; but an analysis which, in all internal thinking, is a mere step to fuller synthesis. Human knowledge of any object begins by appreciating it as a sensible object ; elementary indeed, but qualified with infinite perplexity ; and possessed of a concrete reality only potentially, in regard to the possibility of being known. It is indeed potentially a thing to an intelligence that can know it ; but really a thing only to an intelligence that does know it. This fulness of reality is complex and confused, but eminently simple to a first experience. This fulness of reality becomes known by a putting together or synthesis of experiences conjointly with an analysis which resolves them into distinctness, but then again conjointly with a synthesis which yields by a series of combinations of these separated features a complex once again, a fulness of reality, but one that is no longer confused but determinate. Every experience noticed implies a detachment of it from others, and this involves the double act of analysis, or separation, and synthesis, or combination. The intelligence thus comes to know the thing it previously could know. This is the process of knowledge. Conjoint synthesis and analysis makes things knowable known to men : this is the process by which we get a body of new knowledge to our use and profit: this is the real method of all sciences.

§ 3. *Political Economy must be Provisional.*—It is somewhat appalling to contemplate the vast extent and complexity of subject-matter of any one human science. The attack, so far as any finality is involved, resembles too closely a mere forlorn hope. But there is basis for confidence in the consideration that provisional judgments are of infinite use ; and that their value is enhanced by a recognition of this provisionality. The doom of all achievements of the human intellect is supersession by some other ; nor is this other always in the end a better one. Particular theories founded on such general explanations of the actual as that of evolution, usually proceed on the assumption that what the human mind gains is more than equivalent to what it loses. There is an attractive popularity about such reasoning which, appealing to that powerful lever, vanity, arrests attention for subjects only too often passed by without notice. Yet when we are concerned in strictly scientific investigations it will be well for us if we can remember that procession rather than progression is all that can

be profitably asserted.   We know we change ; can
we say we improve ?   We know we invent and
discover ; but how much do we let go by the way ?
Some have even asked, Do the men of 1880 A.D. lead
more godlike lives than the men of 1880 B.C. ? Others
point out, that though we have steam and scientific
engineering we do not set such marks on the face of
the earth as the Pyramids.   Judging by the past, we
cannot assert that each step we take is one of progress.   If we recognise this, then can we safely assert
that, whether the gain or the loss be greater in the
procession of human knowledge, at all events we
arrive at a knowledge the best under the circumstances ?   We proceed on the basis that self and
matter, man and circumstance, are in a state of perpetual reaction.   Specific experience verified by the
principles of human nature, is nothing more or less
than the human mind forming fresh judgment of
circumstances and interpreting them by former judgment of circumstances.   Man records all of this, that
he remembers, for himself from his own point of view.
It is no wonder then, that the "Laws" he conceives
of are not absolute, but empirical.   He obtains, not
ultimate principles, but explanatory apothegms of
and for himself.   He may observe what to him are
general tendencies ; and such observation will be of
the greatest use to him in his practical work.   He

may be a successful chemist, though he work by the basis of the old-fashioned five elements, or of a molecular theory, or of the latest one-ultimate-element theory. He may navigate the wide seas, though holding to the theory that the sun revolves round the earth. The best theoretic science of the fifteenth century, an epoch of all others reflecting most glory on navigation, gave to the Portuguese all heathen lands they could discover to the east, and to the Spaniards all they could discover to the west, of a certain parallel of longitude. Little did Pope Alexander VI. and his scientific advisers wot they were giving the world reciprocally to the two rival nations between whom they hoped thus to secure peace. But this received theory that the earth was flat did not deter the Spaniards and Portuguese from pushing their explorations till they had girdled the flat earth and opened up the whole world to Western Europe. Indeed, the theory was incentive rather than deterrent.

Our ablest exponents of political economy acknowledge that actually its theory is constantly changing; nor does there seem much present prospect of many of its leading principles emerging from the category of the unsettled. Political economy, then, as being a human science, must be provisional in its nature. The mind may have strong suspicions of the absolute and the ultimate ; nevertheless, the evidence may be termed circumstantial only. Yet is it necessary to base our action upon such evidence as we have ; and such action will proceed with all the greater security and success if this provisional evidence be not mistaken for certainty and for absolute truth. Instead of putting the accused out of this world once for all we keep him in durance, knowing that thus alone is reparation possible on the appearance of other evidence. " Progress of knowledge" is at best merely the process of verification and rectification of this human explanation of human environments.

§ 4. *Political Economy must be Comprehensive.*— When we consider the method, the framework of a science, we at once acknowledge that definition is at once the basis and the crown thereof. A whole treatise on the wealth of nations is nothing more than a homily on the text " wealth ;" nothing other than an amplification of that term. The definition is at once introductory and conclusive. A definition of political economy, or of any science that sets out the resolution or explanation of a complex object, precedes and is all that remains of an account thereof. But it may not be forgotten that this amplification is, in itself, of the highest value. It explains, illustrates, impresses what, in its absence, would be confused, indistinct, and transitory. Hence the high import of a sufficient comprehensiveness in definition.   This is no less necessary in the subordinate than in the principal definitions : but to political economy especially has this necessary comprehensiveness been denied.

Political economy is an integral part of the science of society.   It seeks to explain a definite department of the actual ; it is concerned with a definite division of human knowledge : and, in these its functions, its main duty is to avail itself of all other lights that are the special results and work of other departments of knowledge.   We must recognise as many as possible of the conditions or environments of its subject-matter, if we are to arrive at the best results. It is true the political economist is not called upon to explain and illustrate the mechanism of the steam engine, but he must not, because the engine happens to be the special property of mechanical science, therefore leave its influence in production altogether to the notice of other sciences.   He is not called upon to analyse and explain human motives for action, but he must acknowledge their presence or absence and their influence.   Nassau Senior is among those who would confine the science of political economy to doctrines corresponding with external realities only " in the absence of disturbing causes." It is presumable we recognise these disturbing causes ; and though they are acknowledged causes, yet are we bid exclude them from the cognisance of this science.

There has been much discussion as to the propriety of admitting moral and social elements into political economy. There is at the present a tendency among our leading authorities to give them due place. Professor Cairnes sees the importance of this mental side of political economy. He tells us: "Superior mental power, regarded with a view to the production of wealth, is an instrument of production perfectly analogous to superior fertility of soil : they are both monopolised natural agents ; and the share which their owners obtain in the wealth which they contribute to produce is regulated by precisely the same principles. Men of genius, therefore, and country gentlemen, however little else they may have in common, yet being both proprietors of monopolised natural agents, would in an inquiry into the laws of wealth be properly placed in the same class." It is true Professor Cairnes proceeds to point out the strangeness and incompatibility of such grouping for purposes of science. But he none the less points out the economic importance of the pure mental element in production. It has been said of authors that they should be paid for cultivating ideas on the same ground that a farmer is paid for cultivating turnips. No doubt the ideas have their

material results no less than the turnips. Professor
Bonamy Price sees clearly and distinctly that it is
not only impolitic but impossible to exclude entirely
from political economy the moral and social circumstances of production. He points out, that as it
is concerned with the material it becomes subordinate to the moral. Indeed, it is hard to draw a line
between the two. It is in a certain sense true that
morality can be expressed in the terms of political
economy. For instance, when it is said that Factory
Acts are necessary to prevent the moral evils of excessive work for children, is not this in other words
a statement of the fact, that, by this protection in
their youth, they are enabled to grow into more
capable men and women; more worthy of a place in
the ranks of the great industrial army of humanity?

This view of the comprehensive scope of political
economy is always suggested when labour is considered. Like all other commodities, it must depend
on supply and demand. At once we are brought
into direct contact with important moral and social
elements. We are forced to recognise that the
supply of labour depends on political, moral, psychological and other grounds; on the presence, that is,
or the absence, of personal freedom; of child murder;
of respect for marriage ties; of reproductive power
in the race; and so forth. It is true in such problems

we must rigidly exclude all matter foreign to their
actual solution. It will not serve the purpose of
economy, for instance, to wander to the examination
of the place of labour in a society ; on its ennobling
or debasing effects on the moral nature ; on its
power to develop muscle and health. These may
be moral and social questions, but they do not afford
direct aid in solving the problem in hand.

Perhaps human custom or tendency may be termed
an important social element ; it is certainly a most
potent factor in the solution of economic problems.
For instance, the whole human race exhibits a marked
tendency to set a higher value on the foreign and the
strange than on the home-made and the customary.
This strong tendency, closely allied to man's original
inclinations to traffic and barter ; to explore Nature ;
to increase his knowledge ; may be well regarded
as the natural sanction and incentive to free-trade.

The necessary presence of moral and social elements
is nowhere more distinctly shown than in the consideration of capital. The growth in this element
in production appears to depend quite as much on
moral and social as on more material elements.
Professor Cairnes will show that its growth depends
on "such causes as the external circumstances of
the countries in question, the intelligence and moral
character of the people inhabiting them, and their
political and social institutions."

It is impossible to treat satisfactorily of "wealth" without keeping in view many moral and social surroundings. The exclusion of these, for instance, renders the very definition of wealth palpably insufficient for the purpose in hand. We may see this when the "science of wealth" comes to treat of labour as being productive and unproductive. We are told that a man grows rich by the one and poor by the other; and the trite examples of the two forms in activity are manufacturers and servants. This partial view yields an eminently partial, and therefore unsatisfactory, explanation. We may suppose the case of a manufacturer who invests his capital in a mill and in working it for a year; and at the end of the year has in hand a certain amount of goods he has produced. If, now, he sees no prospect of selling these goods, he will close his mill, leave his plant in idleness, and cumber his warehouse with the goods. He is, according to the confined material view, a productive labourer: it may be asked, does he hereby enrich himself? does he enrich his state? does he enrich the human race? Or, again, we may suppose the case of a man who invests a similar amount of capital in maintaining for a year a large establishment, and his money is expended on a large staff of servants. By so doing he attracts and wins the confidence of his fellows: they may put him in charge of their capital as a paid director, or they may set him to rule over their common concerns as a salaried minister. To the confined material view this is all unproductive labour. Yet if we look further afield we can hardly say such a course of action fails to enrich the man, or the state, or the human race. The labour of his servants, so far from impoverishing, simply enriches all concerned. In short, if we free ourselves from the confined material view, we can see the actual value of this advertisement of his value in his own market.

The fact is, "wealth" includes men as well as things; mind as well as matter. When we discuss "wealth," we are not men judging of things, as chemists "inquiring of Nature," but men judging of men and things. We are judging of the two in combination, and it no more avails to cut out the one than the other. It is held that a true comparative method will judge of everything in relation to everything else. There are theories of political economy, for instance, which resemble certain older theories of ethics, which base the whole system of morality on the motive alone ; results and circumstances are entirely ignored. So would some have political economy base itself alone on "man's desire for wealth at the least possible sacrifice." This one motive is set out as "positively true;"

as the "one unquestionable fact of man's nature."
Yet is it so only when it exists ; only when it comes
into play. It may be true that this becomes the
average motive of a commercial age. Yet in its
absence, whether in an epoch or in a particular case,
we find other motives at work affecting individuals
and politics, even in their strictly economic developments. Social ambition, vanity, lust, often occupy
the place of "desire for wealth." And to omit
these is to beget a popular mistrust in the science
which must rob its conclusions of very much of
their practical value.

Not infrequently we find the aversion to labour
stronger than the desire for wealth. Narrow-
minded selfishness is a fundamental element in
human nature far removed indeed from reasoning
"love of wealth at the least possible sacrifice."
Much human economic conduct is fashioned on the
plea "as much ease as is compatible with bare
existence." As we have said, wealth and poverty
are, as it were, the two poles of economy. And
we can only interpret the one by determining the
other. Political economy is the science of increasing
the wealth of the human race, but that involves
recognising the conditions that operate against this ;
discovering and labelling disturbing causes, not
excluding them from review. Medicine is the

science of increasing the health of the human race, and its first province is disease; its first endeavour to trace those disturbing causes that operate against health.

§ 5. *Political Economy is a particular science for a particular purpose.*—The political economist is, as it were, an expert or person possessed of particular professional knowledge. In other words, he has concentrated in himself all the aids that other sciences yield for the certain specific purpose of ameliorating man's condition. On the one hand, he must guard against a tendency, the cause of much error, confusion, and disappointment, to give the results of a confined science the extended validity of wide philosophical facts. It is this which has brought much discredit on political economy. And, on the other hand, there is a tendency, scarcely less baneful, which leads to a too exclusively theoretical application of the science. This is the special fault of a view that is not sufficiently comprehensive. The confined theory, for instance, which would simply state free-trade to be the right and true condition of exchange, and not deign to allow or account for disturbing causes, at once invokes mistrust in the minds of those who regard the obvious fact that free-trade does not commend itself to the majority of men.

Yet is it undoubtedly the sum and substance of that " desire for wealth at the least possible sacrifice," which we are told is the true base of all economic endeavour. This confined view invites the rebuke that political economy is " scientific but incomprehensible." Men ask for the bread of practical utility, and are given the stones of a confined theory; and usually at the time of the gift, both giver and receiver imagine these dry stones to be nourishing bread.

The political economist is called in to advise the statesman or the merchant. Not infrequently, like the old school of doctors, his advice is couched in phraseology and theory which can but appear pedantic and incomprehensibly scientific to the uninitiated. Professor Bonamy Price is the one political economist who bravely advocates a more modern procedure. Most rightly he insists upon what the world will with far more confidence come to trust in as a common-sense treatment. So, too, in the medical world there has come about a revivalism from the almost superstitious trust, which indeed was but a survival of the days of the medicine-man ; and the patient expects explanations of hygienic and dietary conditions in the place of a mysterious shibboleth and strange concoctions

§ 6. *The scope of Political Economy* is most properly determined by its relations to other sciences. The

whole sum of the subject-matter of human science
embraces the moral and the material experiences of
mankind.   The former are religious and ethical; the
latter social, economical, political: but they are
each of them mere different aspects of one whole.
And this fact is of special importance when we consider economical experiences.   The fundamental
beliefs and dogmas of many systems of religion and
codes of ethics are essentially economical.   The
wisdom of a day of rest commends itself on purely
economical grounds; high-class codes of morals have
their most powerful sanction in the economic
benefits they afford.   All social arrangements are
actually formed on the principle of securing the best
economic opportunities; all political institutions
issue out of the resolutions of men to insure for themselves the best economic conditions.   Thus economic
science appears as the corner-stone of the fabric of
human knowledge.   The question remains, how much
of this human knowledge falls outside the special
provinces of sciences other than political economy.
There are many ways of stating the position.   We
may see that sociology professes to explain man as
living in society; and biology to explain man as
living in nature.   And, again, we see psychology
attempting to explain man's mental environments,
while " natural philosophy" attempts the explana-

tion of his material environments. It would seem, then, that there is a province of human knowledge not occupied by any one of these sciences. This province is the explanation of the actual dominion over Nature of man living in society. The fundamental principles of a science which shall attempt the occupation of this province of human knowledge are the achieved results of the sciences which deal with Nature, and man, and society ; these are the instruments and the aids necessary. Political economy seems fitly to take charge of this science, which explains how the human mind modifies for its own ends the material or physical universe. Political economy becomes the science of human " band-work" or co-operation in respect of the modification of extra-human surroundings. Man is set down in the midst of this world for a time. He has a mind; which involves knowledge, appetite, desire, emotion, and the various " mental phenomena." He has a body ; which involves food, health, clothing, and the various "material" phenomena. He has environments ; which involve travel over space ; the effect of past and the prospects of future time ; communication with others like himself ; contact with what is mentally and materially different from himself ;—the various moral and social and physical phenomena. The art by which he is to regulate these conditions for the best is based on such sciences as political economy. This science is merely a portion of complete science, or of that architectonic νόησις νοησέως, or explanation of the actual, of that perfect knowledge which indeed, at the present, passeth man's understanding. It is by focussing the eye on this portion that we can so much the better understand some of it; but in so doing we may in no wise ignore the fact that it remains but part of a whole. On the one hand it merges imperceptibly into the science of mind, and on the other into that of matter: it cannot sever itself from the sciences of any one of man's environments.

If we define political economy as the "science of the production, distribution, and consumption of wealth" we may not, with the French school, confine wealth to the material products of the earth. And if once we pass on to define wealth to be "anything which can be bought or sold or exchanged, whatever its nature may be," we shall pass beyond the happier terms of the older theory that "the spontaneous co-operation of individuals, seeking each the greatest pecuniary gain to himself, constitutes the best possible organisation for realising the general good of the community." For we cannot assert that every exchange is for the pecuniary good of both parties. This is proceeding on the assumption that the asserted universal motive of this human

love of gain is always the servant of perfect knowledge. That a man may desire gain in every one of
his transactions is a very different thing to his always
gaining by his transactions. And any explanation of
human action based on such a principle will little
accord with the actualities of the present.

We arrive at more clearness in those explanations
which tell us this exchange is based on each man's
absolute right to use and dispose of the articles in
question—articles, as lawyers would state it, corporeal
or incorporeal. But there must exist a desire for
this exchange. The gratification of this desire, when
present, involves a sacrifice. This will be regulated
in amount by the desires of giver *and* taker. Some
have sought to set down the exchange value of a
thing as the equivalent of the labour or service that
produced it. This is indeed the price set upon it by
the giver. But the taker only offers a price which
represents the amount of sacrifice he deems himself
obliged to make to secure the article in question.
From Aristotle downwards we have heard of values
in use, and values in exchange, of values extrinsic and
values intrinsic. A commodity has indeed this double
value, οἰκεῖα καὶ οὐκ οἰκεῖα. But its value in utility is
patent to and enjoyed by its possessor ; its value in
exchange only exists when exchange takes place.
Labour spent on giving a thing value in exchange

is labour wasted, unless the thing is exchanged. A thing is not " produced," does not enter the category of " wealth," until its value is acknowledged in consumption—until it is used. We are told that the economic value of a thing is the quantity of labour it can command; and this is true, provided we remember that " can" means not a possibility, but a certainty. In other words, the value of a thing is the amount of labour it actually saves its possessor, and not the amount it *could* save if exchanged or used. The bootmaker in using a boot is saved the labour necessary to its construction : this is the value of the boot to him. It matters not to him whether he uses it to walk a hundred miles in, or uses it to supply himself with beer for seven days by its exchange. And the same is the case with the publican who uses the boot : its value to him is the labour actually saved necessary to its construction. The supply of commodities gives them value in use ; the demand for commodities gives them value in exchange. A man produces value in exchange ; he consumes value in use.

In popular terms, then, the basis of political economy is man *versus* Nature ; the human known gradually assuming dominion over the human unknown. This attack on Nature may be termed work. What is won may be termed wealth, or more popularly, " stored work."   This only has value when it is used ; when it is taken out of the store and set in motion ; when this stored work can supplement the exertions of actual labour.   In other words, value is the using saved work.

But the term work has a wide content.   It includes, for instance, forethought, knowledge, and advance of stored work.   Thus, by growing wheat in the spring and reaping in the autumn, I have a granary stored during the winter.   If I take of this I save other laborious methods of feeding myself through the winter months ; in other words, of battling with certain material environments.   If another man takes of it, he saves similar labour. But the work thus stored is the result of *" abstinence,"* on my part, in toiling at the plough ; of *knowledge*, in that I trusted the spring rains and the summer suns to arrive in due season ; of the *advance of stored work*, in the wrought wood and iron of the plough and in the seed that was sown.   But those that use of the product pay for this by future exertion.   Each one has to make good the hole he makes in his stored work.   Wages are temporary supplements of such a want ; credit is the use of other people's stores ; capital is the use of one's own stores.   Yet in the use of all these means we only seek to replenish our stock of stored work.

But we must take account of disturbing causes. The very fact that wages exist, that all men possess not equal stocks of stored work, tell us that our subject-matter is heterogeneous. A man does not always save the same amount of labour or work that he expends. Sometimes he secures more, sometimes less. This is the basis of the inequalities we see around us in the prosperity whether of individuals, or of nations, or of epochs. Folly, bad seasons, vice, on the one hand ; prudence, good seasons, virtue, on the other—these are some of the causes of all this. And they are all of them regulating the contact of man and Nature, and must all of them be taken into account if an art is to be based on our science ; if its theories are to have any profitable connection with practice.

We must guard against a too free use of that invaluable instrument, abstraction. It is decidedly a two-edged weapon ; while by its efficient aid we are cleaving our way through the densest thickets of the unknown, we are only too liable to sever by its back-thrust the clue that can alone explain our explorations. We are apt to forget in the relative realities of our experiences that absolute truth is still out of sight. We are concerned with the possible and the contingent ; we are apt to mistake these for the certain and the necessary : or, in concentrating our attack on some definite obstacle, we are blind to the tricks that in other directions circumvent its destruction. It is for this reason that it is necessary ever to be alive to a comprehensive survey—at all stages of the process.

We have seen, then, that the economic environments of men represent their position in regard to "Nature," that is, to all that is not more essentially human. At the same time, man is inseparable from his mind, his body, and his fellows. We may say he thrives by a desire for wealth: but his judgment may go wrong; his energies may falter; his fellows may obstruct; and, in the end, though he triumph over all these, Nature may prove unkind. Thus a science of political economy must not attempt the severance of its connection with the equally developed sister-sciences that treat of mind, body, society, or nature. Psychology, Biology, Sociology, Natural Philosophy—each and all must be laid under contribution if we are to come by a practical explanation of the actual. It will be on these lines that the consideration of Protection will be proceeded with.

D

PART II.—PROTECTION.

CHAPTER II.

PROTECTION AS AN INSTRUMENT OF GOVERNMENT.

§ 1. The True Functions of Government—§ 2. Individual Energy and Unity of Contribution—§ 3. The State Sovereignty—Division of Labour—§ 4. Governments Liable to Error—§ 5. Governments enjoy Highest Knowledge—§ 6. Width of Treatment Necessary—§ 7. Protection an Instrument of Government.

§ 1. *The True Functions of Government.*—Protection, so far as the purpose in hand is concerned, is perhaps sufficiently defined as the interference by a State with the influx of commodities produced in other States, in order to serve certain ends in regard to its own productive energies.

At this very threshold of the subject many authorities have taken their stand, on the plea that such interference on the part of the State is a violation of the true functions of government. To acknowledge such a plea is to cut away all ground for the discussion entered upon in the following pages. It is thus at the least respectful to put forth, at the outset, sufficient reason to justify the rejection of this plea.

The true functions of government have been variously defined. We are told by many that the whole duty of a government is to accord to its subjects security of person and property, together with full liberty for the exercise of their industry and skill in every honest and lawful vocation ; in brief, "the 'protection' of person and property against force and fraud." Within the limits of this theory, protection is and can be no function of government. A yet wider theory simply regards government as that form of the community which undertakes all good works that it is inexpedient for private enterprise to undertake. This would allow of protection, provided it were of itself a " good work."

Again, proceeding to more philosophic. terms, we are tempted to quote the happy description of the true development of mankind in Sheldon Amos's " Science of Law" (p. 119): " It can only proceed through the multiplication of groups, together with unity of contribution." Thus it may be held to be the architectonic function of government to insure that unity of contribution without which the healthy multiplication of groups would result in nothing but a reversion to a primitive barbarism. And a necessary condition to the performance of such function is the continued existence of the healthy action of the individual groups. Many high authorities maintain that protection has an innate tendency to annihilate individual energies. Mill writes: "Letting alone should be the general practice; every departure from it, unless required by some great good, is a certain evil." The eminent Spanish economist, Señor Prendergast, puts it thus : " If you lose confidence in the natural powers of the individual, and call upon the State to substitute its power, it is all over with the individual." Professor Cairnes comes yet more directly to the point: " When once the industrial classes of a country have been taught to look to the legislature to secure them against the competition of rivals, they are apt to trust more and more to this support and less and less to their own skill, ingenuity, and economy." And Bastiat comes to the conclusion that the "best and most righteous economic world will necessarily result from letting things alone."

There is certainly sufficient in this line of argument to make us hesitate in assigning to government so momentous a function. At the same time, it is well to remember that the interference of the State with some phases of individual energy is an absolute necessity. For instance; we are told that this is the case where free competition is impossible ; otherwise private monopolies ensue. Sir Louis Mallet, indeed, replies with much power: " But private monopolies can be controlled and regulated by the power which permits them, and war or revolution can alone control the abuse of a power held by the State." Then is just the objection that this reply is perhaps hardly true theoretically of self-governing communities—that, for example, the abuse of such a power would form a great rallying point for an opposition in our English Parliament. But these various reasonings all serve to point the truth that government interference with the proper objects of private enterprise must be justified by very urgent reasons.

Adam Smith, indeed, would allow the function to government, but hedges its performance round with so much "prudence" in his "lawgiver" as to narrow indefinitely its practical application. When deprecating the " protection" of mining speculations, he tells us, "a prudent lawgiver, who desired to increase the capital of his nation, would least choose to give any extraordinary encouragement or to turn toward them a greater share of capital than would go to them of its own accord." The limits thus set on the principle of interference rob it of much of its specific character.

Nevertheless, to leave individual energies altogether to themselves is to allow a considerable loophole to private initiation, even when it be mischievous, according to the best knowledge of the day, not only to itself but to others as well. Thus at once arises a danger fatal to that other pole of the force, which vitalises and sustains all societies—the unity of contribution.

§ 2. *Individual Energy and Unity of Contribution.*— Merivale tells us: " Every deduction from the liberty of man as a free agent is, in an economical sense, a diminution of his power. This is true in old countries ; still truer in new ones ; it forms the immovable basis of the general argument against public interference with the production and. distribution of wealth." But this is rather to adopt the theory that the citizens of a human society are mere " cannon-balls in juxtaposition." It would make man a mere discrete atom. To assume that every deduction from this "' liberty" of man is a diminution of his productive power, is to adopt a previous postulate that every human being exerts aright that power of his which can be exerted in production. No doubt, in the era of the Vrilya, this may be true, but until the coming race rise and annihilate the present occupants of the earth, it will be, to say the least, indiscreet of statesmen to assume that their fellow-citizens are perfect in knowledge, perfect in the control of their actions, their passions, and their thoughts. Men are curiously sociable. The labourer will thoroughly trust his employer to set him work which is for the economic benefit of the community, so long as the employer does not lower his wages or lengthen his hours. But his view of the economic benefit of the community alters altogether, once his employer lowers wages or lengthens hours And the employer, on his side, will pay wages and buy machinery to carry on an industry, provided his fellow-men allow him to obtain wool from the farmer and to sell his stockings to the shopkeeper un-molested. He will not object to pay out of his profits taxes to secure all this. Right through society there is a pervading principle of dependence : each man leans on his fellow. But to make each a free and unconnected agent, however much it might increase his potential economic force, would by no means, in the present course of human affairs, insure its actual exertion. It would, in fact, minimise the condi-tions favourable to such exertion. Man, in his present position in Nature, is no more a free agent than he is an equal brother. Each petty environ-ment dogs his every action ; a lazy habit of mind, engendered of the associations of childhood, may render a man as much an economic burden on society as a paralytic stroke may render him unable to cope with a healthy rival. The idiot, the thief, the vagrant, become the care of any community alive to its economical interests ; and for the same reasons, even if in less degree, the State has to watch that it educe from its citizens as much knowledge, self-control, and exertion as it may expediently obtain ; and at all events that these qualities be not suffered to lie dormant, and so leaving rampant in their place other human attributes, which a man left entirely to himself as a " free agent" may haply put into operation to the economical loss of himself and his fellows. There are two pillars supporting the edifice of the State above the quagmires of sloth and barbaric ignorance, and the floods of human energy misdirected ; these are unity of contribution and individual energy. The structure can no more stand without the one than without the other.

Thus we see some ground for maintaining that even the threatened annihilation of individual energy by such State interference is an evil which must be faced, owing to the greater imminence of the annihilation of the whole society by an opposite course of action. Thus, while we acknowledge the immensity of care with which such interference, when necessary, must be undertaken, we avoid that other extreme which is to be found in that German school whose mouthpiece is the great writer, List. He advocates protection on the analogy that it is the duty of government to check, for instance, the " industry" of thieving, to turn labour and capital from this to other trades, as being more conducive to the well-being of the whole. This theory, proceeding from the prevention of detrimental to the fostering of non-detrimental industries, is likely, on a strained analogy, to sacrifice individual energy on the altar of unity of contribution.

§ 3. *The State Sovereignty and Division of Labour.* —It may be truly held that a fundamental suspicion actually subsists against any extension of the functional interference of government in private enterprise. Increase of powers means decrease of the division of labour. Government is enticed to other duties over and above that concentrated attention to the collective interests of the community which is its primary function. Especially is this the case under the more democratic forms of government. In these, expansion of power or interference should be most jealously watched. There are two phases of freedom, the one negative, the other positive. The one is represented by citizenship as opposed to slavery ; the other is the mere absence of all restraint. Protection is not of this latter form ; and it is a grave and palpable contravention of the former. A valuably suggestive letter of Mr. Bright's has been published on "Protectionism in the United States." In it he writes : " It is strange that a people who put down slavery at an immense sacrifice, are not able to suppress monopoly, which is but a milder form of the same evil. Under slavery, the man was seized and his labour was stolen from him, and the profit of it enjoyed by his master and owner. Under protection, the man is apparently free, but he is denied the right to exchange the produce of his labour, except with his countrymen, who offer him much less for it than the foreigner would give. Some portion of his labour is thus confiscated. . . . . If a man's labour is not free, if its exchange is not free, the man is not free." Thus America, the land of freedom and democracy, has become first notorious for its slavery, and now noted for its protection : noted, that is, for decided contraventions of the true principles of freedom. It seems that when the people essay to rule themselves there is great tendency to this expansion and extension of the "paternal" powers and functions of the government. And, as England's " crowned republic" is the most advanced type of self-ruling communities, this feature becomes of special interest to Englishmen.

To a student of the best writers on the subject there will always arise the serious question as to the adequacy of the alleged reasons for extending the functions and responsibilities of the central power, when both history and theory point to the conclusion that the more we curtail the nominal powers and duties of government, the greater the actual efficacy of its remaining functions. Sir Louis Mallet wrote : "As the representative system is extended, so will it be more and more impossible for parliament to control the acts of an executive entrusted with vast and complex administrations." And parliament itself, through its leading members, is giving already no uncertain voice as to the over-pressure of business, and of its desire to be relieved of all that can be in any way entrusted to local management, so that there may be time and energy left for its more proper functions. It would seem that the true principle of government interference is negative rather than positive. Its exertion must, so far as possible, be called forth, not "proprio motu" but by means of private initiative.

No doubt in the development of a community some extension of the powers of the government is inevitable, in order to keep pace with a growing complexity of affairs ; yet any overstepping of the necessary mark is an evil of no uncertain tendency. On the one hand, there is a tendency for those in charge to assume tyrannical power ; a danger special to democratic countries. Mill wrote : " When public opinion is sovereign, an individual who is opposed by the sovereign does not, as in other states of things, find a rival power to which he can appeal for relief, or at all events for sympathy." Public opinion, which is sovereign in democracies, seldom escapes thraldom to the specious designs of the cunning, or even the dishonest, and the tyranny so set up is thus of a vitiated type; a thorough παρεκβασις of right sovereignty.

On the other hand, there is a tendency, in this apparently natural extension of the influence of government, to lower the character of the people. " A people," Mill tells us, " who look habitually to their government to command or prompt them in all matters of joint concern .... have their faculties only half-developed." The nation so treated is never weaned from its nursing, never encounters the healthy influence of a bracing independence. And this deterioration of the people enhances the tendency of democratic growths to assume tyrannical forms. " In proportion as all real initiative resides in the government, and individuals habitually feel and act as under perpetual tutelage, popular institutions develop in themselves not the desire of freedom, but an unmeasured appetite for place and power." The most avaricious portion of the public mind seeks to monopolise power; and the more this power ramifies through the society the more is it sought after by the vicious politicians, and the more is it liable to degenerate into a vitiated tyranny. It is remarkable that in the most democratic of the colonies of free England, and in the most democratic form of government any State has yet developed, in Victoria and in the United States, to wit, we have the two most glaring examples of protective policies; and in both the disastrous effects of class monopolies and other forms of democratic tyranny. It would certainly seem that as the interests of a rising community grow in complexity a most jealous eye should be kept on the concomitant extension of the functions of government, to see that these never overstep the boundary line of the necessary ; and to see yet further that they even recede and retire from those provisional positions, which if they must at first be occupied by the corporate power of the society, must none the less in due time be given over to their true guardians of local or personal authority alone.

It is when we consider the growth of young societies we are led chiefly to see sufficient cause for active government interference. The economical sphere of government in such communities is to bring the previous experience of the human race to bear upon the new conditions, and so to forestall and avoid the lengthy trial and consequent misapplication of energy which other nations have experienced. It is a necessary postulate that by protection government gives to national labour and capital a direction which they would not take spontaneously.

In short, " public prudence is substituted for private."
Advantageous mercantile position should result in
the formation of a carrying trade ; the presence of
coal and lime calls for the establishment of manufacture ; a special climate and soil marks out a
country as agricultural, or it may be pastoral in
" natural gifts :" each society will have natural potentialities in respect to products and markets. Will
these potentialities be made the most of without the
interference of the corporate wisdom of the society ?
Can we insure the *timely adoption* of its proper
industry by any community of its own spontaneous
act ; or rather of the spontaneous action of its individual members acting in private capacity; or must
we turn to the government—to the reputed mouthpiece of the collective wisdom of the community?
The question is often put, To what body in the state
can men more naturally look for a timely recognition
of the true conditions and exigencies of local progress?

§ 4. *Governments Liable to Error.*—On the one
hand, it may be asserted that governments, being
human, are liable to error. We may profitably
recall the history of the wine industry at the Cape
of Good Hope. Government there decided that
both climate and soil were eminently suited for
the production of wine for the European market.
Consequent action was founded on the unimpeach-

able plea of giving " every encouragement to honest industry and adventure, and so to establish the success of the Cape commerce in this her great and native superiority." The means adopted were premiums or bounties for the largest acreage of vine-yard, for the largest annual output of wine, for best quality, &c. Government commenced operations in 1811, and in the short space of twelve years no less than a million and a half of capital and one-third of the total labour of the colony had been diverted to this new industry. In this instance government was decidedly correct in its estimate of the suitability of soil and climate; but whether it were from the distance of the European market, or from some in-capacity on the part of the producers, or what cause soever, certain it is that this industry, started under such brilliant auspices, in a short while came to a great and disastrous downfall, involving in its trail a vast amount of widespread ruin and misery. The sole surviving result is a comparatively unimportant industry, doing little more than supplying local wants.

Or we might instance the fishery policy of the French Government. Bounties and heavy duties were put in requisition to protect French fishermen from foreign competition. Thus was it sought to popularise an industry which should give the French navy an inexhaustible supply of practical and hardy seamen. What has been the result ? In the first place, the French people—and this is of special importance when we remember the large proportion of Roman Catholics among them—is deprived of its due share of this harvest of the sea. They have to rely entirely on the efforts of French fishermen. In the second place, the government have actually to enter upon considerable extra expense to send cruisers to the various fishing grounds to see that French fishermen do not simply buy the cargoes of the Dutch and English, in order to obtain the bounties on landing fish cargoes in France. And lastly, the " Inscription Maritime" acts so powerfully as a deterrent, that this highly protected French industry is the one of all others that shows least powers of growth. The corporate wisdom of the human community is, then, not exempt from the human infirmity of erroneous judgment.

§ 5. *Governments enjoy Highest Knowledge.*—It may, however, be held that governments act from a higher vantage-ground than private endeavour. As a rule, they are in possession of the best information ; they may be credited with greater skill than any other body in the community ; they take a view of things more comprehensive, and therefore more just, than that vouchsafed to the individual or to bodies allied together for special purposes. Not many years ago public attention in England was arrested by a loudly proclaimed discovery of a visible end to the coal supply. It was held " the supply of coal is limited ; and with the termination of that supply England inevitably sinks. The coalowners are thus seen to occupy the position of guardians of the very vitals of the country." The State was called upon to interfere ; the supply must be economised ; and there were urgent demands for an export duty on coal. Protection was to enter, and to turn all the capital and labour of the coalminer to bolstering up the manufacturers of England. This was to be achieved at the acknowledged sacrifice of the highly lucrative over-sea coal-trade then in flourishing existence. But· there were higher pleas than these, there was deeper knowledge, there was skill of a more comprehensive order within the country. There were those who could look duly ahead, and see that such measures were, at best, mere palliatives. Once grant the assumption that the coal supply was actually limited, and in due course the end must come : policy could no more than temporarily delay this final event. There were those, too, who could say : these would-be protectionists have further to prove that when this end arrives—and come it will, say they, in a hundred years' time—coal will be the necessity it is at present.

The year 1800 saw coal of little use.   Men went and came, over sea and over land, without the aid of coal.   It is true that at the present moment coal lies at the root of home life.   Our clothes, our food, our light, our warmth, in all their varied stages of production depend on coal.   Specially dependent on coal are we for our means of locomotion.   Yet are there already signs of a coming change.   Nature, in the hands of the chemist and "physicist" is divulging new secrets.   Electricity bids fair early to usurp the place of gas both for purposes of light and heat. Embryo motive powers, making use of water or of galvanic action, are gradually emerging into daylight. Steel is rapidly usurping the place of iron, and is ten times more durable ; nevertheless its production uses up barely one-quarter the amount of coal.   This fact is suggestive when we remember that one-half of the annual output of the pits in the north of England was used for metallurgic purposes.   And it is obvious that even should coal actually fail mankind, there is the probability that it will no longer be a necessity ; there is the certainty that it can no longer be an aid to man.   The steady rejection of such a short-sighted protective policy is the exemplary prerogative of an enlightened government.

§ 6. *Width of Treatment Necessary.*—Many may object to the presence, in the remarks we have to make, of too general a treatment : for it is matter of notoriety that authorities seem strangely loth to allow politics any place in political economy. What is strictly and solely economic at the first blush, is allowed to monopolise the whole attention of the science. But, looking to the facts that come under view, looking to the practice that is, after all, the sole outcome of the theory, we are constrained to admit that to confine ourselves to what is termed "pure political economy" is to confine ourselves to a very partial and fragmentary portion of what must be taken as a whole if it is to be taken aright. When we are told that the sole motive to be recognised in "pure political economy" is the "desire for wealth," we are not to be led on blindly with the many to oust from the scope of our inquiries the endless conditions and environments among which this motive must needs exert itself. It is strongly acted upon by all these. Sentiment is no less powerful than reasoned sentiment. The warm instincts of patriotism have a no less distinct and recognisable effect on the genesis and development of production in a community than the cold logic of "Plutology."

When we talk of economic conditions we must allow the term economic some range. We are told American protectionists have their strongest arguments in what is not strictly economic, in the

" higher interests of humanity ;" such as the theory that town and country must exist in all societies in order to a due *human* development. The same was the idea of the citizen of the United States who expressed himself to Sir Charles Dilke : " I do not want to see the population of the United States reach two hundred millions in the year 1900 ; but I want to see it happy." So, too, with the Chinese immigration into Australia, it is opposed on the ground that it will, if not checked, upset Anglo-Saxon civilisation. Yet it may well be questioned whether even these " higher interests" of humanity are not all in some measure reducible to economic terms; or are, at the least, in intimate and *inseparable* connection with economic development. Mill tells us that national defence is one of the particular cases to which protection resorts when defeated as a general theory. Mill points out in this connection that the Act of Navigation was economically disadvantageous, but may have been politically expedient. It may, however, be asked whether national security and its due maintenance is not one basis of the economical status of a community ; and an element at the least as necessary to the due success of productive energy as natural agencies, labour or capital. If the Act of Navigation prevents the invader from billeting his soldiers on the residents of Manchester and requisitioning the profits of the capitalists, it cannot be entitled economically disadvantageous, even though in its course it do injury to some one industry. It would seem to be the great lesson of this scientific age that it is a task of useless impracticability to draw that hard and fast line in scientific investigation which would separate the one nominal branch from the other. There is an actual interdependence of conditions which can only be left out of consideration with the result of vitiating the whole argument. We seek that architectonic survey, that complete *νοησις νοησίως* or explanation of the actual, which is the end and purport of all right discussion. Abstraction, a mere partial and circumstantial and temporary expedient, is only too apt to usurp the place of an enduring contemplation of the whole. Thus it is that, if we aim at practical results by theorising in the regions of political economy, we must often rather attempt a recognition of economic manifestations than confine our views to phenomena which can be defined as rigidly and exclusively economic.

§ 7. *Protection an Instrument of Government.* —On the whole, then, the conclusion arrived at is the fact that the potential functions of government are "co-extensive with the purposes of union;" and that to say that the government may in no wise interfere in the direction of labour and capital is to take a partial and petty view of the rights and duties of a community in its corporate form. Mill remarks, with much truth : " In the particular circumstances of any given age or nation there is scarcely anything really important to the general interest, which it may not be desirable or even necessary that the government should take upon itself. Providing always that the exigencies of the case require it, government has the duty of interfering, to the best of its ability, in any matter." With Burke, we may exclaim, Government has a right to use such means. We have only to ask, on each occasion, Is government right in using them ? And the true answer is found in the fact that the moral view of an action regards not only its motive, but its result as well. Government must not only take thought as to the best needs of the community, but must in addition see that any means adopted achieve adequate results. Protection is essentially an instrument of government ; a means to an end ; lawful only in the cases where it is applicable, and expedient only in those cases of applicability where it is the best means. It will be our purpose to consider whether on the occurrence of such cases this lawful means is the best means. Thus do we leave these introductory remarks for the main scope of the work in hand.

CHAPTER III.

YOUNG AND OLD SOCIETIES IN THEIR RELATION TO PROTECTION.

§ 1. Structural Developments are very Similar *when* they Occur, whether in Young or Old Societies—§ 2. Young Societies Differ greatly in Character and Antecedents; and there is Equal Variety amongst Old Societies—§ 3. But Young Societies, Capable of Protection, Stand in Intimate Relationship to Older Societies.

§ 1. *Structural Developments are very Similar* when *they Occur, whether in Young or Old Societies.*—A sincere desire to adjust theory to practice makes it above all desirable to thoroughly explore the nature of the material that affords the matter-of-fact evidence on which we build our explanation of the actual. And most theories of protection draw a line of demarcation, more or less hard and fast, between young and old communities. Such a division for many reasons fails to commend itself; the age of the particular community does not concern the motives or the results of any particular protective policies nearly so intimately as does the nature of the industry so protected. There is a comparative method ready to hand by which we propose to trace the

effects of protective policies on societies—their age
will enter solely in proportion as it has to do with
the particular effect under discussion.

We have most of us been struck with Herbert
Spencer's exemplification of his theory of a science of
society.   He holds that though we can foretell, by
means of observed knowledge, the normal development of the physical structure and functions of an
infant, until it pass to manhood and old age ; yet
are we helpless to predict biographies.   With
societies of men no less than with individual men
there are those who see their way to predicting
structural or economic developments even though it
be acknowledged by the same authorities that the
prediction of actual and full-bodied history is beyond
the scope of man's powers.   Thus when the consideration of young and old societies of men is
confined to their relations to protection at once the
field of inquiry is limited to what may be termed in
analogy, structural developments. Political economy,
seeking the fame of a place among sciences, claims to
deal with the more exact, the more organic, the more
mechanical alone of the forces that weld together
society.   It would deal, so to speak, with the physio-
logy of states, and leave to the imagination of the
far-sighted the exploration of that more comprehensive subject-matter, by many considered beyond the

possible ken of the human mind.   Under the ægis of political economy the eyes of the inquirer are shaded from the blinding rays and glare of many of the more confusing, if more attractive, lights of knowledge; thus are they enabled to obtain an insight into a modified portion of the whole, but an insight where want of breadth is amply compensated by great increase of distinctness and detail.

§ 2. *Young Societies Differ greatly in Character and Antecedents ; and there is Equal Variety amongst Old Societies.*—Thus the attention becomes devoted wholly to the structural development of a community. At once, however, the attention so focussed is arrested by the clearly distinct natures of communities ; by the marked differences among them.   Their very antecedents, the natures of their parentage, result in a diversity of conditions which at once multiply the possible structural developments. And to inquire into even the structural developments of communities is at the outset to acknowledge their varied nature.

Such communities may *differ in antecedents.*   They may, on the one hand, be mere developments from the savage state, on the other they may be so many living offshoots of societies enjoying a more or less perfected civilisation.   The men forming the society may be trained in all the cunning of centuries, or they may represent the first banding together, the first seeking for community of effort, on the part of those who previously had led a life of selfish isolation. This latter class we find must be practically eliminated from any discussion as to the effects of a policy of protection. A society under such primitive conditions of existence has not attained to that dignity of political progress which allows it to initiate or even to contemplate foreign policies of any kind; nor has such a society attained to that stage of productive development or skill which can enable it to supply itself with commodities for export; and in regard to a society whose energies are sufficiently occupied with simply providing the means to sustenance, protection is of course an unmeaning term. It is in the other class of communities, in the offshoot of more or less perfected civilisations, that a protective policy can alone find place.

Yet beyond and above these antecedents, the actual *conditions of existence* are a very necessary element to the discussion. Protection finds its field in production. Its sanction is founded on the existence of international intercourse. Yet the history of communities which produce commodities presents us with two distinct classes of such communities. There are those which are dependent, and there are those which are independent. There are the Greek or the Spanish seedlings and cuttings rising in independent and disunited growths, severed entirely from the parent stem, and presenting a series of plants of the same family order, but thriving separately and enjoying entirely distinct conditions of existence. On the other hand, the extensions of the Roman or English race, represent rather the roots of the Banyan, fixing themselves firmly enough in the earth, and instituting so many fresh organisms conducting the fertilising properties of the soil to the branches and leaves, but maintaining a permanent and organic connection with the parent stem. In the one case the young communities enter on a life of actual independence; in the other they remain subject to that fresh cycle of conditions which results from their continued connection with the country of their origin. And this fact it is important should be borne in mind the while historic evidence is sought for theory. Paying no attention to such truths, it would be futile to compare the rise of the lumber trade of Canada with that of the manufacturing industry of Belgium. The one is the direct result of connection with a mother country shut out from the Baltic : the other the direct result of the " home forces" of an independent community.

Such communities, again, may differ in regard to their *prospects of growth.* Population, the essential basis of all growth, may depend for its increase on external or solely on internal supply. The discovery of gold in a country newly occupied at once invests that country with a new population, whose character and numbers radically characterise the nature of its development ; or again, the suitability of the climate and ensuing industries regulate the actual increase of the population by birth. California and Victoria, by the rush of gold-diggers, at once appear before the world as young communities of peculiar characteristics. The British Colonies at Labuan and Tasmania, respectively offering no gilded inducements to a sudden flood of population, yet differ much in their growth by reason of a great divergence in regard to natural increase of population by birth. It is obvious then that any policy adopted or advocated in regard to young communities must necessarily contemplate their particular prospects of growth.

And this is no less true of the *aspirations of any society of men.* The halo of sentiment which surrounds the birth of a new community or the foundation of a young colony has intimate connection with its due development. On the one hand mere existence may be the highest end in view. It may be that the band of emigrants merely seek in a new land the conditions of earning a livelihood. It may be that the new State arises merely as a banding together of neighbours with a view to increased securities of existence. But on the other hand the ends of the union may be of a far higher type ; the new State may regard itself as the nucleus of a future nation ; the sun of a coming political system. The new colony has yet greater inclinations to regard itself as destined to form in years to come the powerful province or portion of a greatly enlarged nation. The policy adopted in either case will be in thorough unison with these aspirations, which indeed tell of that very powerful factor in the development of a community which has been well termed its mind.

But, above all, due consideration must be paid to the *opportunities* of a community. What may be the inherited or " natural" abilities of its people; what the industrial products that its soil and climate offer most freely ; what its position in regard to other communities.. These then are the varieties of character and antecedents, which must needs be recognised if we are to form a just and true conception of such of its structural functions and developments as relate to protection. And this variety is equally present in old as in new States.

It is, perhaps, desirable, in discussing protection and its effects, to recognise the fact that it is in young societies that we find the clearest evidence of the results and influences of protection. Indeed, many authorities, taking their stand round a certain passage in Mill, have regarded young societies as the sole proper spheres of protection. We repeat our view, that it is, perhaps, most convenient to draw no hard and fast line between young and old communities, but rather to deal with the subject matter affected by each case or type of protection. Provided a supreme government determine to foster the industry of making beet-root sugar, similar qualities and results will ensue, whether it be the President of the ancient kingdom of the Gauls, or the local parliament of the newly founded colony of Tasmania : and though the effects of the protection may, perhaps, best be traced in the simpler organism of the colony, yet are they none the less present and effective in the more complex society of the ancient kingdom.

It is true that the conditions and circumstances of old and new societies differ in many vital points, yet these points of difference are of the most prominent value, when forming the basis of a really comparative view of some particular protective policy. And, there is after all, much equipoise of conditions noticeable. For instance, it may be held that in a new society land is abundant, and capital and labour scarce ; whereas, precisely the opposite is the condition in an old country. We shall confine ourselves to the fact, that the effects of protection on these various materials is the same wheresoever they are found.

We again see this similarity between old and new communities, when we consider that in all recorded cases we find signs of an anti-economical waste and squandering, as seemingly the necessary accompaniments of human development. War is the destructive agency most frequently called in both by young and old. But it has at all times become the fashion to substitute for this agency a wrong system of political economy. Any who have studied the history of commerce and industry in the United States for the past twenty years, or in the colony of Victoria for the past five years, will need no convincing on this head.

It may be well to notice that colonial history supplies us with our main instances of young communities capable of protective policies. And, this being the case, it is necessary to remember that these types of societies are essentially and primarily the care of external, though of paternal, government. In short, young societies capable of protective policies must be in many vital respects in close communion with old societies. There is the original motive to render the unoccupied parts of the earth a relief to the overcrowded. And such colonisation is only undertaken by collective action—in other words, by the government of the older community. And it is undertaken on the plea, whether avowed or not, of making due and more efficient use of the productive resources of the earth. No doubt, there has prevailed at one time a bastard type of colonisation. This was during the age when the establishment of colonies was sought for the sole benefit of the colonising state; but in such case the colony was a mere out-post of the home community; a mere detachment of the elder society on special service; and in no sense could it claim the title of separate community, in no sense was it an independent force, battling for its own existence and relying on its own resources. In no sense was it capable of foreign policy.

In the following pages the community, whether young or old, will be regarded as in its essences a society banded together for its own advancement. The prosperity of the community is the end of its existence. In the simplest terms, its whole duty lies in the making the most of its opportunities. In economical terms, the community must win the greatest amount of stock possible from its "natural agencies." This is to be accomplished by the agencies of labour and capital. And these three factors— "natural agencies," "labour," "capital," will conveniently map out the whole subject whether they appear under the conditions of national youth or age.

CHAPTER IV.

PROTECTION IN REGARD TO NATURAL AGENCIES.

§ 1. The Manner of Appropriation and Use of the Soil Determines
the Character of Production in a Community; Specially is this
True in Young Societies; Any Definite Land Policy then
Becomes Protective—§ 2. Free Grant and Low Price seek to
Set up a Peasant Proprietor Class; and End by Establishing
Large Ownerships—§ 3. High Prices seek to Introduce Agri-
culture of a High Type, but Sacrifice all other Industries,
many of them more Profitable.

§ 1. *Land Policies may be Protective.*—Natural
agencies, labour, and capital, may be conveniently
adopted as the three conventional factors of productive energy: their resultants are subject to
the conditions of competition and intercourse; the
marks and outward signs of their activity on trade,
prices, wages; their issue, successful or otherwise,
is regulated by the well-known phenomena of supply
and demand. The influence of protection may be
extended to one and all of these, and a protective
policy may be framed to direct and regulate any one
of them. The resulting effect will influence production and consumption. And though, at the first
blush, a policy of protection is nominally concerned

F

with production alone, nevertheless its economic effects bear upon the citizen in his capacity as a consumer with no less force than in his capacity as a producer.

. In treating of the first of these three factors, we notice incidentally that the field is mainly confined to young societies. The proprietary, or at all events the usufruct of natural agencies in old countries is, as a rule, beyond the scope of direct government or even of legislative interference ; and protective policies can but indirectly affect either the use of or the development of these natural agencies. Land policies in old countries are national and not international in essence ; domestic in motive and scope they have little in common with protectionism. But of the three factors of production natural agencies hold a foremost position in the economical legislation of young societies, and, moreover, are in intimate connection with their development, as nations or communities, in reference to other communities. It is the possession or occupation of land and of other sources of natural wealth, heretofore untilled and undeveloped, that place young societies in so different an economical category to older societies. The due management of the land, for instance, in the best interests of the community, becomes one of its leading corporate concerns. In regard to its land, and that means in regard to all the products that are to be won from the soil by human endeavour, there are many dangers which threaten a young community. If the community as a body do not herein form and act up to a just appreciation of its true natural position in the world of production, the accidental conditions of its existence may involve it in ruin by suggesting courses which shall stifle the right and foster the wrong industries.

The community, in the great majority of cases, disposes of its land to customers ; and thus the market is thrown open to the world with the two-fold object of introducing into the community the other two factors, labour and capital. Both the quantity and quality of these importations, and thus of the productive energy and of the industries so developed, depend intimately on the "land policy" adopted by the community.

Is it then to the economical interest of a young community that free trade should rule absolutely in regard to land ? or, on the contrary, are the bases just and true of that type of policy which seeks certain results beneficial to the community as a whole, by means of protective land policies ?

In disposing of its land the State adopts a system of free gift or of sale at high or low price. In other words, it adopts a protective policy in regard to the use of its natural agencies. Even free-gift is accompanied by stipulations which in reality are payments. For instance, in some cases land is granted free to certain classes of immigrants ; in others again, the conditions are that the recipient fence and build and plant in return for the gift.   In other terms by this "free-gift" of land the community introduces labour of some approved type, or fosters industry of a particular kind.   In short, a protective policy is entered upon to serve certain national interests.

§ 2. *Free Grant, and Low Price.*—The effects of free grant are various, and with them may be linked the effect of sale at low price. The usual plea in support of this policy is the introduction of a peasant proprietor class ; and the establishment within the community of a system of small holdings.   We need not here discuss the motive of this policy, but it is necessary in order duly to appreciate the nature of the action to consider its result. In Lord Durham's well-known report, penned in 1839, it was written : " The whole of Prince Edward's Island was given away in one day, in the year 1767, to about sixty owners"—(this would give an average of over 20,000 acres to each estate)—"and its prosperity was stifled in the very outset of its existence." High authority, having previously determined in principle that large holdings were detrimental, thus passes judgment on the economical prosperity of

Prince Edward's Island. The student of history will however remember, with some misgiving, that in Prince Edward's Island within this same period there came to flourish that species of the Metayer system known as the "Halve's system." In other words, the owners of these unwieldy estates promptly found the introduction of tenants at once necessary and profitable. And a policy both instituted and abused for introducing the system of large holdings resulted in the establishment of small holdings.

Again, in Lower Canada promiscuous free grants of land gave rise to the system of "Leaders and Associates." Each associate and each leader received gratis his grant of land; the associates next proceeded to hand over their grants to their leader for a consideration. The government parcelled the land out in small driblets ; the people accepted the gift, but proceeded at once to make what they considered the best use of the gift. So, too, in Upper Canada, small parcels of land were awarded gratis and with a liberal hand to the patriotic defenders of the soil—to "royalists, militia, soldiers, and sailors;" but in effect, as Merivale* points out, "this amounted to little more than small and variable gratuities in money." In either case the recipients preferred to these cumbersome gifts of

---

* Merivale's "Lectures on Colonisation."

land from the State the hard cash of those individuals who accepted that special division of labour, the utilisation of the soil.

The same tale has been more recently told of the "free selectors," or "cockatooers" of Australia. The governments of many of these Colonies sought to institute a peasant proprietor class by selling blocks of land limited in extent, and at a certain price. And there were regulations preventing one man from owning too much land on this scheme of "Selection." The results, however, have by no means accorded with the intentions. Though there were local variations in detail, the scheme was somewhat on the following basis :—Any man could select where he would crown land in a block not exceeding one square mile. He paid five shillings deposit per acre on allotment. During the succeeding five years he paid the balance of the price, one shilling per acre, by regular instalments. During this five years he had to undertake a fixed amount of building, fencing, and cultivation. And, in many cases, beyond the borders of his own land he had the right of grazing a certain number of cattle or sheep. Here was an ideal prospect of a perfect peasant proprietorship.

But there were certain conditions in the state of the country that had been strangely overlooked. In the first place, the whole of the unsold land of the interior was rented by government to squatters. These men had much capital invested in sheep and cattle, and it was of vital importance to them to secure sufficient pasture for their flocks and herds. Their runs extended over vast tracts of country, much of the wilderness type. Mountainous ridges and valleys alternated; provided their stock had access to *both*, they throve the whole year round. The sheep found the first young grass in the valleys, and in the ridges in the heat of the summer there was shade and cool air. In Australia, again, there exists but little permanent water, and a perennial water-hole, or lagoon, becomes the necessary centre of a pastoral holding. Many a squatter had expended capital and labour in damming watercourses, and so forming artificial watering-places. Again, cattle allowed to roam at liberty are found, like cats, to be strongly susceptible to the ties of locality. They will every night return to the same camping-ground—usually some sheltered valley among those ridges where throughout the day they pick up their favourite sustenance. These cattle camps, dams, water-holes, lagoons, and valleys thus become the very eyes of a run. Without access to these the whole of the rest of the run is well-nigh useless for squatting purposes. When the system of free selection was inaugurated, the squatter at once discovered from practical experience that a few free selectors could, in a very brief space of time, simply, in colonial parlance, " pick out the eyes of his run." In self-defence, then, the squatter commenced to purchase land on a large scale. Instead of being a tenant of the crown he was driven to become a large landowner. Thus the policy inaugurated to set up small landowners forced into existence a class of large landowners.

Nor was this the only unlooked-for result; the bonâ-fide free selectors did not always retain in their own hands the results of their selection. As a rule, it was no hard matter for the steady stockman or shepherd to lay by his ten or twenty pounds out of his forty pounds per annum and his keep. A few years sufficed to place him in a position to yield to the temptation of becoming his own landlord. As a rule, his selection was made in the neighbourhood of his experience. Twenty pounds made him conditional master of a hundred acres. With his family to aid him, he would soon run up a hut sufficient for the time. A few tools and some seed, a score of sheep, a cow or two, and four or five old horses, would not be beyond his means. It was thus temptingly easy to start farmer in his own right. But the selector more often than not had omitted many vital considerations. He would find the soil unsuited to agriculture; he would learn that he himself was witless of farming operations; or would awake to the fact that there was no market within reach for his produce. Then would bitter experience teach him that his venture was his ruin, and in proportion as he was wise, so would he seek to sell out and return to the liberal service of others, a wiser if a poorer man. Multitudinous are the instances of squatters, out of pure charity to their old servants, thus buying up land they would otherwise never have dreamt of owning.

This State policy was further urged along this unforeseen course by selectors of a class certainly not bonâ-fide. Australian experience tells of numerous instances where men "selected" out of spite to squatters. A stockman, "sacked" with a bad character, has been known ere this to select a few acres, picking for the purpose some well-known cattle camp of his former master. This stockman will then reside in a hut, plant his garden, grow some hay, and become shortly the suspected "duffer" of the neighbourhood. In other words, he will appropriate calves right and left. The cattle in Australia, roaming at large, are each marked with the brand of their owner. "Duffing cattle" consists in riding about with one's own branding-iron at the saddle, waylaying young calves not yet branded but belonging to others, and there and then branding them with one's own brand, and thus assuming legal ownership over another man's property. This class of free selectors usually end by deserting their selection, either in the care of the police or in flight from them ; and they do not aid largely the establishment of a class of peasant proprietors. But they do drive squatters to purchase instead of merely renting small valleys in which cattle make their "camps."

Another class of vicious free-selectors are the mere creatures of dishonest squatters : and this is a class which has existed in great numbers in certain localities. The free-selector gets his land cheap, but is not allowed to hold much. The squatter wishes to get his land cheap, but to buy up considerable quantities. To buy land from government implies paying far more for it than the selector pays—consequently a device was hit upon resembling that of "Leaders and Associates," and known as "dummying." The squatter sent "dummies" into the market, trusted men, in his good pay, who selected in his behalf. These new type of selectors picked out the eyes of his run—paid their first instalment ; fenced, built, planted, stocked and paid-up regularly the further sums required. But in the end it was found that these various parcels of land, instead of forming so many homes of so many peasant proprietors, were but the detached domains of the wealthy squatter.

The two chief results noticeable in Australia in its attempt by land restrictions to foster the growth of small land-holdings are, that squatters have become landowners instead of tenants, and that there is an altogether unexpected abundance of forfeitures on the part of free selectors through inability to pay up instalments when due. The first of these results lies at the bottom of the serious political troubles into which the colony of Victoria has been thrown; and the second has produced throughout Australia an earnest attention to land policies, which it is to be hoped may have the effect of inaugurating more just appreciation of the true economic conditions involved.

The same tale comes to us from South America. Mr. Brassey, in his account of his voyage round the world, writes thus of the colonists occupying the grants of land along a line of railway in South America: "Two men will be found, living side by side, who commenced life under precisely equal conditions, having no capital, but with 80 acres of land assigned to them for cultivation. Of these the one is prosperous, the owner of the land he uses, and free from debt. His neighbour will have paid neither principal nor interest on the purchase-money of his land: he will have nothing to reduce his indebtedness for money advanced to him, and at the same time be living in a state semi-starvation and misery." The fact is that proprietorship of land, though feeding the sentimental pride of all races in all times, is, in its real nature, a peculiar possession, of remunerative use alone to the agricultural or pastoral occupant : to the tiller or utiliser of the soil. That primary human principle division of labour reappears here, asserting that the true economical value of land rests on its being duly utilised; and to utilise land is the function of a class, and by no means the duty of the whole of mankind. And to tempt men, by appeals to this misleading pride, to enter upon walks of life for which they are not fitted is to foster a development of industries at variance with the true interests of the community.

We have seen then that the results of "free-grant" or "low price" policies foster the growth of large pastoral proprietorship ; that large agricultural proprietorship tends to correct itself by the substitution of tenant farming. But that when the land policy is one of restriction, when the government decide that land shall be disposed of with a view to introducing agricultural small holdings, we at once see that the means are inadequate to the end. At the same time the plea of attracting labour to the country is one which meets with economical success, even though it be of a kind differing from that conplated originally. Free grant or low price of land attracts population ; and this is an economic attribute of the highest consequence to a young community, even though its acquisition be not contemplated in the policy adopted.

§ 3. *Sale at High Price.*—Passing to the other class of land policies, we find the government of the young community determining to sell land only at high prices. And it is in this class that we have the more thorough protection : in such cases government, by restricting and regulating the disposal, and so the occupation of land, restricts and regulates the productive energy set to work upon it. Of these systems the "Wakefield" is a well-known example. And for the sake of distinctness we may be allowed to include under this title the experiences of the colony of South Australia, though termed by the author himself—" Wakefield's system spoilt by Grey." The primary object of this system was the development, at the highest possible speed, of a sound agricultural industry in a new community. Its plea was : " We must only put such land under cultivation as we have labour and capital duly to open up ;" so shall we attract capital ; and with the proceeds of the land we will obtain the labour. Land was to be sold at high price, and the whole proceeds devoted to importing labour. A minor economical advantage was seen in the definite prospect of devoting this large source of revenue to the best interests of the community. The economic value of this consideration was not inconsiderable. The revenue derived from land sales in a young community is great, and if constitutionally requisitioned for a certain purpose there is, at least, the satisfaction that it will not be squandered by devotion to other sudden, and so, in all probability, faulty projects of the hour.

There were, however, many recognised dangers whose avoidance was sought ; inadequate cultivation and consequent abandonment of land ; sparse occupancy ; purchase for speculative purposes. And there were many beneficial advantages sought ; the introduction of population, of dependent labour, of capital, and of land buyers of the most productive class.

There is great tendency in a new community to cultivate land in very light manner. Wakefield applies the term "earth-scratchers" to single men with small holdings, men in fact, whose labour was their only capital. Such work, though in itself sufficiently productive in most virgin soils, yet inevitably leaves the soils exhausted, and leads to the successive abandonment of the cultivated portions. These then remain idle and useless to the community unless in the rare and distant event of their acquiring a secondary value by the rise of market towns or manufacturing districts. The policy of high prices is presumed to obviate this, and to bring it about that land, if cultivated at all, will be cultivated in thorough and lasting fashion.

The effect of protection in this respect, is to enable a lower margin of cultivation. In young communities, as a rule, such is the exuberant bounty of Nature, that the margin of cultivation stands high. And unless the price of land stands high, there is a great tendency to presume upon this bounty of Nature, regardless of inevitable consequences. Whereas if capital and labour be but once attracted, due cultivation will result, and as this progresses, the margin of cultivation will gradually yet profitably fall as there comes to be less choice of land.

It may with much truth be added that this gives a great impulse to the growth of rent, an economical element, as a rule, of slow appearance in young communities. And the presence of rent under such conditions, marks a secured type of prosperity. We thus see incidentally that free grant and low price have a protective tendency in fostering the deterioration of the productive powers of the soil. This tendency is possible in young communities alone, where the supply of soil is unlimited. And the result is a serious postponement of the appearance of rent. This valuable source of wealth to a community adds, as we are told, no cost to production, yet increases the purchasing power of the consumer. It has been described as an abnormal form of monopoly, which is a good and not an evil. The wages of labour and profits of capital are the first charges on the products of the soil, nevertheless there must remain in some cases an excess of profit of one estate over another ; and rent rises.

We may take rent to be a certain profit on a certain expenditure of a certain amount of capital and labour on certain natural agencies. The manner of advantage of one piece of land, for instance, over another piece, in fertility, accessibility and markets, and other exchange values, is the measure of its higher rent. Natural agencies, in briefer terms, have an exchange value in communities, and the price of this is rent. Rent arises so soon as of two equal outputs of capital and labour on similar natural agencies, the one yields greater actual profit than the other.

Suppose an island, whose extent is 100 square miles ; its soil and climate excellent for the growth of wheat. It is divided into allotments—equal in all respects—in each of which £100 of capital invested in machinery and seed, together with the annual labour of five men, produce a definite amount of wheat. We shall not discover rent till we take into consideration the getting rid of this wheat.

The men who hold these allotments live by selling the surplus wheat each produces over and above what is consumed. Suppose, again, there is but one port in the island. Three allotments surround this. All other farms must need cart their surplus wheat to this port; they thus need roads, horses, and security of passage to and fro. These extra expenses are inevitable in all the farms except the lucky three, and they increase in magnitude as the farms are distant from the port; yet the cultivators, even of the most distant farms, are enabled to make a livelihood by their cultivation; in short, "it pays" to cultivate the distant farms. The advantage enjoyed by proximity to the port, is rent. But this advantage altogether disappears if the island is allowed to be drained of its productive powers by an avowedly temporary method of tillage; which shall indeed successfully cultivate each portion for a time, after the manner of the "earth-scratchers," but abandon each as soon as signs of exhaustion show themselves. There will be the distant farms at work, but between them and the port will come to exist an unproductive wilderness. It will be a system of pseudo-cultivation which shall "sweep in a wave across the land, leaving behind a worn-out depopulated and jungle-covered soil." And it will do away with the possible appearance of rent. In short, the nearness of land to the port will benefit no one, and yet the expense of carrying the wheat from the more distant parts will continue in existence.

Land policies then which are based on free gift or low prices, have a tendency to deprive land of its capacity to yield rent. The excess of fertility is used up by the " earth-scratcher;" this is the wages of his labour, and he passes on to exhaust other land in similar fashion ; " Nature's Bounty" in the way of fertility is squandered; and the community has no means to prevent such waste. There is no landlord to demand rent, and so ensure the maintenance of this original fertility by well-considered " improvement," by rotation of crops, by manuring. Labour and capital find their easiest reward in the cultivation of perpetually fresh virgin soil. But this squandering of the bounty of nature is stayed by high prices, and these produce an effect not usually kept in view ; they enable the early appearance in the community of the valuable element of rent ; which rent eventually more than repays the higher first cost, by ensuring a due profit on the capital invested.

It has been said that the first " point of retardation" in the growth of a young community, takes place when the abnormal productiveness of the virgin soil has been replaced by the more sober results of complete occupancy. This retardation will be but the steps in a downward progress unless some system of land culture has been in vogue from the first, which shall husband and foster and not dissipate thoughtlessly the productive energies of the soil itself. And such a system is that of the High Price Policy.

Again, this high price policy seeks to obviate other ill effects of sparse occupancy. It is often held that the rise of a new community in a new country necessitates for its best conditions the concentration of the population. Thus alone is possible perfected division of labour, the presence of which in any community is an acknowledged lever to success. Thus alone is substance given to that community of wants, supply of which is hereby rendered the easier. Torrens and other supporters of the Wakefield system make this one of their two cardinal points ; "it is desirable to prevent the population of new colonies spreading over too much land." But here occurs once more the vital fault running across this well-laid and otherwise consistent plan. This its cardinal principle, however true for agricultural in- terests takes no note of the other endless objects of colonial endeavour; and runs counter to the whole history of the early stages of human societies. The first portion of nature that falls to the dominion of man, is that which is evident in present effect, viz. : the brute creation. Cattle and sheep are early herded to subserve man's daily wants.   At this stage, land itself is not needed, but the natural produce of land. Man wants not possession, but access.   His end is to feed his stock on the grasses of the earth, not to invest seed and labour in the soil.   A second stage in the attack on nature is the development of agriculture.   Man now throws his energies into the soil itself.   Possession besides access becomes necessary ; the harvesting of the results implies permanent access. Part of the man, in the strained language of the " Humanity" theory, has gone into the soil, and the man necessarily desires to cling to such soil, to possess it.   He needs the land and not its gratuitous produce.   Perhaps the most striking point in connection with a colony in its first formation, is the picture there presented of these various stages of primitive society, existent side by side, and at once. The attack on nature is, from the out-set, carried on in all its points and methods at one and the same moment.   A concentrated population is thus a necessity of agricultural but a scattered population of pastoral interests.   In the one case the land must be possessed; in the other, mere occupancy is the only need.   Thus, a government shackled by a high-price land policy, is bound besides by the necessity of subsidising this policy by some strict system of government tenancy of large tracts for pastoral purposes, otherwise, will the policy run counter to one at least, of the most vital interests of a young community.

And even for agricultural purposes the extent of land necessary for the special object in hand differs immensely. Such a policy would then involve, in addition, the arduous and difficult task of making proper allowance for both varieties of soil and varieties of product. Sugar, Cinchona, Coffee, Tobacco, and Wine, depend on the careful and expensive cultivation of small plots. Wheat or lumber, on the contrary, are products of labour over a vast extent of soil.

Again the policy of high prices is sought as a remedy against yet another evil, that of purchase of land on speculation. Capitalists, of other countries, take up land at low price, or become the successors of those who have received free grants. The price is low and the amount invested comparatively small. The capitalist can bide his time and leave his capital idle, secure of ample repayment when the growth of the young community shall have put a different face on things. Such capitalist is assumedly an outsider, and this reimbursement is the loss of so much capital to the community. And even if in the interval the land be rented out temporarily, yet this rent seeks the pocket of the speculator, and is so far a deduction from the legitimate wealth of the society.

We have said that that state interference with the economical development of the community known as systematic colonisation seeks certain beneficial advantages. It seeks to attract capitalists of the right type, men willing and able to employ a sufficiency of capital in a due cultivation of the soil; and the main inducement it offers to such capitalists is a guaranteed supply of adequate labour. The guarantee of this is the high price at which land is sold. "The one thing needful in young colonies," wrote the South Australian Commissioners, " is to offer high bounties on the introduction of capital." Even a price for the land that was high in the colony appeared relatively low to the capitalist, and the bounty preferred consisted of an assured supply of labour in return for the introduction of capital.

The corresponding benefit sought was the supply of labourers. No doubt was ever entertained, but that increase of population brings to play upon the undeveloped resources of the country, men, with their concomitants, skill and muscle. Systematic colonisation seeks to regulate this supply in regard to kind. Capital may be easily and readily distributed to where it is required, and it is homogeneous in quality; but men are not so capable of rapid transference, and their quality is heterogeneous. Capital may be invested by telegraph; but the labourer must be hired in person. This Wakefield system adopted a vigorous immigration policy, and it sought to ensure "the presence of labour in the best possible proportions to the land." And not only was it sought to procure a due supply of efficient labour by means of the extra profits of high price, but the high price itself prevented the labourer from becoming landowner until he had by some years of labour fulfilled to the capitalist the guaranteed supply. By this means also the idle and the ignorant were prevented from wasting good land by easy purchase, and added to the more proper if less congenial ranks of the wage-earners or labourers.

A noteworthy objection has been urged to this system. It has been maintained that such a scheme makes no allowance for the fact that while much benefit would certainly accrue to those who intended raising exportable produce, yet at the same time an expensive burden was laid on that land which must necessarily be utilised for the immediate sustenance of the people. And this sturdy objection well illustrates the undoubted fact that once the phenomena of wealth are arbitrarily interfered with, whether for good or for ill, clash of interests at once make their appearance.

§ 4. *Free Trade in Land.*—Protective policies in regard to land we have seen divide themselves into two groups.   Free-gift and low price policies have been instituted in order to form a peasant proprietor class.   They have resulted in many instances in large proprietorship.   They ran counter to the natural tendency of mankind to division of labour in accordance with individual abilities and opportunities. And even where free-gift, as in Prince Edward's Island, threatened the creation of abnormally large estates, nature reasserted herself by means of a tenant system.

High price policies, more essentially protective, had for their object the high pressure development of agricultural interests.   But high price policies resulted in a clashing of interests, and were liable to all the evils of a misconception by those in authority of the sum total of the productive powers of the land.

Free trade in land has had many advocates.   The means are sale by auction; thus is land to fetch a value commensurate with a real margin of cultivation. We are reminded of Cobden's desire "to free land like trade from all impediments to free exchange." Merivale has pointed out that free trade in colonial lands accompanies slow and reliable growth, whereas protective interference may result in quick growth, but in growth liable to sudden interruption and relapse. The example however which he adduces in evidence does not carry full conviction on its surface.   In

New England, he tells us, free trade in land prevailed, and New England in two centuries "reached a density of population which old England had only attained in six centuries." In this passage, however, no notice is taken of the fact that a very great portion of this population was the immediate result of migrations from older lands : and in regard to the element of density, New England fast became the metropolitan area of a coming empire, and thus had the benefit of the presence, within a comparatively small district, of the leading ports and cities of a vast State.

On the other hand Mill tells us of the Wakefield system, "wherever it has been introduced at all, as in South Australia, Victoria, New Zealand, the restraint put upon the dispersion of the settlers, and the influx of capital caused by the assurance of being able to obtain hired labour, has in spite of many difficulties and much discouragement produced a suddenness and rapidity of prosperity more like fable than reality." It is possible, however, on consulting colonial history to take grave exception to this statement. Certainly, in Victoria and New Zealand, the assurance of obtaining the requisite hired labour was early and definitively upset, while it is acknowledged on all hands that the rapid rise of Victoria is due to the gold reefs of Ballarat, and that the gold fields of Otago and of the Thames performed the same function for New Zealand. And New Zealand and Victoria have far outrun South Australia in the race of growth, though founded the one five, and the other fifteen years later. In 1878, the population of South Australia was 225,000, that of New Zealand, 414,000, that of Victoria, no less then 867,000.

We have seen that this public interference, when devoted to land, results in a congeries of good and ill, in which it is impossible to arrange a definite balance, save by a due consideration of the particular conditions of each separate appearance of the phenomena. And this consideration is as a rule impossible until after the opportunity for action has passed. And it may well be asked, whether when results are so problematical, it be not more fruitful and safe to leave this balancing and weighing alone, and allow things to take a free course ; allow matters to adjust themselves in natural sequence. Thus, will the members of the young community develop a natural and assured success ; whether this rise from the first, according to the account of the more enthusiastic free-traders ; or whether it arrive only after the beneficial chastening of errors, to a people educated by the lessons of experience to a true manhood of well-directed energy.

When a society of men first forms itself into a state, it is ever among the first endeavours of its government—whether representing the power of a conquering army, or the self-constituted strength of pacific settlers—to assume proprietorship of the soil. Among older societies, save in the now rare instances of arbitrary conquest, the soil has long become by prescription or by right, the acknowledged property of private individuals. But, in newer societies the ownership of the soil reverts to the State. All such new societies, history tells us, part with this ownership, no sooner can they determine on some policy of procedure. We have, then, seen that these policies, whether they proceed on free-trade or protectionist principles, fail to attain all the ends proposed—the one certain undeniable result is the alienation of the soil to private owners. Such being the tendency of human governments, the only recommendation to be deduced from our previous considerations is that land policies in new communities should be based on the two principles, that the great industries, which require land for their development, divide themselves into two great classes—the one requiring ownership, the other mere access. We have seen that occupancy precedes ownership, and that the true land policy of a young community will seek to retain in the hands of the State the actual proprietary right in the soil, till such time as those industries which involve ownership are in need of such soil.

Before taking leave of this part of the subject, it may be of interest to bear in mind, that there are those who would bid the State in its early years alienate no land whatever. By means of long leases they could substitute assured access for ownership. The State is thus to find a true revenue in the rent of the soil. It is allowed that the actual private ownership of the soil is, no doubt, a necessary element in human societies ; nevertheless, the State is to defer the universal appearance of this element for so long as possible—thereby reaping a large harvest, both from rent and from enhanced price—the resultants of its own growth and prosperity. And revenue is thus supported in great measure, without an appeal to the " pocket of the people."

CHAPTER V.

PROTECTION IN ITS EFFECT ON LABOUR.

§ 1. Labour as an Industry; Self-Regulating in Old Societies—
§ 2. Not so in New Societies; When it has to be Obtained
from Outside in Right Quality and Quantity—§ 3. Slavery and
Immigration—§ 4. Labour in New Societies, being more Profitable, Labourers uselessly seek to keep out Competition.—§ 5.
This injures the Capitalist.—§ 6. The right course.

§ 1. *Labour is Self-Regulating in Old Societies.*—
Labour, the second of the three conventional factors
of productive energy, is an industry from whence
large numbers of men derive profit.   To protect this
industry government has to interfere with the competition of foreigners.   The industry of labour is
followed by men in consideration of the wages they
receive ; and the higher these wages the greater the
attractions of the industry.   But it is an industry
that depends for success on the fact that the commodities produced are produced at as low a cost to
the consumer as may be, and of as good a quality as
is practicable.   In fostering labour the State would

strive to secure to the labourer high wages. Price in the labour market depends on available supply. Thus if the government adopt a protectionist policy by allowing no imported labour to stand in the market place for hire, at once the available supply is curtailed ; and provided the demand exists, wages rise. But this very curtailing of the available supply implies the handing over to the local labourers a monopoly of an industry. At once disappears that keen spur to excellence—competition. And again, when labour rises in price so will its products. Thus the commodities produced nominally cost the consumer more ; nor is their quality so good. Next, the demand for them falls ; the profits on their manufacture follow suit ; and in the end the demand for labour itself fails to empty the market.

Seldom indeed do instances occur of such suicidal folly on the part of governments. As a rule, within the boundaries of old countries there is a sufficient supply of labour—which is kept to its work by the knowledge of the plenty of available labour in other lands. This is the great natural check on the abuse of those good institutions Trades' Unions. Such abuse may for the moment hamper local production, but the equilibrium is restored so soon as the capitalist looks further afield for the commodity he requires. Capital is readily transferable ; labour not so ; either in quality or quantity; either in kind or place. Thus when prices fall the capitalist has it in his immediate power to claim as well a fall in wages. Such a fall is naturally distasteful to the labourer, who often indeed is not sufficiently foresighted to look beyond the nominal price of labour: and he is occasionally justified in the fact that no practicable natural sanction exists that the capitalist will raise wages when prices rise. These facts lead to the institution of strikes and other abuses of the combined influence of labour.

§ 2. *Labour not Self-Regulating in New Societies.*— In reference to young communities, however, all is changed, and both the kind and quality of labour required becomes a special charge of government. This is important when we remember that labour occupies the unenviable position of the hardest problem for young communities to solve. Natural agencies are ready on the spot ; capital not only flows in readily but is a plant of the most rapid growth in a young community ; but labour, this it is difficult to attract, and even when introduced it has a tendency to dissolve into fresh forms of human action: the labourer out of the very richness of his work is liable to turn from his labour and become farmer or speculator or tradesman, or what not. Nevertheless, for young communities which are enabled to raise staple articles of produce for foreign markets, the prime necessity is labour. In the words of Locke " it is labour which puts the difference of value on anything . . . . whatever bread is more worth than acorns, or wine than water." It is labour which is necessary to give to the rich produce of new lands an exchange value. And as a new country progresses in growth so will its margin of cultivation fall, so will more and cheaper labour become requisite. The available supply for young communities is outside their boundaries, and thus may it be made greatly dependent on the government; in other words, protective policies may be called upon to regulate it.

§ 3. *Slavery and Immigration.*—Colonists, in many instances, find native populations representatives of a weaker type of civilisation, existing as available supplies of labour. The Spaniards in the New World by their grades of actual slavery, " repartimientos" and " concomiendas" sought the forced labour of the subject races. In Peru for long there existed the "mita" or conscription of native labourers for the plantations and the mines, an industrial army formed on the basis of the Continental war-armies of the present day. Such schemes presuppose the existence of a native population of inferior power. In the absence of these races it was early sought to supply their place by the importation of other inferior races. Slavery arose : labour in such case fell under the rule of a most inexorable protection. The colonists of the West Indies sought the production of exportable commodities ; sugar, cotton, coffee, tobacco ; for which the natural agencies of the islands gave them a profitable superiority. The necessary labour introduced into these young communities was entirely under the thumb of these exporters. As a consequence these industries, protected most efficiently against all free-trade in labour, flourished and grew up to dimensions thoroughly in accord with the interests of the planters, but of no other class in the islands. This fact became disastrously apparent on the abolition of slavery. Free-trade in labour at once deprived these planters of all labour. The emancipated slave found ready sustenance in the lazy cultivation of any small patch of land ; his aspirations, and his energies, never rose to the prospect of production for export ; and the vast industries which strict protection in the matter of labour had so long fostered at once collapsed. This valuable episode gives distinct evidence of the high economic importance of a skilled direction of the labour supply ; but it also most clearly demonstrates the fatal dangers inherent in any system of production which is of an unnatural and forced description.

More modern times have seen one chief method for the supply of labour to young communities at their first start. "Free emigration" is the great modern means. Yet the free emigrant may fall to the care of the protectionist. We have already seen his position under schemes of "systematic colonization." Labour, being personal exertion, needs the human incentive of commercial gain. But this reward once accepted binds the labourer to a contract; and the other party, necessary to this contract, in virtue of offering the reward determines the conditions, and thus regulates the amount and kind of labour. The economist knows well that once labour be secured to a new soil capital will flow in confidently. Thus the development of a new society proceeds, *pari-passu*, with the introduction of labour. And the faster this progress, though with the ephemeral appearance of depressing the condition of the labourer, the faster the production of wealth ; the more rapid the growth of those prosperous circumstances which ultimately make themselves felt throughout the length and breadth of the community.

Most of the English Colonial Governments discharge this function with a vigour that accounts for much of their success. That of New Zealand, for instance, arranges with contractors for large works a scheme for the settlement on holdings of their own on easy terms of navvies and labourers after a certain period of labour. Thus not only are public works of necessity and desirability pushed on to completion, but muscle and sinew are attracted to the country from afar. Free passages and free land grants are plentifully advertised nowadays ; but the quantity of labour thus attracted is also regulated in quality ; now these boons are offered to farm-labourers and dairy-maids ; and anon to cooks and carpenters. The industry of labour is fostered by these Government regulations in regard to the quantity and quality of its imported ingredients.

§ 4. *Labour in New Societies being more Profitable, Labourers seek Uselessly to keep out Competition.*— But labour in a new young community occupies a peculiar position. It assumes a more lucrative position than in old-established societies. This is primarily due to the fact of the increased productiveness of labour when devoted to a virgin soil. And, again, is this state of things supported by the fact that, in the language of some economists, the " market price" of labour is often above the " natural price ;" or as it should perhaps rather be stated, the local market price is higher than the average price in all other markets. And this feature is enhanced when we consider the wages of labour are properly the amount of necessaries, and it may be comfort, attainable by the labourer through his personal exertions. The value of wages is marked by their purchasing power : in other words, by the relative prices of the needs of the labourer. In new communities, with a large margin of positively unoccupied land, the necessaries of life are inevitably low-priced ; thus the purchasing power of all wages is considerably enhanced.

Again, labour in a new community takes up a commanding position, by reason of the fact that its supply falls far short of the demand ; as a consequence, the local or " market" price of labour is placed in a measure at the discretion of the labourer. Ricardo writes : " It is when the market price of labour exceeds the natural price that the condition of the labourer is flourishing and happy, that he has it in his power to command a greater proportion of the necessaries of life, and therefore to rear a healthy and numerous family." The effect of this general law in a young community is to add to its population: and this is one of the most desirable effects for its welfare. But then the very prosperity of the labourer, the very prospect of his being surrounded by a large and hungry (if healthy) family leads to a course which spurns the ladder of his elevation, and seeks the good alone of his individual offspring. The prosperous labourer is found immediately on achieving prosperity to oppose immigration. He becomes at once the violent opponent of the policy which gave him all his welfare He may indeed supply the community with a new source of population, yet as a direct consequence of this very act he seeks to deprive it of its other legitimate source. At once we have the attempted setting up of a class monopoly by means of protection. The labouring man imagines that his profits will be great in proportion as he can rule the local market for his special commodity—labour. If the Government of his community curtail the foreign supply of this commodity he regards his enjoyment of these profits as certain. He says, Let us supply the labour market of and from ourselves—let us have no foreign competition ; and so wages will remain high. Proceeding upon analogy, the labourers in young communities as a rule become the great supporters of *all* protective policies. They say, keep out all foreign competition in the supply of the labour market, and increase the demand for labour by fostering within the community the production and manufacture of all its own wants. Thus in the labour market supply will decrease and demand will increase, and then wages will rise.

But the labourer is early brought to see the dark side to this cloud of his imagination. He finds that though such a state of things raises wages, yet with greater surety does it raise prices, both of his necessaries and his luxuries. Thus it is well if the actual value of his profits even remain the same for all his trouble. Sir Charles Dilke relates the

curious reasoning of certain Australian protectionists
—labourers who, even wiser than their fellows in seeing
the true results of labour protection, actually aver
that one of the great benefits commercial protection
is the stopping the influx of immigrants, by lowering
the purchasing power of high wages. They fear
that immigration would lower wages. They fear
that the fame of their high wages will break through
all Government checks on immigration. They find
that commercial protection lowers the real value of
their wages. And they hope the fame of this fact
will discourage all attempts at immigration. They
do not explain why all this trouble is necessary.
It seems they are content to enjoy nominally high,
but really low wages, saddled with all the trouble
of strict protective measures, to the simpler procedure
of mere low wages, attended by no further complications. Here, again, we have signs that protection
has great charms for mankind, but that after much
trouble, much risk, much energy and much toil devoted
to its manipulation, the same total of results differs
but little, or not at all, from those which would have
come of a pure *laissez-faire* or even essentially free-
trade policy.

§ 5. *This injures the Capitalist.*—And, again, we
may remember that the wages of labour rise in a new
country at the expense of the profits of capital.

This feature has its good side, inasmuch as it aids that one central aim of true economy, the equable distribution of wealth ; the actual available ὕλη is doled out in more equal and fairer portions. Nevertheless, labour being thus amply remunerated at the expense of the capitalist, there may come about a tendency to scare away the influx of capital. McCulloch terms the Wakefield system "a bait to tempt capitalists to buy land, by making them believe that though the land be artificially dear, labour will be artifically cheap." Some bait is necessary to tempt the influx of capital ; capital is the leading necessity of a young society ; commeasurably is it disastrous to have dear labour. It is nothing to the capitalist that the high wages are only nominally so, seeing that prices too are abnormally high. The capitalist seeks to pocket the profits on the use of his capital, and has no reason to desire that these profits should slip through the fingers of his labourers into the tills of tradesmen and others.

In young communities labour then becomes a bone of contention among protectionists. The one class seek the benefit of the labourer, and strive to keep off foreign competition. The other class seek the benefit of the capitalist, feeling that unless he is likely himself to pocket his profits, he will take his coveted capital elsewhere. In either condition of things there inevitably rules an impossibility of free competition in labour. And thus is lost the sole safeguard that, on the one hand, industrial remuneration shall correspond with the sacrifice involved; and that, on the other, capital sunk in investments shall be guaranteed a supply of labour without which its sinking would mean mere annihilation. So long as the community organizes in detail its labour supply free competition is impossible; and there is no guarantee that the wages enjoyed are an equitable renumeration, or that the consumer obtains in return for what he pays an actual equivalent sacrifice on the part of the producer.

§ 6. *The Right Course.*—Nevertheless, it may be advanced with great show of reason that labour will hardly come to young communities unless fetched; and when we see a Government interfering with success, and in spite of the opposition of the labouring classes, so far with the production and distribution of wealth, as to undertake a vigorous immigration policy, we must pause before we condemn on general grounds. It may be said that this protective regulation of the labour supply comes to be protection, not of labour, but of industrial enterprise; it seeks to set capital to work on natural agencies, by means of a necessary supply of labour, of men

of skill and muscle. Yet in reality a vigorous immigration policy is merely the placing a better supply
of a much-needed commodity in the local market ; it
is widening the area of supply accessible to a community. And in so doing it indeed fosters production ; but fosters it on the sure lines of free-trade.
When the result is successful it means an increased
supply of commodities ; and this marks an increased
distribution of the wealth of the community—in
reality, the highest aim of economic statesmanship.

CHAPTER VI.

PROTECTION IN REGARD TO CAPITAL.

§ 1. Capital must be attracted; and used for the best: Protection
fails so to do—§ 2. In Regulating the Production of Commodities—§ 3. In Regulating the Exchange of Commodities—
§ 4. In Regulating the Supply and Demand of Commodities—
§ 5. In Fostering Competition in other Lands—§ 6. Protection
fails in every case.

§ 1. *Capital must be attracted; and used for the best;
Protection fails so to do.*—Capital, the third of the conventional factors of productive energy, introduces us
to the widest class of phenomena affected by protective policies. The stock won from Nature and stowed
up in the shape of capital is the absolutely indispensable lever to the exertions of the labourer. And
natural agencies can only be brought under the
vivifying influence of labour by means of capital.
The presence of capital and the uses to which it is
put are fundamental elements in the economical
success of a community.

To be capable of a protective policy a community
must be capable of a foreign policy. In other words,
the community must exist in a political world wherein
other established systems of civilisation are continuing

in existence. Thus, in regard to our present purpose, a protective policy implies the co-existence of available capital in other lands.

In reference then to young communities we are confined to those that belong to a political world in which old-established systems exist side by side with the newer-formed societies. Thus, the young society in our category is not one that painfully and through long years of labour scrapes together capital for itself by its own isolated exertions; it is rather a virgin field which is first tilled by the aid of that capital which the neighbouring husbandmen have won from neighbouring fields. The oxen that plough have been bred and reared in the neighbouring pastures; the seed that is sown is the produce of the neighbouring enclosure; and the harvest that is garnered depends for its quantity and its quality on the amount of this available aid.

Then, again, in a new society the superior bounty of Nature brings about an abnormally rapid increase of capital. Thus the new society emerges from the leading-strings of external aid with a speed in proportion to the liberality of that aid at the first. That it enjoys the use of capital from its first start is the great condition of its rapid development. Capital is the nourishment which sustains the young society in the speedy development of the power and strength necessary to independent exertion. And the advocates of protection have here their great stronghold ; the Government is to step in, and set up lights to guide foreign capital to the land. It is held that a duly elaborated system of protection is necessary to attract at the very outset that capital without which no new industrial undertaking is possible.

And in older societies capital is no less a necessary condition of energized industry. But in older societies, which are in any degree removed from the brink of a speedy dissolution, there must already exist capital. Its presence is a corollary of their own existence. Thus in older societies there is not so much need for attracting capital as for making the best use of that which is present. Nevertheless, there is the undeniable need to retain for the benefit of local advance this invaluable energizing agent : as in a new society it becomes desirable to invite the presence of capital so in an old society is it necessary to prevent its departure. In either case the presence of capital is sought; and in neither case can it be denied that the end so sought is for the true economical benefit of the community. It is merely a question of the discovery of the true means to this desirable end. Protective policies have been advocated and adopted as a good means to this end both for young and old societies. The question remains, are they *good* means ? This problem forms the main thread of the present discussion.

There is hardly need for the assertion that capital is only permanently attracted to a society provided results prove the field a remunerative investment. If it be found that the industry of sugar-growing "pay" within a community, outside capital will flow in whether free-trade, protection, or any other system rule. We have already sufficiently considered protection, as applied to the attraction of capital. The actual balance of profit and loss accruing to capital from its presence in any given community will be seen in that wider and more congenial field of protection which regulates the uses to which capital is put within the community, and which does not regard its place or origin, though in effect greatly influencing its influx. Protective policies seek *to distribute capital* to certain uses as opposed to other uses ; they have thus great economic effect on the production of commodities ; on the exchange of commodities ; and on the supply and demand of commodities.

§ 2. *In Regulating the Production of Commodities.*— First, then, in regard to the production of commodities. The powers of each branch of production will be in strict proportion to the amount of capital invested in each. The protectionist marks out from all the industries possible in his community some few to fall under his ægis : to these he diverts capital, and thus gives to these an energizing power which is, *ipso facto*, taken from others. Government is thus saddled with a new task. The State is called upon to determine which branches of production shall exist, and which shall not exist, within the State. This forced distribution of capital has then to make good its way against the fallibility of Governments ; against many natural obstacles that arise; and against a wrong balance of deleterious consequences that necessarily ensue from such a course of procedure.

It may be asked at once, Why thus force a new and difficult duty on that portion of the community to which is entrusted its corporate concerns ? There is a homely saying, that the most consummate statesman is not that impossible paragon who makes no error, but rather that best form of human intelligence which makes fewest errors. Why, then, leave open and subject to one of these errors that most important phase in the life of a community—viz., the genesis and development of its productive industries ? The errors of the Government are the errors of the State ; the failure of its policies fall as a burden on the community. The failure of the schemes of an individual, on the contrary, recoil on the individual head alone ;

the errors of private endeavour are felt but by a fraction of the State.

The essential fallibility of statesmanship is perhaps nowhere more clearly demonstrated than in these policies for fostering industries. Canada has afforded a remarkable example of the course run by a protection devised by Governments. During the first years of this century the Baltic States supplied England with timber. At the date of the battle of Copenhagen there came to prevail a dread that this supply would be cut off by political circumstances, and this dread was amply justified. In the seven years, from 1802 to 1809, Memel timber rose from 78s. to 320s. per load. Then the Chancellor of the Exchequer raised the import duties on European and repealed those on Canadian timber. The result was that by the year 1846 the "timber" trade with Canada had speedily assumed vast proportions. Cobden was the first to penetrate these specious appearances. Of this Canadian timber protection, he said it was "calculated to give a forced misdirection, as all such bounties are, to the natural industries of these colonies by causing investment of capital in the preparing and shipping of inferior timber which would otherwise seek its legitimate employment in the pursuit of agriculture." These remarks were curiously confirmed by facts. The evidence of all travellers proved that the protection of this timber trade was disastrous to the farming interest. One or two of the timber-men made great fortunes, but the majority became invariably a drunken and improvident set. And, further than this, the indiscriminate felling of trees brought it about that when the farmer pushed forward to the occupation of the fresh virgin soil he found it cumbered with a dense and useless scrub instead of that "clean" forest which would have readily supplied him with the timber necessary for his houses, buildings and fences. All this added immensely to his difficulties. It is evident that the protection of this timber trade, however much it may have conduced to the fortunes of a few men, and to the productive use of one of the great natural agencies of Canada, nevertheless rode rough-shod over the use of other natural agencies which independent life is now proving to be far more profitable fields for productive energy.

Again, the English Corn-law episode stands forth typical of these things. Both the institution and the abolition of the Corn-laws were advocated for the one identical reason, the increase of the corn-growing industry within England. And the whole history of this episode affords fresh evidence of the fact that few humanly-conceived measures attain to that species of success which was sought by their introduction. A protective policy in attempting to foster some particular industry may either oust some other more profitable one, or introduce one that would otherwise have possessed no equitable or likely claim to entry.

This forced distribution of capital likewise fails to make way against many natural obstacles that beset its path. Mr. Montgomery Stuart has written a a valuable history of free-trade in the Tuscan States. The natural outcome of a policy of protection in regard to agricultural interests has, perhaps, nowhere been more forcibly detailed. The production of corn was sought; and the means adopted were the prohibition alike of its export and its import. Nature continued to provide years alternately favourable and unfavourable to the farmer. But the farmer was unable to profit by the surplus of good years. The requirements of the community for the time once satisfied, the rest of his hard-earned harvest remained a useless burden on his hands; a mere addition of new stores of grain to harvests already superabundant. As a consequence agriculture became unproductive; fields were left fallow; and the fostered corn-growing industry sank to the lowest ebb. There resulted the precise opposite of the end proposed.

Another deleterious consequence is that this forced

production of some one or two commodities, fights counter to the production of others.   There is thus ever present the fundamental objection that the less productive industry may be forcibly substituted for · the more productive. It is also an inevitable economic truth, that of industries protected, those for which the country has no actual superiority pile up loss tending to equal the gain from those for which there are natural aptitudes.   Cairnes well shows that the United States' calico and cutlery competes at a loss with the wares of Manchester and Sheffield. And this loss has to be compensated by the gains of those branches of industry where the United States possess natural advantages.   Mechanical ingenuity, a trait inherent in the "Yankee" citizen, gives the States the command in labour-saving machinery.   Again, Nature pours out of her oil-wells a special product. And the true nature of protection may be seen if we imagine England placing heavy duties on the importation of this oil, under the plea of founding in England an "oil-well" industry. While protection rules there is the danger that labour and capital, devoted to these natural aptitudes, fail duly to increase the national wealth, owing to the balance of loss— loss consequent on the prosecution of those other industries in which foreign competitors possess natural advantages.   In short, taking commodities in the aggregate, a greater expenditure of capital is necessary to produce them than were trade left perfectly untrammelled. Cairnes points out the tendency of free-trade "to turn the industry of a nation into a few channels." Again appears the old, old tale of the division of labour; this time taking its place as an element among nations; as a portioning off of duties and tasks to the whole world.

Moreover, not only do the protected industries stifle other non-protected industries, but they eventually set about stifling one another; and the prospective result is thus the original starting-point—viz., the absence of all industries. The colony of Victoria is again an instance in point. The manufacture of candles, stock raising, meat preserving, agriculture, and the manufacture of agricultural implements, were free industries, which proceeded to receive the anxious, if unskilful, care of a paternal Government. Time is now proving that these protectionist measures, undertaken to foster some one of these, seem inevitably to raise up obstacles in the path of some other. Tallow for candles is unobtainable at anything like reasonable price, because the importation of beasts is taxed to foster stock raising. Meat preserving threatens to come to an utter end for the same reason. The implement manufacturers complain of the high price of labour and raw material;

on this plea they raise their prices ; and as the farmer is prevented by the duties which protect the manufacturer from buying implements elsewhere, he finds himself unable to carry on operations ; and the stock raiser and meat preserver suffer in proportion. The adoption of protection for each of these industries involves the distress of the others.

Policies of protection applied to particular industries result in further deleterious consequences ; they are liable to incur extreme results—to bring in their train an aggravation of the effects intended. It has been said of the protective policy of the United States, " it has become so rampart and universal that instead of being protective, it has become fearfully destructive." The taxes on machinery, on raw materials, and the rest, have virtually excluded them from the use of the manufacturer. And the chief sign of these things is, the inferiority of the article produced. This result is also aided by the absence of the " keen spur" of competition. In 1849, for instance, free-trade was extended to French leather gloves imported into England. The result of the change to the heretofore protected English industry was, according to the report, " the quality and make of our gloves have much improved since they were put into more direct competition with the French, by reduction of duty." Above all does this want of competition injure the producer himself. Cavour could say of his countrymen, "the worst is, that while our producers, under the action of protection, move slowly along, those of foreign countries advance with the vigour of youth, energy, and manhood." Herodotus equally well describes the effect of political freedom consequent on the fall of monopolist or class interests :—" ελευθερωθέντων δὲ αὖτος ἕκαστος εάυτῳ προθυμεῖτο κατεργασάσθαι." Mill talks of the tax which the consumer pays for the laziness and incapacity of the monopolist producer. He adds, "When relieved from the immediate stimulus of competition, producers grow indifferenc to the dictates of their ultimate pecuniary interest." And thus, it may be remarked, there grows up a vested interest in those economic poisons, lethargy and incapacity, which forces the "temporary" protection to become perennial, and makes of the "tentative" duty an endless experiment.

With regard, then, to the production of commodities protection seeks to determine the channel by which capital is to offer its aid. And this results in imposing upon the community a deliberative function beyond its true capacity. The consequences are, that capital is liable to be forced to leave the right and expend itself upon the wrong industries ; the true benefits of the "natural" distribution of aptitudes are ignored; the substantial aid of a due division of labour, as well as the exhilarating influence of competition, are excluded; and, in brief, the natural and only conditions of permanent industrial success cut from under the feet of enterprising ability.

§ 3. *In Regulating the Exchange of Commodities.*—
Other effects of protection on the distribution of capital are seen in its influence on the exchange of commodities. Capital flows naturally to the most profitable investments; and the productiveness of industry is only profitable on the condition that its products are exchangeable. It has been held that will is a mere potentiality; determined only when it is put into action; and determined then by its object. So too of this capital, this useful stock accumulated from the bounty of Nature, it is mere potential force until it comes to be determined by securing an actual value in exchange; and this value is determined entirely by the market in which the product of such stock becomes realised. As a consequence, a community when considering its industrial or productive development, must take into consideration the character of its markets. And this will have considerable influence over the direction to be taken by its industrial forces. It is another question whether the community will judge best of these conditions of itself, individually and

through aid of private enterprise; or whether, on the contrary, its Government must discharge this duty. It is enough as yet to point out that such a duty exists. For instance, it may be affirmed of the Falkland Islands that the pith of their tussock grasses, which luxuriantly cover the islands, is a natural agency of the most perfect efficacy in the production of flesh in cattle. It is not, however, good feed for sheep, contributing neither to the quantity nor to the quality of the wool. And yet it is evident that the community there established should attempt the production of wool rather than the export of beef, seeing that the one potentiality is capable of realisation and the other not; for the one industry the European market is accessible; whereas for the other there is no available market.

Adam Smith writes: "After agriculture, the capital employed in manufactures puts into motion the greatest quantity of protective labour, and adds the greatest value to the annual produce. That which is employed in the trade of exportation has the least effect of any of the three." And again, later on, "When the exchangeable value of the annual produce exceeds that of the annual consumption, the capital of the society must annually increase in proportion to the excess." But it is necessary to notice that neither agriculture nor manufacture can thus increase the aggregate capital unless there be access to markets. It is not labour completed that gives value to a commodity, but the fact that the commodity itself is utilised. An enormous impulse is given to human labour by the fact that exchange of commodities enables two men to obtain respectively what is more valuable in use, in exchange for what is less valuable in use. To cut men off from the possibilities and advantages of such exchange, is to deprive them of their most indispensable aid to progress in the production of wealth. Cairnes writes : " Nations only engage in trade when an advantage arises from their doing so ; any interference with their free action in trading can only have the effect of debarring them from this advantage." It is the cardinal principle of protective policies to interfere with trade ; they have a tendency thus to stifle exchange, and exchange is the principal condition of industrial success.

When we consider the effect of protection in stifling exchange, it is necessary to bear in mind that the presence of markets is necessary to the existence of value in exchange ; that the presence of natural aptitudes, special to localities, is the condition which renders value in exchange possible ; and that the presence of commerce is necessary to the *profitable* existence of both markets and natural aptitudes.

The presence of markets renders possible value in

exchange. It has been to the clear profit of the English manufacturer that he has, in the face of all the world, stood by the otherwise self-evident fact that foreign competition in the home market, consequent on free-trade, may be more than compensated by the reciprocal existence of foreign markets for home produce. The numerous States of Germany in the early years of the century were each separated from the other by protective tariffs. Following the introduction of the Corn-laws in England, Prussia, in 1818, set up a protective tariff. The German States found themselves now stifled by an utter dearth of market. And the first object and first cause of the German Customs Union was the doing away with all local restrictions and the forming Germany into one whole free-trade district. In other words, markets were instituted, and natural aptitudes made the most of. The same policy has to this day marked the endeavours of the United States. However severely protection may bind the external trade with a ring of iron, yet within this ring free-trade is jealously rampant. During the great war the one incontrovertible plea for the preservation of the Union was the guaranteeing free exchange over its vast area. The crucial aid of the people of the West was primarily given in order to retain access for their products to the Eastern coasts. However strict and severe external protection, there exists side by side therewith internal free-trade. The sagacity of the people demands and retains markets for produce. On the other hand, the young communities of Australia are at the present in a less satisfactory condition. Victoria is strictly and avowedly protective in external trade; New South Wales, on her borders, virtually free-trade in external policy. The immediate consequence is an extensive and expensive line of custom-houses where their frontiers touch— their mediate consequence is a useful lesson to Victoria. Bitter experience is proving to her protected manufacturers that the profits of industry are *nil* in the absence of markets. Her agricultural and pastoral industries are crying aloud for change.

The exchange of commodities is then the necessary correlative of profitable production; and all that hampers exchange hampers profitable production. The United States offer an example of the injurious effects of protection in this direction. Commerce is, *objectively* speaking, an exchange of equivalents; thus it is that a nation which will not buy cannot sell. Restrictions upon import eventually become prohibitory duties upon export. Mr. Wells, in his careful Report to Congress, clearly demonstrates the very serious falling off in United States' commerce during the decade 1860–70, as compared with the previous decade. And Mr. Stuart tells the same tale of the commerce of Tuscany.

It may be noted that not only does this commercial fact of profit-in-use benefit the actual producers of the two commodities, but the exchange, being in itself of so profitable a nature, drops wealth in its progress, and enables the rise of a merchant class whose function it is to facilitate exchange. This fact is in itself a crushing answer to certain theorists who hold views of an obtuse "individualistic" type, who force on politics an atomistic arrangement totally at variance with all experience. Mr. Carey, for instance, the great American protectionist, charges free-trade with adding the cost of carriage to the cost of production ; and with some truth adds, that this cost of carriage thus becomes a burden on the production of the world. Yet when we find this burden willingly undergone, we naturally ask, Is there not some overbalancing advantage resulting ? The island of Hong-Kong, one of the " Ladrones," in 1841 the retreat of malefactors and poor fishermen to the number of about 5000, to-day (1879) counts 125,000 inhabitants. In one year there enter the port 25,000 ships of different sizes and does a trade with the United Kingdom of nearly £6,000,000 a year. How then are we to account for the fact that this tract of land, possessing no products or manufactures of its own, has in thirty years come to support twenty-five times the number of inhabitants? The reason lies in a nutshell. " Nearly all the European merchandise which enters China is landed in Hong-Kong before passing to the *line of the Chinese custom-houses.*" In other words, Hong-Kong is made a free port. Actual *free-trade* here usurps the exact field of that *protective* system of trading licences and monopolist factories by which Portugal sought to command to her own use the wealth of the East; and usurps it with a success altogether unknown to the Portuguese. Compare Macao with Hong-Kong. " Curaçoa and Estella," says Adam Smith, " the two principal islands belonging to the Dutch, are free ports, open to the ships of all nations; and this freedom in the midst of *better* colonies whose ports are open to those of one nation, has been the great cause of the prosperity of these two *barren* islands." In Payne's " European Colonies " we find " the tiny Swedish island of St. Bartholomew, bought of the French in 1784, and at once made a free port, rose and fell much in the same way as St. Thomas. With the establishment of free-trade in the rest of the West Indies St. Bartholomew ceased to be worth keeping." Hostile tariffs notwithstanding, free ports flourish all the world over. Sir Walter Raleigh pointed this out more than two hundred years ago in his pamphlet, " A Cleare and Evident way for enriching the nations of England and Ireland."   He says of the United Provinces : " To these privileges of Industry, &c. they adde Smalnesse of Customs and liberty of Trade, which makes them flourish ; and their countries plentiful of all kind of coyn and commodities, and their merchants so rich that when a losse cometh they scarce feel it. . . . . And although it seems but small Duties they receive ; yet the multitudes of all kind of commodities and coyn is so great that is brought in by themselves and others, and carried out by themselves and others, that they receive more customs and Duties to the State (by the greatnesse of their Commerce) in one yeare than England doth in two." And of Genoa he tells a similar tale : " There was an Entercourse of Traffyke in Genoa, and in that City was the flower of Commerce ; all nations traded with merchandise to them, and there was the storehouse of all Italy and other places : But, after they had set a great custome of xxi. per cent., all nations left trading with them, and at this day we have not three ships go there in a yeare." This " Free custome inwards and outwards" is, and has ever been, an unmixed good whenever and wherever it obtains.   And the basis of the success of free ports is the profit of the merchant or middleman in the exchange of products.   Thus we see that the products of one land can be exchanged for those of another with a balance of profit over and above, not only the double cost of carriage, but the profits of a prosperous and proverbially wealthy merchant class ; and that free-trade alone can foster in a community the growth of this socially convenient industry.

The presence of commerce is, moreover, in itself an industry. In order to the existence of exchange a carrying trade is necessary. Nature is again attacked for iron and for timber, and for harbours ; railways and ships call forth a network of intelligent industry ; the production, distribution and use of the instruments of the exchange of products take rank among the most important of the industries of the world. And the hampering of commerce by protective policies, the plea that cost of carriage is an unbalanced evil, at once involves the putting an end to this extensive and productive industry.

Highly instructive calculations come to us from South Australia. It has been found that the large intercolonial trade of that colony yielded but a miserable £1000 profit after the deductions from the natural profit for the costs of the various restrictive measures adopted on the border lines with other colonies.

Instances may be quoted without end of the stoppage which protection puts on trade. In Bengal the Government, some years ago, abandoned the

State manufacture of salt. Forthwith a *new* trade grew up with Liverpool, which lately reached the great total of over 300,000 tons per annum. Victoria is protective. Tasmania and New South Wales adopt liberal tariffs. For the year 1877 the exports from Tasmania to Victoria showed an increase of 10 per cent. To New South Wales they showed an increase of 95 per cent. Such was the increase of trade with liberal as opposed to protective tariffs.

Portuguese history again tells that one of the most trenchant causes of the fall of the Portuguese Empire was a foolish restrictive policy in regard to trade. Her seamen and adventurers, by heroic and skilful explorations, had made her mistress of the water-way to the East. At one time the inhabitants of that small strip of European coast-line held commercial command of all the outlets of native products down the west-coast of Africa round up the east-coast, by Arabia and Muscat to the shores of India; and following these round the whole of Hindostan to the mouth of the Ganges; down Burmah to the Straits and Islands of the Eastern seas. None hoped or dared to dispute their monopoly of the wealth-yielding commerce of the East. But though jealously set on maintaining this ocean monopoly, Portugal handed over to the nations of Europe the monopoly of local trade.   Eastern wealth flooded in continuous streams into Lisbon.   But the Portuguese mariner, carried away by the pride of success, deigned not to serve Europe further.   Others were bid come fetch what they would from Lisbon.   The hardy fishermen of the North Seas were thus driven to discover the lucrative nature of a carrying trade.   Ships and navigation took rapid strides in improvement and efficiency.   The sturdy Dutch and the adventurous English found in the commerce engendered of an exchange of products a wealth-giving industry.   And this industry prospered and grew with marvellous rapidity and developed in these nations the first germs of that power which hinted a means to escape the costly exactions of the Portuguese on their imports from the East.   Dutch and English penetrated of themselves, and on their own account, to the very East itself—and in a brief period drove off the Portuguese from their monopoly of the trade.

§ 4. *In Regulating the Supply and Demand of Commodities.*—Yet a third class of the effects of protection on the distribution of capital appears in its influence on the supply and demand of commodities.   The wealth of the community is primarily represented by its capital.   The individuals who make use of this capital are the producers and the consumers.   The one expends the stock he has won from Nature in further attacks on Nature; the other expends the stock he has won from Nature on repaying the other for his efforts. Yet if there is no due return to such expenditure capital to an equal amount becomes annihilated. In so far then as expenditure is productive, each man with capital or superfluous stock creates a demand for what he himself requires, though offering at the same time a supply of what others may require. The exchange value of the commodities in the market is their price : and the expenditure of capital in the market, if it is not to decrease the aggregate wealth of the State—if it is to vary profitably—must either change its direction or *increase* in quantity. Thus, presuming the increase of wealth is intended, we can see in prices the working of these phenomena :—high prices, accompany inadequate, or decreased, supply, or increased demand ; low prices accompany inadequate, or decreased, demand, or increased supply. The producer suffers most by inadequate and prospers most by increased demand. The consumer suffers most by inadequate, and prospers most by increased supply. In other words, the wealth of the State, as represented by it in its double capacity of producer and consumer, suffers by inadequate demand and supply, and prospers by increased demand and supply. The producer, expending as he does part of the wealth of the State,

K

finds its only profitable expenditure to be in the presence of an adequate market. The consumer, expending his share of the part of the wealth of the State, finds the value in use of the commodities he buys only equal the value in exchange of what he pays for them when there is adequate supply of the commodities required. The farmer will expend some of the profits of his year's labour in growing a harvest of wheat only provided there be a sufficient demand for wheat to enable him to do so at a profit. The farmer will expend some of the profits of his year's labour on a pair of boots only provided he feels that the labour which yields these profits, which he expends in exchange, is equalled by the exertions of the shoe-maker. Protection of its very essence brings about decreased supply and decreased demand.

Decreased supply means at once decrease in production and decrease in consumption : it implies a reversion towards that primitive condition of things when the greater part of the bounty of Nature lay fallow—unknown to and unenjoyed by man. The producer ceases to exert as much energy on producing ; the consumer finds himself less able to enjoy the products of human endeavour. And evidence abounds that decreased supply is the great result of protection. Thus Mr. Wells summarizes the actual present result of the industrial policy of late years

pursued in the United States in the words, " a diminution of abundance ; a premium on scarcity ; a restriction on growth." In our terms these words may
be paraphrased " a decrease of supply ; an impeded
consumption ; an impeded production." And perhaps no more striking proof could be given of the
truth of this conclusion than the petitions spontaneously emanating from Chicago and Boston respectively, after the two great fires in those cities. The
object of their prayer was purely and simply the sus-
pension of the protective import duties on building
materials. Reconstruction was declared, on the
highest authority, to be a simple impossibility at the
existing prices, and with the existing or prospective
restricted supplies.

Mill has written, " defeated as a general theory,
protection finds support in some particular cases, and
one of these is subsistence." But protection distinctly
proves itself a premium on scarcity directly it is
adopted on this plea of rendering a community self-
supporting. The professed object of the English
Corn-laws was to render England self-supporting in
the matter of corn. The country was to be made
independent of foreign supplies. The result, as every
one knows, was a cry for bread on the part of the
poorer classes, which was one of the most powerful
aids to the richer classes when they came to consider

free-trade a good prospect for their own manufacturing industries.

That this contradictory outcome of protection is no vain chimera of theory, may be seen in the history of protection in Tuscany, so ably told by Mr. Montgomery Stuart. The actual food supply was so curtailed by the corn-laws that absolute national starvation threatened the community. As Mr. Stuart puts it: " The protectionist principles dominant at Florence in the administrative department, termed with such cruel irony that of ' Abbondancia,' consistent in their logic, no more allowed the importation of foreign than the exportation of native corn." There was no market for the surplus of good years. As a consequence, farming came to proceed on the principle " sufficient for the year is the corn thereof," and no thought was taken for the coming year. The harvest of 1763 failed through excessive wet ; that of 1764 was little better ; the scanty surplus of former years gave out. There was one patriot in the community, Pompeo Neri, seeking at the time to free his country of its bane—protection. Presiding over the community was its Grand Duke, the well-known husband of Maria Theresa, inclined in his own mind to enlightened principles. The whole community, driven to desperation by the failure of the food supply, was ready to welcome any new scheme. Protectionist principles were no match for practical starvation. The prince was glad to be thus set free, at all events for a time, to follow the enlightened advice of Pompeo Neri. Restrictions on importation were suspended, and the country flooded with imported corn. It is true this application of free-trade principles was but temporary, but the lesson learnt by this temporary abandonment of the policy of strict protection was not forgotten on the recurrence of the corn famine in 1766, and in that year the corn-laws were abolished, once and for all in Tuscany.

On this self-supporting theory a country depends for its food supply on its own soil alone. How if we apply this theory to a country like Holland, where it is said more men are employed to mind the dykes than the corn produced in the country will feed ? It is as though a city were made to depend for its entire water supply on the wells sunk within its walls : with the waters of the surrounding valleys purposely left to their own wilds ; and even the stream that ran past the walls of the city jealously kept from entering the walls. No doubt the city would thus be rendered self-reliant in time of leaguer ; no doubt such a state of things would do well for the un-civilized surroundings of an Afghan fortress : or for the times when the enemy would poison, if not cut off, the water supplies of a city. But in these days we do not starve ourselves in peace that we may subsist during war. We supply our cities with water the cheapest way we can; we drain the neighbouring wilds and conduct their waters to the city; and so with the subsistence of a community we all proceed on the sensible theory that Mill has embodied in the words, " that country is the most steadily supplied with food which is supplied from the largest surface." The community which seeks to supply its own food from within its own boundaries feels to the full every inadequate yield, while it loses the present and prospective benefits of every surplus yield. The selfish instincts of a blind producing class, immediately opposing themselves to the good of the whole community, mediately involve the ruin of the class. They prosper at the first by the decreased supply; but in the train of this there follows a decreased demand, and they find with the vanishing of their market there disappears the prospect of profit. Decreased supply is fatal to the continued prosperity of the producer; and his prosperity is a leading element in the prosperity of the community.

We have, too, to consider decreased demand as resulting from protection; for there follows a decrease in consumption. The practical consideration to the consumer is the price at which he can command any given commodity. Protection renders prices *un-steady* and *high*. The favour of Nature playing variously and capriciously on the natural agencies of the country is uncontrolled by the action of Nature in other lands. Prices of commodities fall and rise to every wind that blows. The stricter the protection, the more inevitable this fluctuation in prices so detrimental to any commercial or industrial activity.

Yet more serious are the *high* prices consequent on protection. The consumer suffers. Cavour once summarized the cost of protection before the Italian Chambers: "With the present system the consumer pays three taxes; one goes into the hands of the Government; the second into those of the smugglers; and the third into the strong boxes of privileged producers." Thus is dissipated the extra capital expended by the consumer. Ricardo tells us that the effect of the English Corn-laws was "to make the price of corn consistently and considerably higher in England than in any other neighbouring country." This enhanced price is nothing more or less than a tax imposed on the great majority for the benefit of a minority. Nor, indeed, is it always for their benefit. It is of course difficult to defend the equity of a system which forces consumers to pay higher prices to the local producers than they would have to pay to the foreign.   The plea of the protectionists is, " by protection we give the producers a higher price for their commodity . . . . and thus . . . . though working at a disadvantage, they obtain the rate of profit current in the country." It may, however, be asked, Why should the consumer be called upon to set right the disadvantage under which the producer elects to labour ? What right have these special producers to exist on the forced contributions of the rest of the community ? We see that the consumers gain nothing by it. They have to pay a higher price for an inferior article. Insignificant examples often have the full anatomic value of microscopical specimens. In the colony of Victoria, strictly protectionist in policy, candles of colonial manufacture, the result of what the leading Melbourne paper terms " State-coddling," were lately quoted in the market at 10½*d.* per pound. Nevertheless to buyers, giving a bond to export the same, the price is 8½*d.* per pound. A tax of 2*d.* in the pound is thus raised by the manufacturer for his own private behoof. Nor is there evidence that the producer gains ; in many cases rise in price does not even succeed in surmounting rise in cost of production, and there is ever present the deleterious result that the consumers, being compelled to buy dear instead of cheap goods, are curtailed in their means of employing labour.

We see then that, under a protective policy, both producers and consumers devote to unprofitable purposes capital which in a healthier condition of things would be expended profitably to all concerned; thus, in a word, a protective policy is inevitably destructive of the capital employed by both consumer and producer.

§ 5. *In Fostering the same Industries in other Lands.* —It is necessary also to notice that protection, in attempting to divert capital to certain definite courses by endeavouring to foster certain particular industries in a country, has another suicidal tendency. The policy is entered upon in order to set going certain industries. But to follow such a course involves, not only the gradual and sure shutting herself out from foreign markets, but it actually fosters the rise in other lands of precisely similar industries to supply those very markets.

It at once deprives itself of certain markets; substitutes other purveyors for these markets, and even raises up rivals and competitors in neutral markets. We may even lay aside for the moment the discussion of the problematical issue that protection will foster in a country the growth of certain industries, in order to bring to bear upon the question other lights. Much may be thrown into new prominence by the incidence of the rays of that light which takes notice of environments. A community, always remembering we can only deal with such as are advanced to that stage of civilization where protective or other foreign policies alone are possible, exists as part of a whole. It has an international as well as a national existence. The German protectionist, List, divides economy into cosmopolitan or international, and political or national. The German Customs Union was in entire accord with his "Nationale system der Politischeœkonomie." But it may well be objected that no nation has existence save as distinguished from other nations ; and progress or civilization, or whatever the term adopted to represent man's environments, shows a network of bonds binding together these individual nations ; bonds meaningless without individuals ; individuals meaningless without bonds. If it have national it must have international existence : if it have "political" it must have "cosmopolitan" economical relations.

Protection, in any community, has certain international effects, indirect and for the most part unintended, yet nevertheless certain. Protection of one industry is not only the driving out of some other, but the compelling the rise of similar industries in other lands. And it is when the mind is given to trace the effects of a protective policy on other nations that the remarkable importance of this fact is given due prominence. In brief, just as it may be held that free-trade encourages the manufactures and raw product of one's own country, so may it be asserted that protection encourages those of other countries. By protection, one community forces another to *supply itself* with definite commodities, and once Force to enter upon the scene, the cue is given for the prompt exit of that natural profit of special aptitudes which is the sure basis of perfect growth ; the single foundation of the increase of the wealth of mankind.

We turn to history for the facts of the case. Cobden wrote of the United States in 1835: "Great Britain now sees in America a competitor in every respect calculated to contend with advantage for the sceptre of naval and commercial dominion." The United States were to succeed England as Holland succeeded Spain and Portugal, and as these had succeeded the Italian Republics. That this forecast should not have come true by this year 1879, is due to various causes. No doubt the American War had detrimental effect. No doubt England still retains geographical position at the gate of Europe, as the bridge between the old civilizations of Europe and the wealthy societies of the New World. Nevertheless, if we cast an eye the while to the history of protection we shall learn of other and yet more trenchant causes. From America came this message to England : " You taxed us into independence, you fought us into a maritime power, and you now enact that we shall be manufacturers." Before the war of Liberation the American Jefferson, with strange wisdom, wrote : " The workshops of Europe are the most proper to furnish the supplies of manufactures to the United States." After the War of Liberation, England excluded American imports from her ports. This rigorous protection forthwith brought about a change of opinion. The same author then wrote : " To be independent in the comforts of life we must fabricate them for ourselves." Cobden noticed the introduction of the cotton manufacture into the United States— " watered by the blood of our ten years' French war, it flourished an hundredfold." A petty policy of revenge adopting protective enactments, fostered the growth in another community of industries for which our own land possessed special aptitudes. " Protection," as Lord Palmerston once said, " is obviously a game two can play at." Manufacturing England, by a protective policy, thus made the United States a manufacturing country. At the commencement of this era the manufactures of England were in decline, and the United States appeared to be stepping into her shoes. In the States, however, there arose in turn a vigorous protectionist school, and their policy, adopted by the Government, in its turn destroyed the rapid growth which Cobden, not without dismay, had watched. The previous balance has since been completely restored by the flitting of the evil genius of protection across the Atlantic.

Of the international effects of the adoption of this latter protective policy in the United States, none are more apparent than those affecting her commercial dominion. Canada herein occupies a foremost place. A thoughtful writer has recently told us: " The protectionist policy which has been so suicidal to the interests of the States has served as a spur to the Dominion to begin, without protection, industries and manufactures which she never thought of before; and from being a mere hewer of wood and drawer of water, a provider of rough raw material to the Republic, she now manufactures and exports for her own benefit ; . . . . . but the greatest triumph of Canada is in the extent of her shipbuilding and carrying trade, which has completely dropped from the fettered hands of the United States." History has shown us Portugal monopolizing the commercial road to India, and thus forcing forward the competition of the mariners of Northern Europe So too the

United States, in command of the direct road to Europe from Canada, attempted to make a monopoly of the fact, and become the *entrepôt* between Canadian and European consumers and producers. Canada has replied in the same manner that Holland and England made answer to the Portuguese attempt. Canada opened the St. Lawrence ; Canada forced for herself a direct path to her markets. She opposed to the "ignorant violence of protection" the calm considerations of free-trade. And the benefits immediately accruing to her own commercial activity became enhanced by the divergence to her ports of much of the trade of the States themselves. From the Western States large quantities of corn and provisions, avoiding the tariff burdened Eastern ports, sought the road of the lakes to the ocean steamers in the St. Lawrence. To the railways and the ships of the States was lost not only the Canadian, but further, a great proportion of American trade. The monopolizing protection of the carrying trade in the United States had fostered the healthy growth of a carrying trade in another community which prospered and overtopped completely the protected home trade.

The effects of the protective policies of the Continent on England afford ample instances of their international results. There were three instructive stages, or eras. Napoleon's Continental system was succeeded by the Corn-laws, and then again by free-trade. The Continental system, coupled with general war, threw endless obstacles in the way of commercial intercourse. The dearth of English supplies from 1806 to 1814 caused endeavours in Germany to manufacture for themselves. But with the peace of 1814 English manufacturers again took their accustomed place in German markets. Meanwhile these few years of forced protection had driven British commercial energy to other fields ; and thus the protective " Continental system," fostering a half-hearted home imitation of English industries (an imitation overthrown no sooner English competition was readmitted), resulted in widening considerably the markets for British produce ; and so, in the best of senses, fostering British industry, by increasing greatly the demand for its products. Asia, Africa, and America brought forth their respective goods in return for the manufactured commodities of the British merchant. And, more important even than this, vast regions of virgin soil became eagerly occupied by the teeming population of England. The governors of Port Jackson reported home—" If we can prosper thus with convict labour, what may not be expected of free ?" And a great English tide flooded Australia. Thus the jealously protected corn-growing of Hungary created for itself the successful rivalry of South Australia, New Zealand, and Canada. Colonial possessions of European countries now lapsed to the care of the British; and Britain, driven from the Continent by protection, developed into that Greater Britain, greater immeasurably in wealth and in power, which excites the apprehensions or hopes of the thinking men of to-day. This is indeed a colossal example of the international effects of protective policies.

The second stage saw the Corn-laws thrust upon England. Already, by the end of the war, England had become the " coal-hole and forge" of the world. But the Corn-laws drove other countries to retaliation. Germany was soon shut up in her own Customs Union. From Lübeck it was written—" The policy you in England are pursuing is making the whole German people your rivals instead of your customers. Cloth manufacture, hemp works, iron foundries, hardware manufacture, are springing up where we used to grow corn." Lord Palmerston saw the further effects of this. " One great evil of our restrictive system," said he, " is that it induces other States to fancy that it is the secret of our prosperity, and thus it sets them to imitate our example." By pursuing a protective policy a similar system is urged on other communities : markets are closed; production beyond mere sustenance is rendered unremunerative ; and a drag, or rather "stopper," placed upon all national and international progress.

During this period England luckily possessed a secret of prosperity which entirely overbalanced the evil effects of this restrictive system, and was in a measure an effect of it. We have seen her, driven from the Continent, open up to her use the whole world. And now we have the third, or latter-day, stage of our historical lesson. The adoption of free-trade now enables England fully to profit by these results of the "continental system," and of its successor, the German Customs Union. Her own corn-laws prompted other nations to copy her restrictive policy, but her abolition of these laws, the saving-point of her policies, has found but few and hesitating imitators.

Thus it is by a consideration of the actual environments of the international life of a nation, that there is gained clear evidence of the ruinous effects of protective policies. Not only are the necessary markets thereby closed; but, while the community shuts its doors and sets to work to bring into being and educate some industry, other lands in want of similar commodities are driven to do likewise. And when this nursed bantling is finally produced in the light of day, other bantlings of equal strength and capacity are discovered forced into open rivalry, claiming successfully portions, if not the whole, of his supposed heritage.

§ 6. *Protection fails in every case.*—What, then, is the balance-sheet of profit and loss resulting from a policy of protection in regard to capital? With respect to the production of commodities, protection limits capital to a few definite industries. Government is thus burdened with a new and hard task, difficult for men to bear; and one, moreover, which if left to itself would inevitably work out its own end. The superior wisdom of governments is found sadly wanting; and ignorance, or more criminal fault, is seen to foster the less at the price of the more productive industries. It is a universally recognised principle of taxation that skill, industry, and abstinence must not be put to any disadvantage. But this cardinal principle finds no place in the theories of the protectionists. Again, exchange of products, that great lever of all human progress, is stayed by the hand of protection, the consummation of whose work is the closing of the markets for the productions fostered. Protection fights contrary to the spread of that network of commerce which stands out the one bright hope in the human future. Again, in relation to supply and demand we find producers and consumers use their capital respectively in producing and consuming. If there be no due returns to such expenditure the capital becomes destroyed, and there is dead loss to that amount of the wealth of the nation. These two "modes" of human exertion prosper respectively by increased demand and increased supply of commodities. Protection results in decreased supply and decreased demand.

While, finally, if we turn from the national to the international efforts, we see immediately that protection, attempting to foster the growth of a particular industry in a community, inevitably sets a premium on the growth of the same industry in some other community, and thus, besides closing markets for its own products and reducing its own purchasing powers, it at the same time arranges for the supply of exactly similar products from other sources, and thereby for the future cuts itself off from enjoying the benefits of its own natural aptitudes or opportunities, to say nothing of the profitable continuance of such industries as it may by such means have endeavoured to found in its own borders.

CHAPTER VII.

IS PROTECTION PROFITABLE ?

§ 1. Protection decreases the aggregate wealth of the State.—
§ 2. It wastes, misdirects, and lessens Production.—§ 3. It
deprives it of its mainspring, Capital.—§ 4. It is merely an
historical phase of social development.

§ 1. *Protection decreases the aggregate wealth of a
State.*—The main thread of the argument is the
endeavour to determine whether protective policies
accelerate or retard the industrial growth of a community. The arguments may be conveniently summed
up in the one question—Is the aggregate wealth of
the community increased or is it not ? To the practical
inquirer the question is entirely one of balances.
It may, for instance, be urged that if corn-growers
or manufacturers are protected by high duties against
foreign competition, it is obvious that the prices
of their products will be high, and at the same
time the corn-growers or the manufacturers will make
extra profits.   The question arises, Are these profits of
these classes in the aggregate greater than the losses
occasioned to the community by the high prices ?   Is

there a resulting increase of the aggregate wealth of
the community ?   Among the most obvious objections
is the fact that avowedly and practically protection
is an obstacle to the equable distribution of wealth.
There ensues a violent tendency of wealth to fall into
the hands of the few.   Thus the majority are deprived, to a vast extent, of a lever indispensable
to increased production.   Again, wealth thus ac-
cumulating in the hands of the few invariably
brings in its train luxury and extravagance.   Much
of this wealth becomes squandered, or, in other
words, economically destroyed.   The hard-earned
winnings of the community are scattered to the
winds, and fresh obstacles are raised to that equable
distribution of wealth which is the great need of
this, as it has been of every other, age.

§ 2. *It wastes, misdirects, and lessens Production.*—
Thus it may be asked, Are these profits of protection,
even .omitting all qualifying phenomena, greater
than, or even as great, as those which would come
about in the absence of protection ? We must answer,
No, if we bear in mind the economic waste of labour
and capital accompanying such policies.   Mill points
out that protection "compels a waste of the difference
between labour and capital necessary for the home
productions and that required for the purchase
of those manufactured abroad."   And Cairns · well

insists upon the fact that protection exactly neutralises all advantage of greater productive capacity of the foreigner. And it is no difficult reasoning that connects with this cause the sequence of a rise in prices. Protection has been called a "mutual assurance against foreign competitors." It is rather "a mutual assurance against foreign aid." For when we ask what it assures to us, we can only reply, a certain deprivation of our share in the benefits of the industrial advantages enjoyed by a foreigner over ourselves. There is a waste of productive energy in overcoming natural unsuitableness in the field of occupation, which results in the fact that the consumer obtains in the home market less value for his money than he would in the foreign market. And when we remember that purchase is, in truth, the exchange of equivalents, we see that the purchaser sacrifices, perforce, a certain amount of his expenditure of his capital or stock. The wealth of the community is thus charged with the profits of the protected manufacturer; and this expenditure is not in proportion to the benefits obtained by the purchaser. In short, in such a community value in exchange is not what it should be—reciprocally realised value in use. In the exchange or purchase of certain commodities the producer has a decided and real benefit in the balance. But under true conditions of purchase each party must be benefited equally, or capital becomes destroyed.

We must answer No, if we bear in mind the fact that protection tends to drive out those industries it does not introduce; to impede those industries it does not foster. Its cardinal principle is to turn productive energy into courses which it would not otherwise pursue; in other words to tempt productive energy from the course it would naturally follow. For it must be remembered that, in effect, protection does not draw its line of distinction between employing the people of the community as opposed to employing foreigners, but between employing the people of the community in certain divisions of labour as opposed to other divisions. The protection of native industry has an undeniable tendency to follow the assumption that the people of the community should attempt the production of those identical commodities which foreigners are already producing. And in this strange attempt to supersede and nullify the natural advantages of different soils and climates theorists involve the community in the loss to productive energy of many of the most profitable industries.

We must answer, No, if we bear in mind that protection lessens production in amount. And the amount of production stands of course in intimate relation to the amount of wealth in any community.

Mr. Wells has made a valuable calculation as to the amount of production in the United States. In the decade 1850–60, with a low tariff prevalent, production increased 86 per cent. In the succeeding decade, 1860–70, with the burden of a high tariff, the corresponding increase was only 52 per cent. In other words, the amount of wealth added in a decade to the national aggregate had fallen by the enormous extent of one-third. Mr. Wells gives us shoes as a particular instance of these general conditions. Shoes, by the way, have since man first begun to think, achieved some mysterious and as yet unexplained connection with politics. The export of shoes in the former decade increasing fast, fell, during the latter decade, to inconsiderable proportions, and the local price had risen 50 per cent. And this illustration is all the more noticeable, seeing that during this latter decade shoemaking machines of very great ingenuity had come into general use, saving an enormous amount of labour, and apparently giving to the United States what was practically a unique " natural aptitude." Thus not only may the non-fostered productive industries be chilled into non-existence, but even those industries that are carefully fostered, may, in the end, in spite of many advantages, prove unable to maintain their place. For in them cost of production frequently rises to prohibitive prices :

demand becomes limited; production disheartened. Under a protective policy, in a word, the aggregate amount of production becomes fatally curtailed, and there ensues a further decrease in the aggregate wealth-producing powers of the State.

§ 3. *And so deprives it of its mainspring, Capital.*— Protection also becomes a premium against abstinence, a premium against the increase of energising capital. To hold that the quantity of wealth produced is lessened is to hold that the rewards of labour and the profits of capital are reduced. This state of things, the result of the pressure of protection, permeating the whole community, works counter to the tendencies of men to save; and, as a consequence, the productive capacities of the community are further curtailed. " To compel the consumers of a nation to buy dear instead of cheap goods is distinctly to diminish their means of employing labour"—in other words, to diminish the energising wealth of the community.

Mr. M. Stuart gives a notable example in the case of Tuscany. Long-continued protection in that State had effectually impoverished the community in every way. And the most remarkable of all the effects of the introduction of free-trade was the reappearance of capital. Nobles, for long poverty-stricken, gradually became again possessors of capital, as their lands once more were duly utilised. Then, too, the rising class of successful tradesmen soon became possessed of smaller capitals for investment, or, in other words, utilisation. The whole community became materially revived by the fact that this new capital reverted in great part to its appropriate field —the cultivation of the soil. And this is the more noticeable when we remember that the previous protective policies had been specially instituted to increase cultivation, but had resulted in a most effectual destruction of that capital which was in reality the essential and sole lever of agricultural prosperity. In Tuscany, the abolition of protection gave opportunity for abstinence, and the costs of agricultural production again became possible. The aggregate wealth of the community increased at a high rate of speed. The same story applies to capital embarked in manufactures of all sorts, and it is to be hoped our fellow-countrymen in the protective colony of Victoria will take this fact to heart betimes. Adam Smith well puts it: " The quantity of industry not only increases in every country with the increase of the stock which employs it, but, in consequence of that increase, the same quantity of industry produces a much greater quantity of work." The consumer is better supplied, the labourer more in demand, the investment of capital more profitable in consequence. And every increase of produce means an increase of aggregate wealth ; and this circle of prosperous progress is continuous.

Dr. Johnson condensed the most approved floating opinions of his time in the dictum " a man cannot increase his store of wealth without making another poorer." This strange individualistic theory was the basis of the policies advocating the principle of the balance of trade. Their object was to draw to a country the precious metals, and so to enrich it at the supposed cost of other countries. Protective policies were the logical outcome of this strange reasoning, which arrived at the production of commodities required by a country entirely within its own boundaries, in order to retain its wealth for itself. As in the one case the man is to sell all he has and fill his house with gold and silver; so in the other, he is not to sally forth and buy, but to make all he requires without going abroad, and to let as little as possible leave his house. In either case he has no incentive to acquire stock with the intent that he may use it, for he can have no use for it ; he has no incentive to that profitable abstinence which surely improves his ability to produce ; and he will find in the long-run that his gold or his commodities *per se* are insufficient to enable him even to exist. He omits to notice that the true source of the increase of wealth is the bounty of Nature, and not his individual self alone ; he fails to see that a due use of his own increased powers of production means an increase of stock won or to be won from Nature to the use of man ; and that he must, if he seek real truth, exclaim, "a man cannot increase his own store of wealth without aiding other men to become richer."

§ 4. *It is merely an historical phase of social development.*—If we look to history we shall see that protection is merely an historical phase in social development; and the abnormal accompaniment of that original or "natural" equity which, after all, fundamentally regulates men's actions. All whose thoughts have gone below the mere surface of things ; all who have attempted, in plain language, to think out such problems as we are now engaged with have always caught sight, with more or less distinctness, of a certain and sure connection between the moral and the useful. Those who have explored further into the secrets of Nature—the Huxleys, the Lyells, the Argylls—whether they view what they perceive with the spectacles of pure materialism, of "revealed truth" or of dogma, nevertheless one and all bear witness to the existence of what the human mind conceives to be Laws in Nature. They may even dispute concerning the δι ὅτι ; they may differ as to the τι ἐστι; but one and' all agree in an affirmative answer to the εἰ ἔστι. And so it is with the reports of those minds of higher calibre which have attempted the exploration of the secrets of those phenomena which Spencer discusses under the head of sociology, which Aristotle deals with in his ἐπιστήμη πρακτίκη—his science of society as being the human realisation of a virtuous life. However much authorities may differ in the circumstantial variety of their discoveries, yet do these all point to evidence of the existence of a substantial substratum which seems to be nothing more nor less than an identification of the Good and the Useful. This identification, it would appear, is beyond the practical recognition of the majority of men. It may be that it must remain unrecognised save by more thoughtful minds : nevertheless there it is, working on as the powerful even though silent regulator of the results of all human effort.

Cicero wrote of old, " Nos vero, justissimi homines, qui Transalpines gentes oleam et vitem serere non sinimus, quo plures sint nostra oliveta nostræque vinæ ; quod quum faciamus prudenter facere dicimur, juste non dicimur." These words, "juste non dicimur," are well descriptive of the conscientious objections to protective policies which are present, however vaguely, in the minds of most men. On the other hand, we find in modern times the first successes of free-trade happily described as a "legible record of the dawning conviction that the good of each nation is the good of all." Thus are we brought to recollect that free-trade and protection, as with all human things, have their place in history. Perhaps there are few branches of human inquiry that have made such sudden progress as those theories of society which within the last few years see in the history of man the fact that he is a πολιτικον ζωον. Society begins with the individual man struggling by himself. He next herds with the opposite sex from the first instincts of a brute nature ; but his higher intellectual capacity gives a permanence to mere lust, and the family arises. Then his herding with his own offspring from a dim consciousness of increased strength against human or animal foes, develops the tribe out of the family, and there ensues a marvellous and rapid intellectual growth in customs and principles of relationship. Thus man passes from one stage of isolation to another. In the first, the man stands by himself, an individual at war with all the world. In the second, he groups himself with others, and stands out again, a group by itself, in isolation, and at war with all the world. But with the mental growth of man came what in popular language may be termed fresh conquests over Nature. Men grew and multiplied, and the consequent dispersion

over the face of the earth brought in its train such
fresh accessions of power as new methods of communication and new natural products. In time,
from the tribe developed the nation, and a third stage
of isolation was reached : a stage from whose leading-
strings we are not yet free. Each nation, like each
tribe or each original "man," became a being by
itself in isolation, and at war with all the world.
Nevertheless, for long mankind has striven to carry
out an apparently innate even though unavowed
tendency to overcome this spirit of isolation. These
efforts have taken the shape and visible form of
far-spreading conquests or of far-reaching religions of
ever-increasing nationalities. The German national
idea of our own time, the Catholic Church of
the Middle Ages, the Roman legions of old, are
types of these efforts. Protection, in its full sense,
is nothing but the old principle of isolation, the
"selfish" idea of the isolated tribe or of the
strongly individualistic human unit. The opposite
principle, that of free-trade, is the one which
leads man to unite with his mates ; which leads
tribes to combine when common effort is salutary,
which leads nations to ackowledge that they may
actually gain more themselves from the friendship
of other nations than from their enmity.

A most practical instance of these desirable results

is seen in the consensus of all authorities in the fact that Adam Smith and Turgot, Cobden and Chevalier, were mainly instrumental in bringing about the thorough breakdown of the ancient, long-lived and hostile antagonism between French and English. The more nations come to acknowledge this principle the more they discover they are aiding their own prosperity by aiding that of the whole world. By allowing full and proper development to the bounties of Nature the most is made of them ; and the free-trade principle thus fosters the best and greatest increase of the productive powers of the world ; an increase felt to its remotest corners. Cicero would have had cause to write " prudenter facere non dicimur" in addition to "juste non dicimur" had he experienced what men now know. Men will readily do the good if they find it coincides with the useful ; they will avoid the evil no sooner than they discover it is identical with the unprofitable. Ricardo advocated on behalf of free-trade " the pleasing conviction that we can never by freedom of commerce promote the welfare of other nations without also promoting our own." The converse of this appeals to a higher morality and is of equal truth : " we can never by freedom of commerce promote the welfare of our own nation without also promoting that of others." And the principle of protection is the very opposite to the principle of this freedom of commerce.

If, as we have seen, protection is so destructive of wealth, it may well be asked how is it that man, the basis of whose productive action is selfishness, has so long endured such an infliction. And the answer is, that protection is the inevitable accompaniment of a certain stage of what is commonly called growth in civilisation. Free-trade and protection are the opposite poles of productive endeavour; and they are the outcome of different stages of commercial development. The period when first there has been gathered a sufficiency of stored wealth to set men's minds a thinking as to the best uses to be made of it, is the epoch of the rise of economical policies. Then there first appears as a prominent principle the regulation of individual labour and skill to ensure national prosperity. This epoch arrives with either of the two stages of isolation attained, as we have seen, in the life of communities. Tribal custom was evinced in the rhythmic laws of the Norse—

> " If thou yieldest a step, take thy leave of the band."
> " 'Tis the law, and so do as thou wilt."

He that would not do as the tribe does, must leave it altogether, and becomes a foe and no longer a friend. Again, when England had reached the isolated nation stage, we find the protective policy a favourite with the statesmen among whom Lord Bacon figured. And yet, as if to protest against this human perversion of a "necessary truth," we find the leading intellects of all ages opposing its very principle. Many leading authorities, though abhorring protection, have yet allowed there may be some excuse for it in the case of young communities; but the intellect of Lord Bacon could pierce the mists of his own age, and enjoy an insight even clearer than that of many of his learned successors. He could write of a young colony, "Let there be freedom from custom till the plantation be of strength; and not only freedom from custom, but freedom to carry their commodities where they may make the best use of them." This is what the most advanced would now term a sound political economy; and yet we children of this nineteenth century vainly talk as though political economy were our own creation and a blessing unknown to our benighted forefathers. Bacon tells us even the young community must not be hampered in any way in developing its productive energies; not even are Customs duties to be laid for those purposes of revenue, or rather tribute, which were at the time the end and aim of all colonial policy, and this for fear they should *hamper the free growth of the young community.*

Curiously enough, too, in the same period, Sir Walter Raleigh stands forth as a prominent and persistent advocate for the full freedom of productive energies. The principle he contended for was, that each man should employ his labour or his capital in the way he might judge most beneficial to himself. In the House of Commons itself, speaking against the proposed compulsory cultivation of hemp, his words were, " I do not like this constraining of men to manure or use their grounds at our will, but rather wish to let every man use his ground for that for which he finds it most fit."

And there was yet another lesson in store for mankind when nations first emerged from what has been termed the isolated nation stage. One of the first economic truths that dawned on mankind was that of division of labour. By this means production in particular directions rapidly exceeded the local wants. It became evident, then, that unless the native energies were allowed to push beyond the frontiers of the nation an important amount of the national labour was rendered useless and unprofitable. This became painfully apparent in the more primitive systems of colonization adopted by the States of Western Europe. The protection afforded by mother countries to their colonies took the form of the monopoly of both the export and import trade of the colony. This policy was, in reality, based on the plea that the mother country and the colony should each lose much in order that each might gain a little.   And as Mill has shown, " There is a loss on the whole to the productive power of the world, and the mother country does not gain so much as she makes the colony lose."   When once nations felt the pressure of other nations there crept in the idea of international production ; and men were forced to allow that a selfish isolation, lessening the productive powers of mankind as a whole, lessened the productive energies of each portion thereof.

The value of combined effort on the part of all mankind came home with no uncertain teaching as soon as communications between men were rendered easy.   The rich Eastern merchants of Venice, and afterwards of Lisbon, soon found the value of sharing with the Dutch and the English the rich harvest of the North Sea fisheries.   To Roman Catholic populations this economic discovery was of great importance.   These economic convictions spread; and protection, instead of passing as the inevitable accompaniment of human energy, began to find in the first place apologists, and in the second place, and at no long date, those violent supporters who, by their very vehemence and rage, prove the inherent weakness of their case.

Protection was all-in-all in the absence of free-trade.   Protection became possible and popular when nations first turned to industry ; and protection flourished as the concomitant of faulty and inadequate communications between men. A nation by keeping itself to itself had then the best security to support itself in those days when the arm of trade was short ; when possibilities of locomotion were extremely limited. England might well seek jealously to grow her own corn and make her own ropes when she knew not of any lands that could be trusted to supply her with these things. But, taking the history of Europe, when once commerce burst her Mediterranean bonds, when once the command of the sea opened up the whole world to mankind, policies of protection lost their meaning and their use. The tribes of the world, heretofore living in jealous isolation, guarding with zeal their peculiar herds and crops, were suddenly awakened to a new state of things by the possibilities of roads and locomotion. Traffic arose, development was given to that original human propensity "to truck, barter, and exchange one thing for another . . . . common to all men, and to be found in no other race of animals." Protective policies were the swaddling-clothes with which barbarous and unskilled nations sought to foster the growth of their infant industries. But on the widening and deepening of man's ideas there ensued a more healthful opinion as to the treatment necessary. It was found far better from the first to allow the limbs free and full play, and not to forbid contact with the outside world. It was found best to allow normal and natural developments of every form of growth untramelled opportunity. And the good results have been amply apparent in the green tree; older nations have been inspired with a renewed vigour of youth. And such treatment has never failed when applied to the sapling.

CHAPTER VIII.

LIMITED PROTECTION.

§ 1. Limited Protection is Advocated by some, Provided it be *Temporary :* but this is Impossible.—§ 2. Or Tentative : and this is Impracticable.—§ 3. Or for Young Communities; but here the Means of the End outdo, in their accompanying evils, the good of the End.

§ 1. *Limited Protection is Advocated by some, Provided it be Temporary : but this is Impossible.*—Many authorities, endorsing to the full a general and just condemnation of protection pure and simple, yet hold that modified or limited protection has its time and its uses. It has been urged ere now that the evil effects of protection are minimised and the good enhanced by a due regard to certain conditions under which a protective policy becomes a benefit and not an evil to a community. But when this plea is adopted by good authorities, it is always with the proviso that this limited protection must be rigidly temporary or tentative in character.

It must be temporary they say. Those who have studied the results of protection know full well that its inevitable effect in the long run is to impair the equality of the distribution of the results of production ; or in other words to tax the many for the benefit of the few ; " to make the rich richer and the poor poorer." Ricardo tells us of France, " the fortunes of the iron-masters and cotton-spinners increased enormously under a system of artificial prices, while the condition of the mass of the people advanced less rapidly than in any other country in Europe." But, it is urged, these and all other sad results only appear by lapse of time. To maintain that skill degenerates through lack of competition, to hold that prices rule high by reason of diminished supply—is to assume a long life to protection.

Multiform are the reasons advanced in support of this theory, that, provided it be limited in point of time, a protective policy may be made to conduce to the good of the community. It is undeniable that in order to take up a profitable position in the family of communities it is necessary for a society to have within it in working order some industry wherein, owing to natural advantages, it surpasses some other communities. And a protective policy, rigidly limited in point of time, is advocated as the best means to this desirable end. " Protection," according to the covertly ironical definition in MacCulloch's Dictionary, " is the protecting or bolstering up of certain branches of domestic industry." By this pillowed support the young industry is introduced to life, and the genesis of such industry is an unqualified advantage, an undeniably beneficial end. The question, however, remains,—Is this means possible and practicable ?

The possibility, the practicability, of a temporary protection is founded on the economic plea that "Protectionists lose their strength as consumers learn their power and their interest." The economical theory involved may be perfectly sound. That the consumer will object to be taxed for the private benefit of the producer is only natural and reasonable. But that his objection will meet with success history tells us is highly problematical, if we look alone to the vast political power of the force known as vested interests. Society is not ruled by abstract laws of economy, but by the economical interests of those who for the time grasp political power. We must bear in mind that, generally speaking, every citizen is both a consumer and a producer. In the Middle Ages we meet with instances of thriving commercial cities despotically governed by a close oligarchy ; the industrial policy of such a city necessarily followed the interests of these few, and that of the many but incidentally, and, in cases, not at all. And yet the many are equally producers with the few ; and where the many govern we find the consumer still at the mercy of the producer. And not only so, but with that suicidal shortsightedness of the ignorant or the thoughtless we may often see the labouring man, in his character of producer, figuring in public as the elector of "Protection" candidates because they promise him high wages; and suffering in private, in his character of consumer, because of the high prices ensuing. Taking is everywhere a more powerful human motive than giving. A man will go through endless pain and trouble to amass wealth, but in the squandering of it he will take no heed. As a producer he will concentrate all his energies on success; as a consumer he is only too ready to rest and be thankful. When he sets his mind to the government of his community he will lay aside his position as a consumer, and take his firm stand on his rights as a producer. It is with men as producers and not as consumers that the ultimate issue lies.

Mill gives as one of his conditions for the introduction of this modified protection "certain abrogations of the duty after a fair time of trial." It is difficult, from what we know, to imagine the probability or even the possibility of the carrying out in practice such a condition. Men as consumers may see their unfair position, but as producers, each one, tasting of the joys of protection in his own branch, will put forth all his strength to keep his hold of the cup.

The Emperor Napoleon III., affording the rare historical instance of a despot forcing free-trade on an unwilling people, experienced to the full the effect of this "vested interest" opposition. Cobden has recorded Napoleon's expressed opinion on this point :—
" The difficulty is this—the monopolists may be few, the minority ; their interests are not to be compared with those of the nation ; but they are an organised body, a disciplined army, and the great consuming public is only a mob." The manufacturers, labourers, employés, and their widely ramifying connections, reaping the benefits of the protected industries, have interests of their own as producers ; these are opposed to the interests of consumers ; their own private good, their palpable advantages as producers, is directly at variance with the public good, the general advantages to consumers. But their interests are uniform and compact; the interests of consumers, quâ consumers, are multiform and heterogeneous. Force in the one case, small in the aggregate, is condensed and strong ; force in the other case, large in the aggregate, is dispersed and weak.

The consumer, as a force in the politics of government, is far inferior to the producer. The policies adopted come home directly to the producer ; the consumer feels their effects indirectly. It needs no thought on the part of the manufacturer of axe-heads to see that it is for his benefit that the importation of foreign axe-heads is forbidden. It does require thought and calculation for him to discover that this extra profit is dissipated in the enhanced prices of a thousand and one articles of consumption. So, too, the labourer at the manufactory readily sees that if axe-heads are sold in the country which are not produced there, he will not be paid for making axes; he does not see, or understand, or think of the fact that these extra wages of his vanish in the hard economical fact of a reduced purchasing power. Thus it appears to be outside the region of practical politics that protective policies, actually temporary in character, shall be successfully instituted.

§ 2. *Or Tentative: but this is Impracticable.*— For the same reasons we find the institution of tentative protection impracticable. It is certain no industry should be planted in a country concerning whose independent after-success there is the smallest doubt. For an industry once planted becomes forthwith a vested interest. And yet, sad to say, there is the undeniable truth that the introduction of an industry even of an uncertain future has a great experimental value. "Nothing," we are told, "has a greater tendency to promote improvements in any branch of production than its *trial* under a new set of conditions." The success of such a trial in a country is forthwith a productive advantage not only over its own previous status, but even over the former homes of the industry. Russia's long-lived hostility to Turkey has forced a trial in the East Indies of the hemp-producing industry. And now the Russian supply of rope fibres is greatly supplanted by the East Indian. No doubt this experimental value is an end devoutly to be consummated. In this chapter it is sufficient to point out that protection, as a means to its end, fails, even when limited in its design as a purely tentative measure— and this for the reason that, however good the design, the result brings in its train such destructive conditions as vested interests.

These evil effects are specially visible when we remember that the outcome of an experiment may be negative as well as positive. To introduce an industry as an experiment is, on the part of the wise, to admit the duty of destroying it if the result be in the negative. But in the practice of politics this has not been found practicable. In one of Mr. Bright's speeches occurs the passage : " The extraordinary distress in the United States is almost entirely to be attributed to their mistaken protective system ; to their having misdirected so much capital ; to their having, on the strength of high tariffs, promoted a great extension of business which could not be permanently sustained." Much of this protected misdirection was originally undertaken for strictly tentative purposes ; it has resulted in the setting up of various vested interests of a sort that " cannot be permanently sustained"—under, it may be added, true economic conditions.   The very perfectness of protection gives means and strength to vested interests ; and where protection is *tentative* the industry set up as an experiment is found so firmly set up as to defy knocking down.   The gravity of the issue is apparent when we remember that the claims of vested interests are specially persistent and dogged in those cases where the wrong industries have been fostered ; where the experiment has had a negative issue.   The producer becomes the more loth to yield up his claim on State protection for his venture the more he is persuaded that the industry so set up will never face with success the keen air of free competition.   Thus a fresh burden is entailed on the community either of undoing its own gratuitous labour, or of abiding the sufferer of its own acts.

§ 3. *Or for Young Communities ; but the Evils of the Means outdo the good of the End.*—Much plausible argument has been promulgated that at all events this limited protection is an unmitigated good for a young society.   Though protective policies are alone possible with societies living in communion with others, and though young societies, in which protection policies are likely and possible, are offshoots of older societies, nevertheless the young society is no mere facsimile of the parent. However old the civilization of the colonists, yet a new community encounters new conditions ; a fresh start of society is entered upon. Many of the conditions are similar to those of the old country ; but again there are other conditions superadded which are entirely different. And it is on this ground that authorities have argued that, whereas protection is originally and fundamentally an error for old countries, yet may it be a good and useful institution for the young. Protection is thus regarded as of the nurse type ; good, aye indispensable, for the youthful, but neither needed nor desired by those of maturer growth.

Here again we discover the discussion of *a* means as if it were the only means. Authorities should strive to balance the acknowledged evils of the means with the undoubted benefits of the end. We have seen the impracticable nature of the temporary and tentative theories. But the goodness of the end is certainly more visible when the industry fostered is a true natural aptitude : and the means look specially tempting when we are told they actually give a country a balance of advantage over some other of similar natural aptitudes. Adam Smith wrote—" By means of such regulations, indeed, a particular manufacture may sometimes be acquired sooner than it would have been otherwise." When one country has natural aptitudes similar in every respect to those of some other, by starting the given industry first, it gains great vantage ground; the prior acquisition of skill and experience gives it a start which may even effectually counterbalance some inferiority in the bounty of Nature. Here again we have an end enhanced in utility. But are there no better means than one that is all the while avowedly incomplete and faulty and detracts considerably from the total of benefits resulting?

We are told in dealing with young communities we have no vested interests of long standing to deal with. If this limited protection does set up vested interests, their suppression will not be so grievous a wrench to the young community. In old countries legislative interference with industry becomes occasionally necessary as the country marches along the road of scientific change. In the old countries of Europe the theoretic good of free-trade could not be set on foot without previously uprooting large vested interests. France, since the day when Colbert, in 1667, prohibited the importation of manufactured articles, raised up for herself a mountain of formidable prejudice and fallacy to support the great class interests engendered of protection. Under the

Second Empire we witnessed the curious spectacle of a government in great measure vainly defending its subjects from themselves. The one great obstacle to the action of the government in accordance with the best spirit of the day is these vested interests. Why, then, set them up in young communities? The sole logical reply possible is that there are certain ends we all know are good and desirable, and protection is the sole means to them. In a future chapter we shall ask, Are these avowedly bad means the sole means?

Protection coming upon young communities is an evil. An able article in the *Colonies* newspaper thus summarised the advantages possessed by young over old communities ;—" speedier roads to wealth, exemption from the grinding poverty which so frequently disfigures old States ; larger political freedom ; absence from mischievous vested interests to hamper the progress of society; the sense of strength; and vast confidence in the future. . . . . But they have little leisure for scientific study ; thinkers among them do not wield the authority they possess in older countries ; the true nature of measures cannot be accurately examined ; the immediate results assume a too disproportionate importance." The consequence is a tendency to which they are specially prone, of running counter to the experience of others. Among the manifestations of this tendency none is more prominent than protection. And yet is this the very antidote and opposite to each one of the advantages peculiar to a new community. It cuts up, turns, and destroys the natural roads to wealth; by mal-distribution of wealth it fosters the growth of a pauper class; it avowedly seeks justification for its gross interference with political freedom; and its sure outcome is the erection of powerful vested interests of a peculiarly mischievous character : it brings in its train a sense of weakness in the society, and soon produces a distrust in the future which disheartens and discourages fatally the enterprise of a society.

In judging of protection by the results of history, it must be borne in mind that young communities are peculiarly tenacious of life. "The plenty and cheapness of good land," wrote Adam Smith, "are such powerful causes of prosperity, that the very worst government is scarce capable of shaking altogether the efficacy of their operation." The very men become a type of excessive vitality, and possessed of a boisterous energy and superabundant confidence which renders them reckless of others' experience; and which combines with the natural agencies to give to the constitution of the community a hearty vitality which the most violent distemper of protection may scarce endanger. It is for this reason that nations have been so much misled by appearances. But with the older established United States things are different. "The great fact that the tide of immigration which once flowed so steadily towards the great Republic is now turned back to Canada, and even to Great Britain, proves that even the enormous resources of the United States cannot long bear the strain caused by artificial and unsound restriction. And this ought to modify the idea that protection and prosperity go together." Though failure is eventually in store for such young communities as adopt protective policies, yet for long their great vitality enables them to conceal the symptoms of the disease until it has taken so sharp a hold on their system that the indications of a coming break-up of the constitution appear with a suddenness which prevents all remedial measures.

Why should a colony for instance put in force its corporate power to start manufacturers of a special type within its boundaries. If labour and capital find more remunerative employment when left alone, where is the good of their being forced to divert their energies to the production of goods which other countries can supply them with at lower price? Natural growth will develop those altered conditions in which labour and capital turn naturally to manufacture. For instance, in the Australian colonies at the present day there is a population about half that of London ; yet the country in its occupation is nearly as large as Europe ; and so far as yet occupied, is fertile in every sense. Wool-growing, cattle and horse breeding, mining, wheat-growing, these are the branches of production most profitable under the circumstances. And to attempt to force the immigrant to stay in the port of arrival as a factory hand is to mistake altogether the true channel to success. Protection has no less evil effect in new countries than in old. If it differ in kind it is no less real in effect. Its only claim to consideration is on the assumption that the good end sought is to be attained by this means alone. And even this means is acknowledged to be accompanied by many undesirable effects. What if there be other means to the same end not similarly circumstanced ?

CHAPTER IX.

§ 1. Protection as a means is Inefficient—§ 2. Yet there are other efficient means to the same end—§ 3. Protection in other Communities—§ 4. Some Bounties—§ 5. Free-trade ; in the Genesis of Industries, and in the Discovery of the most Lucrative.

§ 1. *Protection considered as a means to its end is inefficient.*—When weighed in the balance of economical results, protection is found wanting. The end sought by protection is the fostering of industrial energy ; the increase, in other words, of the productive industry of man ; of the results of his labour ; of the profits of his capital. And the means adopted by protection is the exclusion of the competition of other societies of men outside the limits of the particular community seeking thus to develop its own resources. Yet even when plausible successes attend particular efforts the gross balance is always found to be on the wrong side.

§ 2. *There are other efficient means.*—These results which we have detailed might be deemed a sufficient condemnation of protection. But there is another and entirely different class of arguments, which perhaps best demonstrate the essential uselessness of protection. It is found that other means actually attain the same end without that probable surplus of loss by the way which protection involves. It may with reason be asked what is there in the conditions of the existence of a community which calls for the adoption of measures directly regulating the indirect freedom or " natural course" of circumstances. Is there any reason or necessity for throwing on to the burdened shoulders of government such, at the least problematical, means to an end as protection ? A distinct negative to such a question is forced on us when we are brought to consider that any and every good effect of protection may be, and has been, brought about by other means.

Many advocates of protection. appear to proceed entirely on the assumption that the end sought is good in general principle, but that in particular applications we must make concessions to circumstances. They tell us protection fosters industrial energy ; but, in so doing, in its train it will bring about in some cases a balance of good results, and in other cases a balance of evil ; and before we condemn it for thus risking evil results, we must remember that it is possible for it to bring about good. The end is good. But such a line of argument necessitates the tacit assumption that protection is the *only* means to the end. Were this so it might, of course, be correct or right to apply the general principle, trusting that particular circumstances would turn out favourable. But if there are other and better means to the same end, why trouble ourselves with a means which is acknowledged to be at best but problematic in beneficial effect ? In the advocacy of protection as good for young communities, though bad for old, we find this fallacy ruling. An analogical line has been taken. We are told that though protection is bad for old communities, that is no reason why it should not be good for the young. Pap is bad food for grown men; but good for children. To deny this is as illogical as to argue man is a flesh-eating animal, therefore feed a baby on meat and not on pap. But suppose it is found that revalenta arabica is far superior to pap in developing all the proper growths in the child, are we still to feed children on pap ? Pap may be bad food for the grown up ; but the question none the less remains, is it the *best* food for the young. Protection is adopted as a means, but no question is asked as to whether other means are not far superior in every respect.

The main advantage credited to protection is the genesis or origination of industries within a community. Yet if we look to history we shall find the

most unexpected industrial fields opened up, not
only without the aid of protection, but often because
of the presence of its opposite, free-trade. Saxony
and Switzerland have become flourishing manufacturing countries without any kind of legislative interference ; and this, in spite of the fact that both
countries are under great disadvantages in regard
to industrial production.   Means of transport,
whether for the supply of raw material, or for the
export of the manufactured articles, are far inferior
to those of other lands, and yet these industries
rise and flourish. Again, take the case of Lyons—
far distant both from the places which produce the
material, and the places which consume the commodities of its manufacture—this city nevertheless
flourishes as the centre of a most profitable industry.
Sicilians grow silk and send it to Lyons to be
returned to them to deck their bodies withal. Again
what system of protection could ever have started in
Dundee the profitable industry of marmalade
making? Oranges travel 2000 miles to feed this
industry. Dundee, too, is the meeting point between
tropical India and the Arctic circle. Whale oil is
the best natural dressing for rendering jute service-
able as a foundation for cheap carpets. Free-trade
enables a large shipping interest to bring these two
products of distant climes face to face. Natural

capacities and the aptitudes of experience bring about far more incongruous results than protection can even dream of. The truths of untrammeled nature are stronger than the fictions of benighted visionaries.

We may take three exemplary types of other means which bring about the boasted good results of protection: yet are burdened by none of the objections.

§ 3. *Protection in other communities*, it has frequently been noticed, has a tendency to promote in the one community precisely similar industries to those protected in the others. There is, as it were, a natural lex talionis ever on the watch to adjust matters naturally. Man proposes, Heaven disposes, or the " Reign of Law" would be a meaningless myth. Suppose the manufacturer of some new commodity of general use—say telephones—be rigorously protected on the Continent of Europe in each separate State. The prices of telephones will rise in each community in proportion as such community has to overcome difficulties in obtaining the requisite materials, experience, and skill. This rise in price naturally leads the inhabitants of, say England, to despair of obtaining their telephones from the Continent, and to set up and start making them on their own account. And the telephone manufacturers of many of the countries who were inferior in this particular industry will eventually carry on the manufacture only at a loss to themselves and to their community. Whereas the people of England find developing in their midst a new industry through no policy of their own.

§ 4. *Bounties.*—A second exemplary type of the "other means" is to be found in duly regulated systems of bounties. These means are specially applicable to the circumstances of young societies. And they are in accord with the true theory of government interference. Mill well says that government is in duty bound to do "those things which are made incumbent on it by the helplessness of the public—in such a manner as shall tend not to increase and perpetuate, but to correct such helplessness." The assistance of government must not be a substitute for man's own labour, skill, or prudence, but merely the adjunct to insure to him, if possible, the road to success by these legitimate means.

There are two methods of procedure open to government to influence the conduct of the citizens. Mill classes these two methods under the heads "authoritative" and "non-authoritative" interference; a division which brings to mind the Kantian "categorical" and "hypothetical" "imperations." The one issues a command, and confirms it by penalty : commands, threatens, sanctions ; ἃ μὴ κελενέι ἀπογορευέι. The other proceeds by means of advice, information, incentive; "what the law does not forbid it sanctions." It is this latter class of interference which alone is beneficial and healthy in economical questions. Protection belongs to the former class.

The main point of the system of these bounties is that it leaves the responsibility of success or failure entirely with the individual. The plea of the fallibility of governments fails to apply. No expense is entailed on the community from any errors of expectation : if the industry fails to thrive, or, in other words, to enrich the community, there is no loss to the State. The whole burden falls on the individual. He may listen to the exhortation of the government incentive or not as he will; yet failure rests on his shoulders alone; and if he is successful the community in fact repays to him in the shape of a bounty part of those new profits which his enterprise has enabled the community to enjoy. And though it thus burdens the individual with the responsibility of failure, yet it is a properly active type of government interference. It is not that passive type of which Adam Smith speaks, "which affords to industry the only encouragement it requires—some tolerable security that it shall enjoy the fruits of its own labour." It is not a limitation to that policy of "masterly inactivity" or negative protection which is based on the adage, each man in doing the best for himself is doing the best for the State.   This system in addition conceives that the State has corporate duties towards its individual citizens as representing the unity of which it is composed, beyond those of mere protection of life and property.

The basis of a true bounty system is that there are pecuniary risks incident to the attempting new industries, and it is held that the wise community will collectively set up some premium to induce enterprise to run this risk ; though the risk is borne by the individual in the event of failure.   An industry that is successful yields profit to the individual who undertakes it; yet in so doing it yields profit to the community at large, and the system of true bounties is the addition by the community, out of its share of the profits of something, to the profits which legitimately fell to the individual.   The introducer of the industry thus gains more than his due share of profit, and is thus enabled to run greater risk.   At the same time if loss ensue the community does not suffer as a body.   But the loss comes directly home to the individual alone ; and this will insure more individual caution and labour.   As a consumer the whole community will barely notice the enhanced prices which bolster up protective manufacture.   But as a producer, seeking the aid of the community, each individual will endeavour his utmost when he knows that his receipt of this aid depends entirely on the success of his own efforts.

Other systems of bounties have been advocated. It has been proposed, for instance, to tax an article when imported, but to give a drawback of equal amount on the article when exported. Taking corn as an instance, each imported bushel pays so much duty; and then on every·bushel the farmers can grow and export they receive a drawback to the amount of this duty. Thus the farmers are induced to grow wheat for the home market, because foreign supplies are prohibited. And then if the farmer has any surplus yield he can undersell the foreigner by reason of his receiving this drawback. The question remains, who pays the duty on the imported corn, and who pays the drawback on the exported? And the answer is the consumer. The consumer, if he would buy foreign corn, has to pay an artificially high price for it; he has further to reward his farming country-men for the benefits they enjoy in "good years" in the shape of surplus harvests. And then paying the duty on imported corn tends to lessen the imported supply, and paying the drawback on home-grown corn sends that out of the country, and tends to lessen the home-grown supply. This decreased supply sends up prices. Thus on the whole there is a very con-siderable loss to the consumer. In other words, the aggregate wealth of the community is seriously lessened.

Bounties of the right type are *temporary* and *tentative*; but they are *incentive* and not *protective*. They are indeed a government interference with capital and labour; but their influence is national and not international. A bonus on the first cargo for export of some particular commodity, or on the " discovery" of " payable" goldfields is, eo ipso, temporary. It is awarded no sooner than the industry has started on a successful course ; and when awarded it ceases. It has thus nothing whatever to do with the institution of vested interests. A bounty of this type is a definite and certain sum to be taken from the pockets of the people only after the industry has proved of intrinsic value to the people. The consumer only pays for his commodity when he receives it in proper condition. The community says it will give £500 for the discovery of a " paying" goldfield within its estate: men may bring " Chinamen's diggings" and other inadequate discoveries, but the community will none of them. No expense is entailed until the actual commodity required is handed over to the State.

To determine, for instance, that soil and climate have scientifically a capacity for tea-production, and to determine on the payment of a definite sum of money, as bonus or bounty on the successful production of a first cargo of tea, is a healthy and sound economical plan for developing the industry of tea-growing. Carlyle well says in reference to protection in our colonies,—" No country under the sky has ever got manufactures except by spending the funds of the State to plant them, and, unless Australia does that she will get no manufactures." Where " countries under the sky" go wrong is in their system of spending the funds of the State. Protection by both duties and high prices takes money out of the pockets of the community and hands it over to one class of the population, without necessarily receiving in return the benefits of *successful* enterprise, to distribute again among the pockets of the people.

Bounties may be established in kind. Thus the Government of New South Wales, in order to encourage wine-growing, authorises any owner whose vineyard exceeds a certain acreage in extent, to set up a private still and enjoy the proceeds thereof. But such a bounty encroaches upon, if it does not touch, that hard and fast line of demarcation which must jealously subsist between temporary and permanent bounties. These latter become nothing more nor less than class protection. A striking example is that of the English linen manufacture. In this trade, bounties to the amount of £400,000 were annually awarded for nearly a century. This was nothing less than permanent protection. When these bounties were abolished, this particular industry was of sufficient strength to face successfully all competition. The question remains for how long had the national funds been annually made presents of to the lucky class of linen manufacturers. Undeniably vast sums had left the pocket of the nation for the coffers of the few. This evil state of things died a stubborn and a lingering death, because of the concomitant growth of a network of vested interests of varied character, which the very success of the industry had brought into being. Government aid may originate, but it may never perpetuate, industries.

§ 5. *Free-trade.*—A third exemplary type of "other means," which accomplish the end sought by protection, is free-trade itself. Protection seeks, for instance, to introduce manufacturing industry. Free-trade lowers the price of raw materials in a country; and this price is the main regulator of the profits of manufacture; in other words, of the success of manufacturing industry. Among the very first effects of free-trade in England, was the fact that the British manufacturer was enabled to undersell all others in the markets of the world, because of the repeal of all duties on manufacturing materials. This repeal thus enabled the inhabitants of England to make use of their great natural advantages in the possession of coal and minerals. In short, free-trade directly fostered the growth of a manufacturing industry which had lain entirely dormant in the embrace of a strict protection.

Again, protection is advocated as a means to the genesis in a country of its true industries. But it is free-trade which determines at once which industries are the true industries ; and it is entirely clear of those errors of anticipation, which must always form a large ingredient in the devised policies of an essentially fallible human nature. It is thus a safe means to an end to which protection is at best but a lucky means.

History points this fact with telling emphasis. We have seen that in the development of a community, protection is a phenomenon of an advanced stage of isolation. Thus, in the history of communities there is a period wherein protection has had a lengthy reign. It has fostered and built up certain industries. Yet for many of these other countries have a greater natural aptitude, and, as the recognition of them among other qualities of neighbouring communities begins to prevail, so do those who personally prosper by these wrong industries feel that unless protection be preserved they will suffer personally. In a word, vested interests prevent the community from enjoying the benefits of the better natural aptitudes of neighbouring countries. Thus, protection has a tendency, even if to foster the right industries, in the same breath to neutralise the benefits of this by setting up cheek by jowl with them the wrong industries. Free-trade not only fosters the right industries, but it destroys the wrong, if they are previously set up. And, seeing that in practice economical developments belongs to economical history—free-trade usually steps in in its place as a successor to protection.

The introduction of free-trade has however been opposed on this very ground. It is acknowledged that free-trade may be a better means to the end than protection—but it is advanced that free-trade can only come in over the fallen bodies of many established industries. This has been the great argument of all first opponents of free-trade. They say, the benefits you free-traders promise will not repay the destruction involved in its introduction. Such an argument involves an obsolete theory; one indeed which fits well with the obsolete ideas of an obsolete age of isolation. In the realm of political economy as in that of the physical sciences there is not nor can be annihilation of force. The destruction of a trade or industry is, in reality, the transference of its economical forces to some other form. The actual body or corporation, the class or the individual, may even suffer extinction, but the force passes to other and more lucrative opportunities of usefulness.

Perhaps no more notable example of this is to be seen than the introduction of machinery in aid of human labour. Hand labour at the first stands aghast. Prophecies are rife that with the introduction of reaping machines the industry of the reaper will be destroyed. We may see this fallacious argument still appearing in the public statements of high authorities. Many a time do we find agriculturists boasting of their labour-saving machinery; many a time do we hear of the supersession of manual labour by machines. Yet, if we look with unprejudiced eye on the true state of the cause we shall find that human labour is every whit as necessary. The reaping machine does not save human labour—that is still as necessary as ever, but it enables it to accomplish with certainty what before was uncertain; to accomplish with speed what before demanded much time; and in every way, in short, not to do away with labour, but to render it more profitable in results, and consequently to raise its value.

Again, when railways were first introduced into England, learned were the prophecies throughout the length and breadth of the land that an evil day had come upon England's horses, and that all the profitable industries connected with these hitherto indispensable animals—that horse-breeders, horse-food growers, post-keepers, inn-keepers, and all concerned—were ruined men, whose special industry was destroyed. Yet in spite of these learned prophecies there arose a demand for horses far greater than had been known before : and the prices of horses rose to an unprecedented and previously inconceivable height. These learned prophets had omitted to notice that railways facilitated carriage a hundred-fold : and there resulted from this the opportunities of an immensely increased production. Markets were placed within easy reach of every district, of every product. The industrial force embodied in the horse had been driven from the industry of the carrying trade, but not with annihilation ; the same embodiment of force had found other and more remunerative employment in the economy of the State. From his former field of energy he had been driven by a far more effective competitor : but this superior effectiveness of energy opened up for his energies the various other fields in which, by the gauge of price, we find his energies to be more profitable than in their old place in front of the slow-travelling waggon of the last century.

The transference of economic force may be brought about either by free-trade or by protection. But in the one case the forces *must* proceed to the most profitable field for their energy ; in the other their transference is entirely arbitrary, and has no actual connection with the profitable nature of the ensuing results. An arbitrary transference may of course be instituted on plausible pleas, but in its very nature it is a forced transference, bound in the bonds of interest foreign to the purpose. The horse is a type of the forces which free-trade sets loose ; which protection retains in bonds. Capital, labour, natural agencies, are ready to turn to their most profitable uses once free-trade allows of their ready transference to more suitable fields. But their transference is not their annihilation ; economic force is indestructible.

Nor are these prognostications of the learned any less liable to the human imperfections of bad logic than the decisions of governments. Indeed, what are classed as " fallacious modes of reasoning" in logic books seem to prevail in the " working" intellect of the average man with far greater frequency than the "correct modes of reasoning." Facts, practical results, are the only reliable touchstones of theoretic schemes. And these are to be experienced in production by freedom and not by restriction. Unless different powers be compared together who shall say which is strongest of them ? The rigid protection of the Napoleonic Continent fostered in English hands a great carrying trade. On the reappearance of peace and the repeal of the Navigation Acts, the English were found established as the great sea-carriers ; they had set up claims on

the confidence of the world in this capacity; serious
competition seemed beyond the hope of others. The
English Protectionist school could not understand
this prosperous result of freedom; its existence was
fact; and they had perforce to content themselves
with vague prophecies of its ultimate failure.
Sir A. Alison wrote, so late as 1852, "The
repeal of the Navigation Laws in 1849 have given
such encouragement to foreign shipping in preference to our own, that in a few years, if the same
system continue, more than half of our whole commerce will have passed into the hands of foreign
States." But a sufficient answer to this is the fact
that English shipping has increased four-fold *since* the
throwing open of her trade to the competition of the
world. The fact was that in this case England,
through the rigid protection of others, had developed
an industry which the open air of free competition
showed to be the proper development of her natural
aptitudes. Her large proportion of coast afforded
ready to hand sea-going material in skill and muscle,
and her geographical position aided all this. She occupied the most eligible site for the port of Europe.
The long waterways of the Baltic and the Mediterranean meet in her; and she stands out to command
Atlantic trade. And to more distant quarters the
Suez Canal, the Atlantic, both North and South, and

the coming Panama Canal are the three great routes ; and these again centre in England. Free-trade has thus brought England to her proper position. Her commercial greatness is the outcome of natural aptitudes ; but an outcome which might never have been realised had the ideas of a certain school prevailed, and had we selfishly supposed that freedom for our shipping should not be permitted, seeing that it involved as well encouragement to foreign shipping.

Again, Canada now takes rank as the fourth of the great mercantile communities of the world. This is no small result to have been brought about within half a century. It arose under the pressure of protection of other lands. The rising commerce of England when cut off from the Continent, obliged her to seek elsewhere for that supply of ships which Europe refused her. Canada happened to possess the natural aptitudes for the supply : inexhaustible forests ; a long coast-line ; a seafaring and hardy population. At once ship-building and sea-voyaging became her distinctive characteristics. It may be noted, too, that the best seamen ever come from northern climates. This may be in the main due to the more boisterous nature of their native-elements. Far more seamanship and hardihood is called out in struggling with the continuous gales of the north than in making the most of the trade winds of more temperate zones. The Dutch and the English and the Americans—fed by contingents from Norway and Sweden—the seamen, that is, of the more boisterous seas have acquired a vast supremacy in the struggle of the survival of the fittest at sea. Spaniards, Portuguese, Italians, Arabs —each at one time in undisputed possession of the ocean trade—have had to yield before these nations cradled in the wild waves of the North seas. This fact has no doubt aided the Canadians to retain a supremacy over their brethren in the United States. And combined with this cause we notice the effect of that " protection in other lands" which arose out of the Great War in the States.

Thus we have seen free-trade accomplish well what protection accomplishes ill. It follows that nothing, not excepting the speciously obstructive power of vested interests, may for one moment be allowed to stand in the way of the ready flow of capital and labour and energy to their most profitable uses by the means of freedom and liberty.

CHAPTER X.

§ 1. One-sided free-trade—§ 2. Reciprocity illogical and impracticable—§ 3. The true statement of the case.

§ 1. *One-sided free-trade.*—We have hitherto seen that protection is the bad and free-trade the good means to the end of assuring the best success to industrial energy. In other words, there must be free production and free exchange of commodities if the higher form of productive success is to be attained. What is known as cheap production is the secret and basis of industrial success. But the producer is himself a consumer; and cheap production depends ultimately on the power of the producer to obtain freely and cheaply what he consumes. In some thoroughly scientific articles in the *Colonies* newspaper the whole case was stated with admirable clearness. The rationale of free-trade is most succinctly set out in the following quotation from one of these articles :—

"The foreign producer is not the rival, but the "friend and benefactor of the colonial labourer and

"merchant; just as the man who makes shoes for us
"at a moderate cost does us a valuable service. A
"shopkeeper who cried aloud that the shopkeepers
"in other trades were his rivals and enemies would
"be thought fit for Bedlam; yet this is precisely
"what the protectionist does. We buy of others
"because we get our goods in that way more cheaply
"and of better quality than if we were to try to
"make them .ourselves; and the fact that we do
"buy rather than make, is a complete proof that we
"find a clear profit and advantage in employing
"another man's labour for making those goods in
"the place of our own. Buying of a foreign country
"is the same identical process with buying in
"shops in our own country. All trade, of whatever
"kind, large or small, across the street or over the
"ocean, is nothing but an exchange of goods of
"equal value. It knows of nothing else but the
"things exchanged; it is profoundly unconcerned
"with geography, nationality, or any other idea than
"the worth of the things exchanged. In every act
"of trade—and every purchase, even of a penny
"roll, is an act of trade—both sides gain : each
"prefers the goods he receives to those he gives
"away. The colonial purchaser of European manu-
"factures finds that it is more profitable to him to
"make colonial goods to send over to Europe in
"exchange, than to manufacture them for himself.

" He sets to work on those articles which he feels
" he can produce more efficiently and more cheaply
" than the European ; he spends less time and cost
" on them than he would have laid out on manufac-
" turing the European goods." But there remains the
grave question, Is this desirable free-trade possible in
the world of to-day ? Do these other shopkeepers in
other trades act to us as rivals or as friends. Is it not
rather a fact that we, the shoemakers, find the bakers
willing indeed to sell us their bread, but obstinately
set upon making their own shoes as best they may ?

In England during the transition period from protection to free-trade it was acknowledged that there
must necessarily be two parties to any system of real
free-trade. This latter system came in in 1846 on
the expressed basis that "The commodities of other
countries are clearly as useful to us as they can
possibly be, whether other countries get paid for them
directly, by giving reciprocal freedom to our English
goods, or prefer to let the account balance itself in
some of the thousand indirect methods which constitute the untold resources and the new power of
modern cosmopolitan commerce." It has, however,
been objected that in this use of the term "cosmopolitan commerce" there is implied the fact that the
whole world is acting on the principles of this free-
trade. Provided all the shopkeepers abide by the
truths of division of labour, and each produce alone

his special class of commodities, no doubt there will reign a true cosmopolitan commerce, whether the baker gets paid for a week's bread with a pair of shoes, or whether he receives the ten shillings which the butcher has paid for the shoes.　But if the baker determine to make for himself inferior slippers and to feed inferior mutton in his back-yard the commerce of the community will not proceed on the same or similar principles.

If we are to continue to be supplied by others we must supply them; and if we are to continue to supply them they must continue to supply us.　If we supply others we hand over to them what is to us the result of our labour: we give to them so much of our own "stored work."　If they supply us they give to us so much of their own "stored work."　But the fund of "stored work" to be drawn upon depends on the proper activity of productive industry.　We may buy provisions from America with our cutlery—but we can only continue to do so so long as we continue to produce cutlery.　A country may be possessed of an enormous fund of this "stored work" of capital.　With this fund it may for a long while pay for the enjoyment and use of the "stored work" of other lands; but in the end this fund must disappear unless it is replenished by continued exertion and productive industry. The one condition of this continued industry is the fact that its commodities will be taken in payment by those who supply the other wants of the producer. Unless this is the case the producer is proceeding on a course which can but end in the impoverishment of himself and the enrichment of those that supply him. He will merely transfer to them gradually the whole of his stock of "stored work" without in the meantime filling its place with other wealth. So is it with nations. We may profitably picture the case of one nation living in a community of nations among which it alone adopts the principles of real free-trade. The other rigidly protectionist nations supply it with greater facility than it can supply them. This lesser facility—on its part implies a greater expenditure of "stored work" of wealth—in payment of what it is supplied with. And in the end it might be supposed that this nation would be impoverished, and all the other nations share the enriching division of its own original fund of "stored work."

If we look to these features alone we should at once conclude that a free-trade policy is fatal for a nation so circumstanced. But history tells a different tale. England was so circumstanced from 1846 to 1876 ; and yet England became enriched to a far greater extent and with far greater rapidity

than the surrounding protectionist States. The fact is that free-trade favours and protection hampers production. The free-trade nation obtains more of what it consumes for the amount of " stored work" it pays away than does the protectionist nation. And much of what it consumes of food and raw material is a direct energiser of its productive capacity. The " bounty fed" sugar of France under-selling Bristol sugar in the English market, raises all workmen's wages throughout England. But the tax on English iron entering Germany lowers all work-men's wages throughout Germany. A day's labour will purchase four pounds of sugar at 6*d.* per lb. ; but it will purchase eight pounds of sugar 3*d.* per lb. A day's labour will purchase one hammer for 1*s.* 6*d.*, but it will purchase two if iron. is so cheap that hammers can be made at half that price. Again, free trade increases indefinitely the area of supply, and so the steady income, and reliable quality of all the manufacturers' and the consumers' needs. It is only if we omit to notice the fact that free-trade favours and protection hampers the proper activity of productive industry that we can bring ourselves even to face the question of discussing protection in the same breath with free-trade. Reason and experience prove free-trade to be an unmitigated blessing : and show that this is the case even in its very partial and semi-fulfilled application to one free-trade nation existing in a community of protectionist nations.

But people are blind to these facts, and they become specially liable to this blindness in seasons of commercial depression. We want peace and confidence, let us say, in South Africa : to establish this we are told, we must go to war. Free-trade is a blessing : But to establish this we must adopt protection. In either case it is a question of balance. If the war cost 20 million sterling, but yield, in increased production, 200 million, the war is economically a justifiable means. But when have we any guarantee that protection can achieve a similar balance? The question is indeed much discussed under the plea of the introduction of reciprocity.

§ 2. *Reciprocity illogical and impracticable.*—What then is the nature of this reciprocity, this substitute that is proposed as the efficient, because the only possible, means of securing all the advantages attainable in a free-trade direction, when free-trade itself can only be one-sided. Its supporters, in common with all advocates of the application of any theory, lay claim to the title of common sense for their theory. If common sense be anything more than an unmeaning name it is that natural sagacity which combines fact and theory *aright* : consequently to say of a theory that it is a common-sense theory is to assert of it that it is in true accord with right practice. The base of reciprocity is to do to others as they do to you : free-trade for free-traders ; duties for those that impose duties. There is a taking simplicity about this theory which commends it readily to that large section of public opinion which for want of time and knowledge mistakes semi-informed and thoughtless conclusions for common sense. We are told this theory is the common meeting ground of the free-trader and the protectionist. And those who agree with Bastiat that reciprocity is merely a form of inconsistent protection are met with the rebuff that it is in reality merely a form of inconsistent free-trade necessitated by peculiar circumstances. If we endorse Adam Smith's declaration that by adopting a policy of retaliation "the sneaking arts of underling tradesmen are thus erected into political maxims for the conduct of a great Empire," we are met by the retort that, in days when free-trade is impracticable, it would seem true that great Empires are composed of underling tradesmen, and must mould their policies accordingly.

Again, some advocates of reciprocity point out that Adam Smith himself admitted that if a foreign government, by granting bounties or by prohibiting the admission of the products of another country, interfered with free-trade, to that extent the country whose trade was injured was absolved from the doctrine of non-interference. No doubt the country thus treated is absolved so far as the equity of the case is concerned ; but this is a very different thing from saying that it is absolved so far as the economy of the case is concerned. It is no doubt true that were France to prohibit the admission of the products of England into France, England would have equitable justification in refusing to admit French goods. England would have right on her side; but she would not have reason. She would simply be depriving herself of much that she needed, because Frenchmen chose to follow a similar suicidal course.

There is much kindliness about reciprocity ; it is not always retaliatory. Friendly discriminating duties have been imposed by two or more communities in favour of one another: and this of course necessarily includes the exclusion of all other communities. Such results prevailed in the latter stage of the old-world colonial policies—when the great end sought was the monopoly by the mother-country of the whole trade of her colonies. In reality this was an unconscious tribute to the benefits of free-trade ; a modification by way of protest, of harsh protection. The markets of both mother-country and colony were so far circumscribed; both demand and supply were arbitrarily interfered with. The real result of this policy was that the mother-country and the colony each consented to forego much possible profit in order that each might enjoy a certain little. The mother-country and the colony, by confining their intercourse to themselves, no doubt shut out the products of other countries ; at the same time they closed to themselves not only other foreign markets for their own products but also other and probably better sources of supply of the raw materials and other necessaries of consumption. Such policies could be rightly based on but one plea ; and this was that foreign markets not only would be, but actually were, closed against them by agencies over which they had no control. It was held that the policies regulating foreign markets were such as to render the possible larger profits of a more generous policy of so problematical a nature that the certain little gained had a higher actual value. This historical phase of the question readily demonstrates that human nature strives to secure assured opportunities of exchange, even upon most adverse conditions.

In such instances reciprocity is seen to be set up as a means of escape from protection ; but it is seen at once to possess the spirit and body, even if not the form, of protection. It is simply a plausible system which under a veil of equity conceals the nakedness of a vicious system. If we tear away this veil we find that restrictions are placed on the entry into one country of the products of some other, in order that similar products may be produced in that country. This is naked protection. And it induces all the obvious evils in its train. It courts retaliation : and by its means an industry is fostered, and by the same act the markets for the commodities of the industry are closed. Before the union, Ireland thus protected her industries. England was driven to retaliation, and confined Irish commodities to the Irish market ; glut was the result ; supply exceeded demand ; and widespread ruin and waste ensued.

But though reciprocity is protection, it is necessary to bear in mind a class of duties which public opinion often wrongly classes with those imposed for the purposes of reciprocity. There are duties, discriminating directly between home and foreign productive energy, which are not protective ; and for the reason that they are imposed for purposes of revenue alone. Thus a duty is laid on the importation of a foreign commodity because of the existence of an excise tax on the home production of the commodity ; otherwise would the untaxed competition of the foreign article have no other effect than the destruction of the home industry, for the sole reason that it was burdened with the task of supplying revenue. If a brewer pays a tax on the malt he uses it is obvious that if a foreign brewer, contributing no malt tax to the revenue, is allowed to compete without let or hindrance, the native brewer can no longer brew. The rationale of this policy has been much questioned. Ricardo declares such a duty to be little else than a bounty paid to the foreign producer by the home consumer. If such a tax is set on hats the foreign manufacturer obtains the normal market price, and in addition he pays his entrance into a new market with the addition to this price the local duty rendered necessary, and which is paid by the local consumer. But these duties do not preserve or foster an industry; they simply enable revenue to be raised from such sources as can best provide it. Indeed, if it may be said of them that they foster any industry, it is that of the foreign competitor; and by introducing such competition the consumer should be benefited.

Duties imposed for purposes of reciprocity, on the other hand, discriminate between articles of foreign and home production, for the express and avowed purpose of fostering the home production. But there are two types of reciprocity. The one type is a naked evil. It simply seeks to save from the natural and wholesome doom of open competition some industry that has shown itself inferior to that of the foreigner. This is simply to establish a poor-rate for the support of certain unprofitable workers. The citizens at large contribute from their hard-won profits to make up the deficiencies of a few of their number, who are devoting their energies to work that does not "pay." The other type has much more plausibility on its surface : it is based on the argument that when a foreign country gives to its own producers unnatural advantages men must take some means to counteract the evil effects of this action of outsiders on their home production.

But this is to ignore the fact that such unnatural advantages, and they are specially designated unnatural, must in the end bring upon themselves their own destruction. And this destruction must come upon them with greater speed than the indirect effect of their competition on industries flourishing under truer or more natural conditions. Such is the undoubted logic of the question ; and such has been the teaching of experience. The thinking community will notice the existence of hostile tariffs, but it will say with Carlyle, "hostile tariffs may arise and shut us out, but they will fall and let us in." Times of commercial depression teach the worthlessness of protected industry by the fact of the far more intense distress which prevails in lands where protection rules than in those presided over by free-trade. All authorities set down the distress in England from 1839–42 as ten times greater than that suffered in the commercial depression in 1877–9. And there is no doubt but that policies of restriction raise prices and curtail supplies, while more liberal policies have an exactly opposite result ; and low prices and abundance of supplies are the main instincts to the alleviation of commercial depression.

Reciprocity involves much difficulty of collection, especially in the task of discriminating the origin of commodities. Trans-shipment in foreign countries may bring goods through clear of harsh duties. And again, reciprocity involves much treaty work and continued revision. This would impose upon trade a most ruinous uncertainty ; and would bring the producers of each country most directly under the local political struggles of distant lands. These difficulties have been found to operate with sufficient evil effect even when only one country imposes duties ; and these difficulties become doubly complicated when two countries are involving themselves in rival duties.

The great defence of reciprocity rests on its being a practicable alternative to impracticable free-trade. But that it is practicable or in any sense an alternative, has yet to be shown. Free-trade has come into most profitable existence ; the sole complaint, even of the advocates of reciprocity, is that free-trade is not universal. The very success of free-trade seems to generate opposition rather than belief. And some advocates of reciprocity base their advocacy on the hope that reciprocity is the means to instilling a belief in free-trade. They have not yet shown cause, however, why a nation which has enjoyed unparalleled success, and which has passed through great commercial depressions with far less misery and distress to itself than that endured by other nations, should turn aside from the prosperous course, on the vague chance of attracting others to follow a course from which it has itself turned aside.

§ 3. *The true Statement of the Case.*—Lord Lytton's Mr. Caxton gives us an able disquisition on the " life integral" and the " life fractional :" the one being that portion of life we spend altogether on ourselves, and the other that seized upon and invaded by other people. It is in the " life fractional" that man becomes of direct use to his fellows. So with States, their highest economic value is in their "life fractional ;" where that is, in other words, they combine with other States in energising production. But such a life is only possible provided other States live also lives fractional. For, if they shut themselves up in themselves, however much we may deplore the waste of human opportunity, it avails nothing for us to hold ourselves free and ready to combine. The last thirty years have no doubt advanced nations far along the road that leads away from the stage of

national isolation ; they are fast realising the attainment of the idea that they are members one of
another. But they fail to act up to this idea.
Absolute free-trade will become fact when all
nations live lives fractional and not integral. And
at a stage when the tribes of the world are guided
by a ruling spirit of integral selfishness, absolute
free-trade is not to be looked for. But in such a
stage, when there is, too, every sign of a transition
period being in active progress, there need be no
despair of an increasing partial free-trade. The
secret of productive success is that man be supplied
from the largest surface *possible*. And this is the
true basis of all commercial policy ; proceeding
indeed on the lines of free-trade, but neither hoping
for nor expecting the perfect results of a universal
free-trade, when partial free-trade is all that is
possible under existing conditions. The nation is
forced by environments to live a "life integral" in some
cases, but in all others, whenever and wherever
possible, the best commercial policy will invite others
to join with it in a world-wide "life fractional."
Reciprocity is the sign that man has reached a stage
when he is consciously dissatisfied with the restrictions of isolation, and when he is in the transition
stage from protectionism to free intercourse, from
isolation to combination.

PART III.

COMMERCIAL DEPRESSIONS.

CHAPTER XI.

THE TRUE CAUSES OF COMMERCIAL DEPRESSIONS.

§ 1. Real Relation of Cause and Effect—§ 2. Fallacies concerning Commercial Depressions—Morbid view of the present and of the future; Special cases given too much prominence; Distrust in Scientific Knowledge is engendered—§ 3. The true causes of Commercial Depressions; i. Waste of Capital; ii. Waste of Labour; iii. Failure of Natural Agencies; iv. Closing of Markets; v. Glut of Markets.

§ 1. *Real Relation of Cause and Effect.*—Commercial depressions are recurring phenomena. All communities of civilised men have felt their weight. And they are perhaps, of all other instances or examples, the most explicit and clear concerning the relation of so-called cause and effect. We have mapped out for us by history the tale of many a commercial depression. And, if we illustrate each present instance by the examples of the past, we are led to the conclusion that a commercial depression is a mere sum-total of conditions in a state of simultaneous existence. Yet we find numerous authorities entirely misled by following a course piloted by those who maintain effect and cause to be a relation of sequence, of antecedent and consequent. Such pilotage invariably leads us to confined channels, where each man's special horizon is bounded by his immediate environments. In such case one theorist will hold that commercial depressions result from free-trade ; another will substitute " protectionism" as the cause consequent on which *follows* depression. Or, again, we have the politician, taking modern instances, who tells us our latest depression is the consequence of reckless expenditure of the party in power. Yet others, looking round within the walls of their manufactories and warehouses, tell us, " All this has nothing to do with policies or politics, it is simply that we producers have been producing too much, and the consequence has come upon us of widespread commercial depression."

It is this temporal idea, adopted to explain phenomena, which, not unnaturally, glamours even acute intellects. The mind that has set itself to think out that bone of contention, " time," will acknowledge that time is ultimately the creature and the tyrant of man. Yet few have given the necessary power of thought to remembering, in the every-day events of life, that time is for human beings nothing more than a mere method by which man's mind in its present stage of expansion finds it can agreeably account for much that it experiences. And this provisional method is the reality pressed beyond its due limits; and made to embrace many phenomena merely included in it for the sake of popular convenience. The mind recognises the pain of placing the finger in the flame; the act of placing the finger in the fire and the act of feeling the pain are each of them. phenomena which the mind habitually connects with the idea of time. But chained in its habit of thought, the mind is led astray to hold that the pain was consequent to placing the finger in the fire. The child will be told—your finger will be burned if you put it in the fire ; and with excusable confusion of thought the child argues—such effect will follow such action. Very little thought suffices to explain that there was no interval, even of this so-called time. How does this effect of a burnt finger come about ? Take the finger of a live human being, the mind of the same human being, matter in condition of combustion; combine these three, and there will exist *ipso facto* a burnt finger. The effect is there, then, and at once. We can say the finger would not have been burnt till the finger was put into the flame. And the popular expression may be correct enough that the pain of a burnt finger is caused by putting your finger in a flame. Yet if we would prevent this pain, this " time" explanation is at once seen to be insufficient. We must influence the mind with the fact that a portion of the human body attached to a human mind, placed within matter at a certain temperature, is then and thereby put in pain. And all the mind has to see to is the avoidance of such a combination of conditions.

Again, it may be asked, if effect is only consequent on cause, when does the one begin and the other end ? Where is the line of demarcation between the cause of putting the finger in the flame and the effect of " pain." So is it with commercial depressions ; we must seek what conditions in combination constitute the effect so named. It is this view that alone can tell us the actual diagnosis of the evil. When we know those conditions, the sum-total of which actually is the effect, then can we, each one of us in our sphere, so group these conditions that the effect shall never be in existence.

Instead, then, of seeking a temporal relation of cause and effect, we turn to the more satisfactory inquiry what *is* commercial depression. We shall see that commerce is the sign of the presence of energised productive forces ; and that commercial depression means that men expending new work and stored work on the varied bounty of Nature are unable duly to profit by their exertions. Proceeding more into detail, history will tell us that the conditions of this state of things are continually shifting and different. To superficial notice one commercial depression looks very like any other; so much is this the case that many authorities hold they proceed in cycles. To this argument much colour has been lent by the fact that one great condition of productive success is the kindliness of Nature. Many observers deem they have sufficient evidence to prove that the rainfall on this earth has, at all events for some time past, increased and decreased in eleven years' cycles. Australia, where wool-growers feel most keenly droughts and rains, is a most prominent witness to the truth of this contention. Others, again, point out that the sun-spots vary in quantity by the same periods. And though we may not see our way to asserting that the quantity of rain is the measure of commercial success, yet we can remark with much certainty that the abundance or the want of rain has a very great deal to do with the productive energy of certain communities, occupying certain parts of the earth's surface. But, this cyclic tendency is, we can see, only *one* of the conditions whose co-existence means commercial depression. A certain state of the sun's envelope does not cause commercial depression; but there is a tendency for commercial depressions to assume a cyclical period, because of the fact that one of the conditions of which they are made up has, in human experience, a cyclical periodicity.

§ 2. *Fallacies concerning Commercial Depressions.*— There is every reason then to clear the ground of many illusions and fallacies which, on a first view, cumber a soil fit in every way for more useful growths. A vigorous crop of fallacies is the inevitable accompaniment of commercial depressions; and this crop hides from cursory view the real features of the case. Thus it is in the very nature of human beings, when "bad times" arrive, at once to find fault with their actual surroundings. At such times loud cries are raised, declaiming against the commercial policy that happens to prevail at the time. Free-trade is the scapegoat in 1879, just as protection was in 1846. Reciprocity and protection again in 1879 found advocates in free-trade England, as they did in the "bad times" ten years before. And then men are only too apt to mourn over their personal miseries, omitting altogether to notice that other communities are equally or even more burdened. Thus is it that in free-trade England men cry for protection as a remedy, but do not go afield to learn that protection has done far less to mitigate or prevent "bad times" in other lands then free trade has in England. As Mr. Bright wrote to America, " in ' bad times' there are always quack doctors ready to prescribe for the sufferers a course of protection, as though it had never been tried and discarded in England long ago, and as if it had been found a successful specific in other countries."

Again, in many of these fallacies there is a strange misregard of the teachings of the past. Commercial depression acts on the political brain much after the fashion of the liver on the physical. It appears to induce morbid and melancholy views of the present and the future ; views utterly at variance with actual fact and actual experience. Thus, in all depressions, far too much heed is given to the cry that the country is obviously on the downward road to proximate failure and ruin. This cry, no doubt, becomes a salutary check on thoughtless or reckless productive energy ; but it has little to do with the real conditions of the phenomena of commercial depressions. If people in England in 1879 studied facts, they would discover that England had actually gone ahead instead of fallen back, according to the usual forebodings of ill. Productive progress in England, as in other countries, proceeds in waves of profitable energy. Comparing dates when the wave was either high or low, we get at facts that show distinct, steady advance. But, if we compare dates when the wave was high with those when the wave was low, we may come to most disheartening conclusions ; but these conclusions are far removed from the truth.

A morbid view is often induced by a prejudiced study even of statistics themselves. In England, in 1879, men found that there was a falling off of 30 per cent. in the imports and exports. They forthwith embraced despondency. But with less pre judiced eye, it was pointed out that with this fall in values there was no concomitant fall in bulk. And quantities exchanged are a truer index of industrial status than values exchanged, seeing that the bulk is real, but the value merely set out in nominal terms, and liable to a vast variety of fluctuation. It is obvious that the using statistics which are set out in the terms of money-values and not bulk, will lead to most erroneous conclusions if the mind is morbidly blind to the fact that prices have changed. And in times of commercial depression this fall of prices will be expected by those who attend to experience. In 1850 and again in 1868, as in 1879, there was a great fall in prices. But prices fall or rise from a multiplicity of causes, some of which are intimately connected with the phenomena of " bad and good times ;" while others have but little direct connection therewith. Of this latter class is the appreciation or depreciation of the precious metals ; this is a fluctuating, uncertain, and temporary condition, which must only be taken into account when it actually exists, but which is by no means the only basis of price. Again, good harvests, improved production, improved facilities for and freedom of exchange— these phenomena of good times—all lower prices. Whereas such phenomena of bad times as over-speculation, extravagant competition, or over-production, likewise lower prices. Thus the money-values of statistical reports prove most misleading guides, unless real values be attended to at the time. And statistics rightly viewed are invaluable. When the appeal came from the sugar industries in England against the invasion of French competition, it was deprived of its whole force by the statistical fact that there was no diminution in the amount in the market of sugar manufactured in England.

Again, a morbid view is taken of the future. Englishmen, for instance, see that the United States in 1858 drew nine-tenths of their manufactured articles from England : and in 1879, Americans not only manufacture for themselves, but export largely. Thence they argue that England is on the downward road to ruin : they forget that, at the worst, it is only the closing of one market to Englishmen; and of a market that must eventually re-open, or Englishmen will not be able to pay for what they take. If England possesses natural superiority or special aptitude in any division of human labour, this must eventually assert itself; and that she does possess this is seen by her steady progress on the average.

Many of these morbid views are due to the fact that men, in times of depression, have a tendency to confine their view to their own one class of production. For instance, sugar-refiners are loud in their complaint that the French bounty on sugar, though it is paid by the French taxpayer and finds its way into the pocket of the English consumer, is, nevertheless, damaging to the British sugar industries. No doubt this action of foreign nations, like bad seasons and other causes, does occasionally cause great damage to some specified industry. But in times of distress these special cases arrogate to themselves all attention. People go astray following the adage, "ex uno disce omnes." And in bad times much countenance is given to these suspicions by the fact that commercial energy is so complex in its ramifications that one trade can hardly suffer without affecting in some manner other trades. Yet it must be borne in mind that different industries depend for success on entirely different conditions, and that, therefore, if one industry is very much oppressed, there is reason for hoping that others must be prospering in proportion. Agriculture, for instance, depends intimately on the weather and the seasons ; a succession of bad years inevitably diminishes profits in this particular industry ; but, at all events in England, over-production or undue increase in the power of production are not causes which could ever cause depression in agricultural industries. The precise converse is true of such an industry as that of cotton manufacturing. Actual weather has, nor can have, nothing to do with its success : over-production may completely ruin it. Thus, conditions that engender a too active production, aid the one if they injure and kill the other. There are industries, again, which depend entirely on the amount of capital that is invested in them. The iron trade is intimately connected with capital. Thus, in times of war, States do not set about inciting capital to be spent on various productive public works. Again, in times of distress, individuals are loth to invest " fixed capital." And yet it is with the supply of machinery, of railways, of ships, that the iron trade is chiefly concerned. Moreover, in times of inflation, plant is erected frequently in excess of actual requirements, and for all these reasons the iron trade suffers, and even continues to suffer, after other trades have recovered—until productive energy has again recovered itself so far as to employ all plant already in existence, and so to require renewed supplies.

To argue, then, that because of the fact that the iron trade is depressed everything else is, is not consistent with a true explanation of facts. Yet is it tempting to the morbid views of bad times thus succinctly to explain matters. That three or four large industries should suffer in particular and concomitantly, is a necessary accompaniment of commercial depression; but that they all suffer from the same causes is evidently far removed from the truth. Nor may it be forgotten that in manufacturing countries there are endless productive energies at work, most of which are affected in the most indirect and slight manner by the depression in others. And it is this fact which is the reason that a country of energetic industry always pulls through periods of depression "with astonishing ease."

Another reason of this is often lost sight of. The panic, created by periods of crisis, does insure the saving of capital. Caution is then readily instilled. The failure of the City of Glasgow Bank will save millions of money from the risk of unlimited liability investments. Again, thrift is greatly encouraged in times of depression. Not only are palpable evidences given of its benefits, but the consumer enjoys the one-sided advantage of exceptionally low prices. The glut in the market, which often lies at the foundation of the depression, allows the consumer to reduce his expenditure, owing to the fall in prices. This renders thrift possible, and this means that capital will accumulate ready for investment when dull times pass away. Thus there is a tide in productive energy. Over-sanguine production floods the market with a spring-tide of commodities, and there is a consequent ebb running in its violence below average tides, but gaining thereby an additional impetus to bring the waters forward again towards prosperity.

Men, in times of depression, are liable to cry out against the words of the sages. Lord Dufferin, in one of his speeches, eloquently consoles colonial governors who are attacked by local politicians. " Sometimes, no matter how disconnected his personality may be from what is taking place, his name will get dragged into the controversy, and he may suddenly find himself the subject of criticism by the press of whatever party may for the moment be out of humour ; but under the circumstances he must console himself with the reflection that these spasmodic castigations are as transitory and innocuous as the discipline applied occasionally to their idol by the unsophisticated worshippers of Mumbo Jumbo when their harvests are short or a murrain visits their flocks." So, too, in times of depression, we hear that political economy is all theory, and that however good in the abstract, it is all vanity and vexation in the concrete. Assuming Mumbo Jumbo to be an anthropomorphic presentation of the powers of Nature, we can set down his treatment by his worshippers as simply due to the fact that he is the impersonification of their own ignorance of the powers of Nature. So, too, when political economy is declared to be no better than a blind leader of the blind, this castigation can readily be set down to the ignorance on the part of her assailants of her actual character and nature.

Such are some of the types of fallacies that spring up with a mushroom-like vitality in times of depression, and though they have their uses they must never for one moment be allowed to cloud the view—that is, to survey the whole conditions and so strive to account for " bad times ;" and in so far as possible rob depressions of their sting.

§ 3. *The true causes of Commercial Depressions.*—We turn then briefly to group the actual conditions which, when in unhealthy conjunction, become commercial depressions. We may group under five heads these conditions, under any one or more of which productive energy becomes unprofitable—or, in other words, man's attack on Nature no longer repays him for his exertions : his expenditure of " stored work" diminishes instead of increases his store.

We shall discover these conditions group themselves naturally round the three factors of productive energy—capital, labour, and natural agencies. And it may be observed that in regard to capital and labour, the conditions may be described as national in origin and effect, whereas in regard to natural agencies and the further results of supply and demand, the conditions are better described as international in origin and effect. The five groups taken in order will class themselves as :—i. Waste of Capital ; ii. Waste of Labour ; iii. Failure of Natural Agencies ; iv. Closing of Markets ; v. Glut of Markets.

i. *Waste of Capital* is primarily a national error. The stock won from Nature, and which remains the prime lever of future productive exertions, may either be destroyed by a faulty system of action, or it may be tied up in a napkin and laid away hidden and useless. The actual destruction of capital arises under vicious systems of industrial or commercial endeavour. Thus the German iron trade was given extension with a supreme disregard of the future. No notice was taken of the fact that other countries boasted undeniable superiority in natural agencies and aptitudes. For instance, Great Britain enjoyed such advantages as superior quality of ore, superior quality of coal, absence of compulsory military service, great superiority of communications, home and foreign. And yet, in the face of all this,

Germans invested capital as though Germany were to become the iron-shop of the world. And the fated consequence followed. Of thirty-two companies floated with these views, representing a capital of £16,000,000, in a few years only six paid any dividend whatever. It is not difficult to see in this case a gigantic dissipation of capital : a vast mass of plant, machinery, buildings, training, and, generally speaking, expensive exertion is for the most part simply annihilated.

A similar waste of capital arises from a vicious commercial system. An instance of this is seen in that unwholesome Eastern trade, which, arising out of abnormal financial facilities, led such firms as that of the Collies to transactions of an apparently reckless character. Or, again, it is seen in the undue spirit of speculation which results often in "good times" especially, among the younger commercial houses. Such are tne business systems which proceed on the principle of large profits and large risks ; for in such, when the risks predominate, actual waste or annihilation of capital results. Such was the reckless enterprise which led to the financial crisis in the United States in 1873 ; and brought about the gigantic failures of Jay Cooke, and others. Of older date are the South Sea Bubble episode and numerous other instances of profligate waste of capital on perfectly worthless, and indeed visionary undertakings.

Times of inflation lead to waste of capital in increased or extravagant domestic comfort, in the growth of luxury, as well as in the too great impetus given to speculation and enterprise.

The very conditions of "good times"—increased production and increased facilities of exchange—lead men to that abnormally active use of capital which can only force men to outrun their strength, and so to court the eventual destruction of much of this capital. Times of depression no less drive men to an abnormally active use of capital by means of the reckless desperation they often engender. Thus there is much reason for the vigorous manner in which England, of late years, has sent out her "stored work" to other lands in the shape of loans. Much of this went out in actual "stored work;" and though it is true that a great deal was repaid by actual work in England in the construction of ironclads and locomotives and rails, nevertheless a vast proportion of these loans actually left England. A vast amount of the "stored work," that resulted from the favourable productive opportunities which culminated in the year 1873, found its way to North and South America, to Turkey and to Egypt. A vast proportion of this stored work has been simply annihilated, and represents merely so much capital wasted. And it must be further remembered that this wasteful employment of capital gave a fictitious activity to certain branches of trade and commerce. A large carrying trade of locomotives and railway material sprang into being; vast colonies of labourers were started along the wilds that the railways were to traverse. And much of the result of all this labour "will not pay ;" and vanity and vexation and waste are all that remain. It is said that Englishmen have contributed one hundred millions sterling to railways in America that pay but insignificant or nominal dividends. This represents an enormous amount of "stored work" simply dissolved into its original elements ; an enormous amount of wealth dug out of the earth and buried again in the soil it came from at so much dead loss. Capital is simply the possession of value-in-exchange, but the usufruct of this possession is conditional on this value-in-exchange becoming value-in-use. This value-in-use may have two issues ; the one developing, and the other destroying the continuation or reproduction of the value. In the one case there is annihilation, in the other recuperative fertility ; in the latter case capital is used, but in the former capital is wasted.

Capital is wasted when it is laid uselessly by.

Capital includes all the profits of man's "attack on Nature" which are laid by for future use. But the longer capital, in this acceptation, lies by idle, the longer is the world of production deprived of so much of its main instrument to success. Capital, under the control of men's minds, may be wasted when it falls to the charge of excessive caution or dull stupidity, no less than when it is squandered by criminal speculation. In either case its productive use is denied to man; and to such degree is man disabled in his making the most of his industrial opportunities. In times of commercial panic or of war, much capital is thus abstracted from profitable existence.

ii. *Waste of Labour* is another of the errors confined within the national frontier. This waste may take a variety of forms; on the one hand we may have unproductive labour, and on the other we may have deleterious abstention from necessary labour. Unproductive labour is that which fails to increase or even to maintain the fund of "stored work" that man accumulates by his exertions; and which enables him to triumph over his environments. All labour that diminishes this fund is unproductive; but it is a fund of *stored* work, an accumulation of the results of productive labour. And in the absence of these results, and they must be absent when labour is absent, there is also an inevitable drain on this fund of "stored work," an inevitable diminution in this accumulation of the results of productive labour. This fund is not equally shared in by the individuals of the human race. Man, as being the sum total of his antecedents, finds himself with a sufficiency of this fund or without such a sufficiency. His first law is self-preservation; and such a sufficiency, whether temporal or permanent, is the only basis of self-preservation. A sufficiency is capital; the winning a sufficiency is labour. Many men are in such position and of such character and environments that they spend their whole lives winning a sufficiency. These men make up the labouring classes of any country. Men fall into and rise from this class, but there are certain human characteristics which make such a class a large factor in human production.

There is the old practical theory that there always exists an urgent need of considerable incentive to overcome man's natural inclination to non-exertion. And of a certainty when once personal exertion, through extrinsic or other causes, reaps anything approaching a surplus reward over and above the mere needs of any particular type of existence, a baneful spirit of idleness inevitably makes its appearance. Luxury for the moment competes with this newcomer. On the first arrival of " good times" there is an inevitable inflation in the liquor traffic among the labouring classes ; and those acquainted with manufacturing districts know of the high prices paid by labourers for strange and incongruous luxuries. Factory girls will expend fifteen or twenty guineas in sealskin jackets; colliers will refuse £50 for a good fighting-dog. Yet sloth soon proves mistress even of luxury ; and her chief handmaidens are the modern Furies that preside over strikes. Entering with the specious excuse of raising wages and so increasing the means to luxury, they soon alter their syren-song to shortening hours of labour, and thus beguiling the labourer with the prospects of idleness. Thus these direct accompaniments of "good times" rob the world of production of its great energiser—labour.

It is in regard to the true nature and functions of strikes that political economy has a special field of most direct usefulness. Strikes are adopted as a means to an end. The end sought is good; it is an end that should be attained. It is sought to place the workman on an equality with his employer in settling the price of his labour. It is sought thus to secure to labour its due reward ; to attempt, so far as may be practicable, to insure an equitable distribution of the profits of exertion. The capitalist, the human being who makes use of the work he has stored, employs "labour" when he deems that further human exertion will maintain or increase his own fund of stored work. This "labour" is exerted by other human beings in consideration of his handing over to them that portion of the whole fund of stored work resulting from the combination, which may be set down as the product of their assistance. A man may sprinkle a bushel of wheat over a field with his own hands—a certain proportion will germinate and give him, say, 100 bushels of wheat in the harvesting. But, if he gets other men, and is thus enabled to plough and delve and weed and protect against birds and thieves, a bushel of wheat sown in the same field will give him a harvest of 1000 bushels of wheat. Some of this extra profit accrues to himself, but some accrues to the men by whose assistance he obtains any extra profit : and this is the wages of labour, as we have them in the world of to-day. The labourer of to-day suffers from the fact that there is no practicable national sanction that the price of his labour will continue in proportion to the profit derived from his assistance. But, on the other hand, though the labourer cannot secure a rise in wages accompanying a rise in prices, the employer finds he cannot secure a fall in wages when prices fall. This is the present dilemma.

The attempt to escape by means of strikes causes grievous waste of labour. A coalition to cease working is justified on the plea that the labourer supplies a certain commodity—labour, to wit—and that he has a perfect right to withhold his commodity from the market when he thinks he can benefit himself by so doing. Thus strikes considered as a means are said to be good ; but this abstract attribute fades before the concrete fact that as a means they are lamentably unsuccessful. In the first place, they seldom attain their ends ; and in the second place, in the rare cases where the end is attained, it is found that the cost involved is greater than the good achieved. In the year 1878 there were 277 strikes in the United Kingdom. Of these no less than 256 failed altogether, and only four attained their object. The remaining seventeen, most of them of an insignificant character, resulted in compromises. Such is the tale of actual experience of these means.

That the result is thus eminently unsatisfactory is not to be marvelled at when we bear in mind the gross misuse to which this means must ever remain liable, from the circumstances of its existence. The management of strikes must fall for the most part to the care either of the ignorant or the designing. They are the instruments of a combination of labour, and labour is the heritage of the unsuccessful in this world. Labour precludes leisure, and want of success precludes benefiting by familiarity with the best knowledge of mankind. This lack of knowledge amply explains the fact that a majority of strikes take place under conditions hopeless for their success.   There is frequently an entire ignorance of the circumstances even of their own trade.   And not only does this apply to the origination, but in still greater degree to the continuation, of strikes.   Thus at the conclusion of a period of inflation, with prices and prospects falling, educated capitalists know that there must for the time be less profit on the application of present or of stored work.   But if they attempt to reduce wages the labourers strike, and reduce themselves promptly to unnecessary misery. The same is the case when prices fall, as they do, for instance, when freedom of exchange and of production bring about the best industrial conditions.   The labourer has no knowledge to see that when prices fall wages may be reduced, yet he will be possessed of more purchasing power than before.   With this lack of knowledge, not only are labourers liable to rush in themselves where the knowing fear to tread, but to follow the seducing cries of interested misrepresentation.   In his hands he holds a weapon which he has fashioned for himself, to regulate the rewards of his labour; and thoughtlessly and in ignorance of its effect he uses this weapon in an illegitimate cause, and suffers accordingly.

This lack of knowledge, for instance, on the part

of the labourer hampers the well-informed capitalist in his attempts to improve production. An English silk manufacturer, when asked why he continued to use certain machinery which had been superseded on the Continent, replied : " If I were to make the alterations mentioned, I should set fast some thousands of pounds, and as soon as it was seen that I was making a better article than before at a smaller cost, my hands would all go out on strike for an increase of wages." Lack of knowledge would prevent these hands acknowledging that this extra profit was merely the interest on the extra fixed capital invested. And yet such investment would " improve the business" to the eventual benefit of all concerned ; but it was prevented by the threat of striking on the part of ignorant labour.

This lack of knowledge on the part of the labourer, reduces the profits of all engaged in production by curtailing productive energy. This limitation of production is often the avowed object of strikes ; it is usually the direct result of such as are successful. Shortened hours of labour or increased expenditure on labour equally imply lessened results in quantity. But here, as in all things, there is a happy mean. A human being can work profitably and well a certain number of hours per day ; to curtail this number is to encourage the idle non-use of labour power ; but to overstep this number is to detract from the efficacy of labour. We have here the chief reason for the value of Factory Acts : they maintain the efficiency of labour by placing a limit to its abuse. At the same time, to shorten hours of labour for such a reason as the prevention of over-production, no uncommon pretext in support of strikes, is entirely to misconceive the economy of the question. Hours of labour may be shortened profitably, only when the efficacy of labour is thereby increased. The bricklayer who idles twenty-three hours a day will not build the house within the year. The bricklayer who sleeps eight hours each night will be able to labour the whole year round. Hours of labour may be lengthened profitably, only when the efficacy of labour is thereby increased. The bricklayer that should attempt to labour without sleep for a week would find himself unable to work at all. The labourer reaps a greater harvest for himself the greater the production per head of those engaged. His true economical aim is the increase of the "stored work" from which he derives his reward.

It has however been asserted, with some truth, that strikes are an efficient means to their end, inasmuch as the employer, as a matter of fact, from dread of strikes, no longer attempts to dictate his own terms. He can calculate to a nicety the cost to him of strikes ;

the loss on plant standing idle; on orders not executed; on reputation for reliability gone. But this calculation does not always enable him to accede to the terms proposed by his labourers. The state of the market, when prices are falling and labourers refuse to see wages fall in proportion, not infrequently indicates to the employer that his best course is to close his mill and await better times. His capital can carry him through, at a loss it is true, but not at a loss enhanced by the payment to labourers of wages above " cost price."

Or, again, this suicidal tendency of strikes is exhibited in the fact that manufacturers are driven in self-defence to devise other expedients wherewith to supply the place of the unruly labourer. Not long ago a writer in the *Times* gave one notable instance of this result of strikes. His words were :—

" About fifty years ago it was the custom in those factories where cotton warps were made, to employ women to attend to the machine or mill on which the warp was being wound, such machine being, of course, turned by the steam engine; but as the warp was too heavy for women to take it off the machine when completed, men were employed for this purpose. In one of these factories the men became discontented, and demanded to be employed on the whole work and the women to be dismissed ; to which, however, the master demurred, and, as a consequence, the men turned out and the factory was closed.

" During the interval of the turn-out the master set his wits to work. and he succeeded in inventing a very simple machine, something in the shape of the human arm when bent, by which he was enabled to take the warps off the mill by the same steam power that turned the whole of his machinery ; and then, being independent of the men, he reopened his factory, and employed only women for the whole work."

When we pass on to consider those rare cases when the end is attained, we do not discover even then the balance to be on the right side.   On the one hand, it is evident that supposing a strike succeed in raising wages or keeping them high in the face of a surrounding fall, the only effect will be to attract fresh supplies of labour. In the two years 1871 and 1872, when wages were kept high, the number of persons employed in English coal mines increased from 370,000 to 470,000. And this increase at once overstocked the local labour market, and there was much subsequent suffering and disappointment among the labourers. The capital invested in that particular industry could only employ profitably a certain amount of labour ; and the more men there were ready to perform this the less was the portion earned by each man. Unless strikes can be universal in effect, they will, in proportion to their success, generate conditions fatal to a continuance of this achieved effect.

On the other hand, we may consider the cost of strikes. This, of course, falls ultimately on the labourer. While he withholds his commodity from the market the commodity yields him no profit; and when he again puts it in the market, assuming that his strike has been successful, and that he sells it at an advanced price, he must reckon up whether this advance covers the losses of the idle period. If a labourer earns 15*s.* a week, and goes on strike for five weeks in order to obtain 15*s.* 6*d.* a week, it is obvious that he will have lost 75*s.* Supposing the rare case of his strike turning out altogether successful, he will then have to work for 150 working days before he has recouped this expenditure by means of the extra rise in wages he has been holding out for. Thus before he can benefit by this successful strike he will have to work some five months or more at the increased wage. If during that period wages fall, or if they rise, his whole labour will have been in vain. So that the chances of his ever gaining anything by striking are very small.

The worst point about strikes is that these facts do not come home to the labourer—he pays his subscription to his union as a matter of course, and when he goes out on strike the union pays him. He has parted with his money, and when it returns to him it comes in the guise of a fresh supply. He does not imagine that he is virtually and actually spending some of his own earnings that he has not yet spent. He does not understand that until by future extra exertion he recoups this outlay he will not be in the same position in regard to those other excellent purposes of his union, the relief that is given in sickness and old age. Strikes are simply a robbery from this beneficial fund to forestall the extremely problematic gains to be achieved by strikes; gains which, in the majority of cases, never are achieved.

It may be said, "but take away strikes and there is no method left whereby labour is to have prospect of asserting its due rights." And there is very much reason in this statement. Co-operation, which succeeds so well with consumers, fails when applied to production. This is no doubt the result of the radical attributes of human nature. Men desire wealth, but they desire it at the least possible sacrifice. The consumer seeks the attainment of what he desires always at the least possible sacrifice; that is the common basis of procedure among all consumers. But among producers there is no such common basis; their desires differ greatly, and with this difference there arises a great difference in the amount of sacrifice necessary. It is practically impossible to assess correctly the proportion of profit that belongs of right to each worker in a concern where each works and aids according as it pleases him best.

Other methods proposed have called in the valuable aid of extrinsic knowledge. Much practical success has actually attended appeals to the arbitration of high-principled and well-informed men. Much good has been done by Boards of Conciliation, by means of which, in the prospect of dispute, employers and labourers meet to discuss matters, and thus come the better to understand one another. Actual advance has been made in some cases by the mutual setting up of a sliding scale, wages following the rise and fall of the price of the staple commodity; but on behalf of the labourer there is the stipulation that the wage shall never fall below a definite level; and on behalf of the employer that it shall never rise above a certain level. It is certain that it is to the economic benefit of all concerned that there be a fair day's wage plus a fair day's work. But the one must not exist without the other; and the problem yet remains unsolved as to how this happy union is to be established definitely and universally. The proposed remedy of strikes is, as we have seen, simply and purely waste of labour; and as such highly detrimental to the real interests of labourers and employers.

iii. The other groups of conditions, extending both in origin and influence outside the frontiers of the nation, become essentially international in characteristics. Foremost among the efficient factors of production stand natural agencies. Man depends intimately on the co-operation of Nature for the success of his productive exertions. A "good year" gives to the same expenditure of capital and labour a far greater amount of produced commodities than a "bad year." And corresponding is the effect on all those many industries which are directly connected with the kindliness of Nature.

It is by adopting this one group of conditions as though it were the sole group, that many are led to seek remedies for commercial depressions on the ground that they proceed in cycles. Professor Jevons has shown that the price of wheat in India, recorded since 1763, reaches a regular maximum in ten year periods, and these periods coincide in a startling manner with the periods of commercial crisis in England. No doubt the teeming populations of India and China have long supplied Europe with many commodities ; taking, of course, in repayment a considerable amount of the products of Europe. Years of scarcity in the East mean a lessened production of these exchange-values, and the West becomes thus affected by the kindliness of Nature in the East; and in so far as there is periodicity in the kindliness of Nature in the East so far is there a tendency to infuse periodicity into such of the productive successes of the West as may be directly connected with the Eastern markets. Astronomers have long been at work seeking a connection between the periodicity of the sun-spots and the rainfall on the earth.   Incidentally their tables exhibit periods of ten years or thereabouts.   It cannot be doubted but that a variation of solar radiation, which it would seem must occur with the variation of the sun's surface, must affect the amount of solar heat actually received by the earth.   Recorded experience on many parts of the earth's surface reports a periodicity of about ten or eleven years of bad droughts. But whatever may be their periodicity, " dry-times" and " wet-times" do succeed to one another over the whole surface of the earth : and either extremes benefit certain types of production and harm other types.   Thus the dryness and wetness of the seasons have a vast effect on the success of man's productive energy.   And not only is the kindliness of Nature thus intimately bound up with man's productive success, but he himself, with his proverbial trust in the future, seems resolved always to live as if all seasons are good.   The Australian sheep-farmer will take possession of a run and stock it with, say, 20,000 sheep.   They will thrive there in good years, but a succession of droughts will render the run no longer capable of maintaining even 10,000, and 10,000 will be starved off the run. So, too, in all times of inflation, every one builds and spends as though a golden age were commenced, in which bad times could not exist. It is well known that Nature is variable in her gifts, and yet when she is in a bountiful mood so delighted is mankind that no regard is paid to the sure certainty of her changing presently her bounty to niggardliness. Thus even good seasons lead men to waste the kindliness of Nature; and when seasons are bad men suffer most from this withholding of her bounties on the part of Nature. And in addition to bad seasons there are many freaks of Nature man cannot as yet account for or obviate. Vine disease has frequently neutralised the best human efforts over wide districts. The various cattle diseases have done the same. Nature thus often involves man in an extensive waste of both capital and labour.

iv. The fourth and fifth groups of conditions are connected intimately with the supply and demand of commodities. The fourth group, embracing the *opening and closing of markets*, gauges the actual demand by which alone the producer can command profit for his exertions. And among other conditions of commercial depression none are more telling than the closing of markets. This is often an international question. It is the action of other nations which, in these days of world-extended communications, usually opens or closes markets to the producer.

In the first place, some markets may be closed to the world's trades by the self-will of those who control it. Under this category fall the influences of protective policies. The non-admission of English goods into, for instance, American ports, cuts off the English producer from a large market; as a consequence his productive energy has a lessened area for exertion. So far the demand for his products is lessened, and in so far his activity curtailed.

In the second place, some markets may be closed to the distributors of the world's productions by the misfortune of those who control it. The famines which desolated Hindostan and China brought in their train a sad decrease in demand for manufactured commodities over large portions of the world's surface, and similar is the effect produced by war. So long as the manhood of France and Prussia were devoting their capital and labour to the service of political ambitions or national antipathies, so long had they little to spare for the attack on Nature; so long did productive enterprise languish; so long did local supply fail to pay for local demands.

And a secondary result of this temporary withdrawal

of forces from productive exertion was the creation of a false stimulus to production in other countries. This false stimulus, bringing about false good times, always has an evil effect on the productive energy of a nation. The labouring mind only notices the actual prosperity of the present, and the speculating mind is heedless of all other contingencies but the making of hay while the sun shines. Since free-trade was inaugurated in England war has successively devastated and overcome Russia, Turkey, Austria, Italy, the United States, Spain, and France. In other words, the whole manufacturing world of the present day, with the sole exception of England, has been, at one time or another since 1866, the scene of actual war. This, no doubt, gave England her opportunity of developing her manufacturing powers ; but the resulting effect was not all good. Her capitalists and her labourers alike abused their opportunities ; and alike were blind to the effect of returning peace in other lands. Thus war has a duplex effect on protective energy ; it is disastrous to that of the nation where it actually rages ; but beyond this does it create in another nation a false impulse to a hurtful productive excess.

v. Turning to the fifth and last of the groups, we consider chiefly the supply of commodities, and again find a distinct international character given to the conditions under examination. We have seen Nature affect the supply of the markets ; and in scarcely less degree does man. There is such a thing as over-production, which results in a *glut* of commodities. To the producer this means profitless expenditure of capital and labour. In other words, a destruction of the products of industrial energy—a distinct waste of force. Over-production is a result of good times. In England a notable instance of good times were the years 1869–73 ; prices rose, first the profits of capital and then wages of labour felt to the full this buoyancy of upward tendency. It was not, how-ever, till this state of things was confirmed and obviously assured, that means and facilities of produc-tion followed suit. Yet when once a start was made, mills, furnaces, shafts, cultivation, railways, ships, all the means to production fell to increasing their capacities, regarding only this upward tendency. The sober requirements of consumption were entirely un-heeded in the race for the magnificent rewards of exertion apparent on all hands. In the same epoch the United States had barely tided over the waste of the great local war, to find themselves chilled in the embrace of protection. The various manu-facturing centres on the Continent were at a com-parative standstill ; recent war, proximate war, actual war—the vague suspense which held Europe in the unproductive condition of an armed camp—were the conditions under which this standstill became possible. Thus her environments aided to blind England to her true interests, and she stands forth a notable example of the evils of over-production, for presently the grievous fact became evident that the capacities for production had altogether outrun the real demands of consumption. And of late years the revival of manufacture in these other lands has only added to the already glutted condition of the markets. Over-production corrects itself by effluxion of time. But glut of markets embraces as well that dearth of profitable exchange which is one of the leading results of commercial restrictions, and which in every way intensifies commercial depressions.

Such, then, are the five groups under which the conditions of productive depression may be ranged. It will next be our task to seek what action on the part of the community can modify or prevent the occurrence of these conditions.

CHAPTER XII.

PROPOSED REMEDIES FOR COMMERCIAL DEPRESSIONS.

§ 1. Protection as a cure or preventive—§ 2. Reciprocity as a cure
or preventive—Partial Free-trade as a cure or preventive.

WE have seen in previous chapters that some of these
conditions of commercial depressions are, strictly
speaking, national, and others as strictly international.
Nevertheless, in ages of civilisation, all productive
effort has, of necessity, an international character.
It is for this reason that all policies, by which those
who lead communities in their common efforts seek
to benefit such communities, have an international
leaven. If, then, we propose to consider how the
community is to ward off commercial depressions by
its action as a whole, we find at once that its action
must in some measure influence its communication
with other communities. Policies that regulate productive effort may be distributed over a wide line,
and the two poles of this will be protection and free-
trade. And for the sake of distinctness it will, perhaps, be well to take protection pure and simple and
free-trade pure and simple, and to group the various

modifications intervening under the head of retaliation or reciprocity.

§ 1. *Protection as a Remedy.*—First, then, will *protection* cure or prevent commercial depression ? The cry for protection arises in times of depression in free-trade communities ; it is in reality a mode or form of that lever of much human action—discontent with the present; it is but the expression of that yearning after something which is not, without which human effort would probably come to a standstill. Protection has been ere now compared to physic ; there is a cry for it when the nation becomes sick ; yet is it a medicine of that type that if once given it becomes a necessity, and health disappears in the prospect of a chronic valetudinarianism which can only end in disease and death.   In free-trade England the cry has been heard; but it is a cry popular only with a generation that have forgotten the ills and disasters from which the country only emerged when protection was finally laid low.

It may be asked, Will protectionism cure or allay *waste of capital?*   Will it stay faulty application of capital ?   Will it stay the idle storing of capital ?   It can hardly be looked to to stay faulty application of capital.   We have seen that it saddles the community, as a whole, with the indiscretions and ignorances which must for centuries to come mark all human endeavour. In other words, the successful are made to pay for the failures of the unsuccessful : and this is tantamount to a pure throwing away of stock won from nature. We have the witness of the cry of the iron trade in Germany. Starting on the sarcastic abuse of " Manchestertum" the ironmasters cry aloud for protection. The trade was thrown open in January 1877, and before two years were over this fostered industry threatened to dissolve altogether in the fire of outside competition. The ironmasters acknowledge that England has an advantage of facilities of communication both with supplies and with markets equal to 28*s.* a ton ; they acknowledge that the United States far and away surpasses them in mechanical arrangements : and therefore they cry aloud for protection to this industry. It would be difficult to find a more glaring example of conscious misapplication and waste of capital than this.

But this instance teaches us another lesson. The complaints of these ironmasters incidentally bring to notice the fact that their industry for the four years immediately preceding its being thrown open to the whole world had experienced a disastrous shrinkage. The number of mines in work fell one-quarter ; there were employed one-fifth less miners ; and corresponding was the shrinkage in the furnaces and their workmen. The presence of this demanded protection itself had already failed signally to bolster up the industry.

There is undoubtedly in protection a tendency to stifle industries ; it may indeed be a power to set them in motion, but it is a power of a negative type, which sets them in motion but for the end of destroying them. Thus protectionism sends capital to industries which were presently to die away carrying with them much capital invested. And further than this, protectionism becomes the annihilator of capital properly applied, for the industrial suffocation resulting is not confined to any one industry, but spreads over the whole land its blighting influence. The logical basis of this is the fact that protectionism is and can be an undivided blessing to only one industry at a time. Farmers may say,. prevent the importation of foreign food, but by all means let us have cheap ploughs. Manufacturers exclaim exactly the reverse, prevent the importation of foreign ploughs, but by all means let us have cheap food. The fact is protectionism is food to the producer, but poison to the consumer—and each man, doing his work in a community, is both producer and consumer. If protectionism affect him in his capacity of producer alone, well and good, but if it extend its influence to him in his capacity of consumer, evil is the result. And the cry for protection is a cry that eventually permeates a community with the certainty of leaven. If the community taxes itself to support any one industry, at once is set up an equitable claim on it in favour of any other industry, and the natural greed or ambition of the individual is always ready at once to assert this equitable claim. The cumulative result is that the community becomes more and more taxed to support production. Fresh burden is added in enhanced prices, and, in short, the community as a consumer puts its hand into its pocket to pay away without profit what it earns as producer. This is what is alluded to when we are told of the "plunder of the American masses by a few New English manufacturers." Capital is put into industries under conditions which preclude its securing any reward or profit ; and, under such protectionism, if it is advanced that the idle storing of capital is impossible, the answer is that the impossibility arises from the fact that all the capital of the community, all the stock won from nature, is wasted and dissipated by being applied to industries which in the end must be stifled. For be it remembered, the march of protection advances logically till all industry is protected, and the nation as a consumer is sacrificed eventually at the shrine of the nation as a producer. And with that event the nation is no more.

It may be asked will protection cure or allay the

waste of labour of which we have spoken ? How does protection effect that reward of labour which is a chief incentive to productive exertion ? At the first blush, by the introduction of industries, protection appears to increase the amount of capital expended on labour, but to look further into things is to see that this phenomenon represents the sum total of the good effected, and that this asset is miserably small in comparison with the liabilities otherwise accruing. On the one hand, protection destroys capital ; there is consequently so much the less to be devoted to the reward of labour. And on the other, the community, to support a protectionist policy, has to contribute in enhanced price the duties which forbid the flow into the country of the bounty of nature in other lands. In other words, protection curtails to an indefinite extent the purchasing power of the wages of labour, robbing labour thereby of its due reward. As a consequence, labour is driven to seek by every means what is known to the world as a rise in wages. To this end labour, in protectionist communities, is greedy of political power ; and by such means labour is more than ever liable, under the stimulus and opportunities of good times, to attract to itself an undue reward. As we have seen, the inevitable result is first unproductive luxury, and in the end disastrous idleness. And the economical reaction to bad times is thereby rendered all the more disastrous to all concerned.

It may be asked, will protection in any way counter-balance or lessen the evils of the *failure of natural agencies?* A community is dependent on nature most directly for its food and its clothing. The raw materials of these two essentials are, more than anything else, intimately dependent on the bounty of nature. A good harvest and the absence of the potato disease are the forerunners of cheap food ; plentiful pasture, kindliness in the weather, absence of destructive murrains, are the forerunners of cheap wool and flax. And however much statistics may prove that good and bad seasons recur in cycles, they are yet more explicit in the fact that seasons differ in different countries ; that if the harvest is bad in England and Hungary it will be above the average in California and South Australia ; that if the sheep in the Cape and South America suffer from scab and drought, Australia will be blessed with rain and health. In short, in the long run, nature provides a constant supply ; and as a consequence that community is best supplied from the bounty of nature which reaps its harvest from the largest surface. It need scarcely be added that the one main result of protectionism is to confine the natural resources of a community by its own frontiers : and history abounds with examples of the sad and fatal consequences of man's endeavour to found his State on the protectionist plea of independent subsistence.

It may be asked—Will protection in any way cure or prevent that fourth group of conditions, whose result is seen in the *closing of markets?* Protection has for its main aim the prevention of commodities of foreign origin entering the community ; in other words, it is the actual closing of one international market. And to close one's own market to the entry of others is surely to invite others to close their market to one's own access. So far as protection goes it is an all-round shutting up of markets, an all-round attempt to curtail the opportunities of producers to profit by their productive energy. Protectionism endeavours to foster productive industry in a country, but omits to notice the fact that man's energies come to no profit unless they are expended on work which gives him a superiority over some other band of men. Mere naked subsistence may indeed be gained ; but mere naked subsistence has never been the sufficient end of human endeavour. It is therefore idle to argue as if man could be forced into some theoretical state of happy savagedom. Again, we can by no means ignore the influences of the bounty of nature. When they find that petroleum lights their long winter evenings better and cheaper than seal-oil, Icelanders feel they had best get their lights for their long winter evenings from America. When it is determined to have a necklace of cats-eyes, Ceylon or Queensland must be sent to for them. When the London lady wishes for winter warmth, she sends for furs to Archangel or Port Nelson. To profit by what nature yields men are driven to go to different parts of the earth's surface. But protection bars this intercourse, and in so doing shuts out the products of each country from the profits of value-in-exchange. History affords many examples. There is the well-known instance of the silk weavers of Coventry and Spitalfields. In times of distress they successfully clamoured for protection. This supposed efficient remedy only made matters worse; and the culmination of complaint centred in the threatened disappearance of all markets for their products. The name of Huskisson appears as the advocate of the despised remedy of free-trade : and since his successful endeavours this particular silk trade has entirely recovered itself; and English silk finds a world-wide market by means of its fame for a unique durability.

It is, however, when we consider the last of the five groups, that we notice the utter inadequacy of protection as a preventive of commercial depression. Protection, according to the measure of its success, results in *over-production.* Assuming it to be adopted by all nations, and this is the logical outcome of its advocacy, foreign markets are all closed. This is indeed the extreme result; but it is a result which must exist in modified form in due proportion to the modified adoption of this principle. Again, within the community itself, protection seeks to set going productive energy, and in proportion as its intentions are crowned with success, so will there come about a mass of produced commodities. For these, then, there is no outlet, and there will necessarily ensue a glut in the home market in exact proportion as protection is adopted with success.

Protection, then, encourages waste of capital. Protection leads labour altogether astray in its applications and its aspirations. Protection ignores altogether the benefits derivable from superiority of the bounty of nature. Protection avowedly shuts up the markets for the commodities of productive energy. Protection, in so far as it is successful, in so far brings about glut in the markets under its command. Thus Protection magnifies and intensifies every one of the five groups under which we have ranged the conditions of productive depression.

§ 2. *Reciprocity as a Remedy.*—We turn to a brief view of the various modifications of productive policies which intervene between the two poles, protection and free-trade. There is the old tale that when extremes prove to be impolitic, the "media via" is the safest course. In the present case of commercial depressions we are told that protection is impossible, and free-trade impolitic; and we are urged to consider the fact that the mediatives that are furthest removed from the impossible and yet approach nearest to the impolitic, will turn out to be those presently expedient.

Most of these mediatives fall under the title retaliation or reciprocity. These have been somewhat aptly described as "protection in a fancy dress." It is, indeed, impossible to see many traces of free-trade among their principles, while their great essential is protectionism in some shape or form. But they come decked in the alluring expediency of the moment; they come cloaked in the superficial attractiveness of a much-needed relief.

We are told in regard to the prevention of the waste of capital and labour that reciprocity will insure to a workman his wages and to the capitalist his profits. That we will do unto others as they do unto us, and, in short, adopt "quid pro quo" as our motto in our dealings with other communities. There is a plausible logic about all this, and an enticing clearness of enunciation. If thought is not allowed to busy herself too much, the whole argument seems consistent and well rounded off. But the political economist at once exclaims, this is all perfectly true of the producer; but as a matter of fact the producer can only produce by being a consumer; and the "quid pro quo" theory, until the days of a universal free-trade, is nothing more nor less than the taxation of the consumer to support the producer. In actual theory, every member of a community is both producer and consumer; the practical exceptions are due to such human frailties as idleness and stupidity; or such misfortunes as failure of health or miscalculation. On the Saturday night the carpenter, as a producer, receives his wages into his right hand and places them in his pocket. At the public house, at the bacon shop, he dives his left hand into his pocket, and his wages disappear in his capacity as consumer. As a producer he has manufactured the wood for the bar and for the shop-front. If he is blinded by reciprocity, he will say, Canada will not admit my woodwork free. I will not admit hers free. And he will pay more for his wood, and so charge the publican and the grocer more for so doing. But the publican and the grocer each have the equitable right to say, Germany will not admit my barley malt free, the United States will not admit my bacon free—neither will we theirs. And barley and bacon, supplied with all the uncertainty of a restricted acreage and with none of the advantages of vast tracts of virgin soil, rise in price. And the labourer receiving an extra shilling a week for his work, pays an extra shilling, and more if he be not lucky, in enhanced prices.

And reciprocity can do little to alleviate the waste of capital. Reciprocity implies closing of a multitude of the right avenues of investment. This tempts the capitalist of energy to speculation; and the capitalist of caution to low profits. Reciprocity fosters both the classes of conditions which lead to a waste of capital.

And will reciprocity in any way allay or prevent the failure of nature's agencies? Can this be asserted of a policy which has for its aim the lessening of the area of supply? Its advocates tell England she is no longer the workshop of the world, other States shut out our exports; other countries have their manufacturers; it is too late to hope for much from lowering wages and profits and prices; all we can do for our struggling selves is to repay others in their own coin, and shut out their exports. Reciprocity would thus cut us off from foreign supplies. And some advocates, attempting rather to advance towards the free-trade pole, tell us free-traders are perfectly right in establishing free-trade in corn and tea and wine—in the necessaries of life, but they are wrong in throwing away all protection to native industry *before* they had good reasons to know what the course of other nations would be. But even this modified reciprocity still cuts off the nation from *some* foreign supplies. And every foreign product cut off is a curtailment of the area of supply ; an addition to the opportunities for the operation of the failure of natural agencies.

As for obviating the loss of markets, reciprocity in any shape or form is avowedly useless. Its prime principle is the closing our own markets to others because they close theirs to us. It has indeed the convenient boast that we are ready to open ours if others will open theirs, and this is a promise which might, under certain circumstances, prove effectual. But the principle involves none the less loss of markets. Trade becomes restricted if the French refuse to let English goods into France, even though we allow French goods into England. Such restriction will be done away with if the French let our goods in free, but it will be disastrously increased if we, in our turn, refuse to let in French goods. Again, it must be borne in mind that protection can only affect directly the land of its adoption. The Germans can prohibit English iron entering Germany, but they cannot prevent English iron from competing with German iron in all other markets.

Reciprocity then, in whatever form, is, as it were,

protection justified on the principle that universal free-trade is impossible. It ignores altogether the fact that partial free-trade attains to many of the undoubted good results of universal free-trade. And it is the outcome of a species of spite which comes of the baffled desire of men for the unlimited benefit of universal free-trade.

§ 3. *Partial Free-trade as a Remedy.*—Turning to the opposite pole of the policies which regulate productive effect, we ask will *free-trade* cure or prevent commercial depression? Arguing from the abstract ground of pure theory, acting in the sphere of the human energy of the present or of the future visible to us, free-trade will effect all that human endeavour can effect to prevent productive depression. But the world is not regulated by abstract theory. And when we turn to a more practical or prosaic view of things concrete, we come to two propositions. The one that free-trade in its entirety cannot exist under present conditions, and the other that free-trade, even in practical realisation, boasts a preponderance of good results.

Now this first proposition is the main fact for statesmen of the present. The various communities of men do not all allow of free-trade. It is true enthusiasts see a dawning of a new era. It is said nations are passing from a stage of isolation to one of union ; a passage similar to that from the stage of tribes into that of nations. And if for the immediate present the spirit of selfish isolation still dictates the policies of the short-sighted, nevertheless there is a shadow already cast over the world, recognisable in the network of finance that extended commerce is throwing over the world; recognisable in the increasingly distinct shapes assumed by international law ; recognisable in the prospective denationalisation of religions ; recognisable in the uprising of a common morality ; a shadow cast by the coming events of a world-wide union for purposes of human advance- , ment by the advent of an era of union succeeding to an era of isolation. Nevertheless, for the present there are various causes in active operation to aid this spirit of selfish isolation. And many of these causes have little in common with it. This spirit in itself appears in the world of to-day as a patriotism which seeks, after a somewhat spurious fashion, to satisfy the greed and the ambitions of citizens. Each community endeavours to rival others in the race for wealth; each wishes, with true human selfishness, to garner for its own citizens a lion's share of the vast profits of human energy. But there are other causes at work which are the incidental allies of this spirit; and foremost among these are the political actions of communities. These actions are, indeed, often wholly confined in intention within the frontiers of the community, and it may be accepted as a sign of that future of which we have spoken that these actions, avowedly and intentionally national, have great and lasting international effect. A minor instance of such action is the compulsory military service in such favour on the Continent. This purely parish policy is one great basis for the outcry of Continental manufacturers against free-trade competition with England and America—both of them free of this uneconomical burden. Or, again, we may see a complexity of local politics leading even acute minds in the States and Canada to look for a commercial union between these two tracts of territory, to the exclusion of the rest of the world. Again, the purely·household politics of France afford yet another instance. Free-trade was the highly lucrative policy of the second empire. On the over-throw of the empire the reaction to a republican form of government brought in its train a reaction towards protection ; and, with true ochlocratic inconsistency, the men who blazoned on the ruins of the Tuileries the magic word égalité in the same breath foster an extravagant inégalité by enriching with their protection the few Lille and Rouen manufacturers from the poorly lined pockets of the masses. It will be perhaps sufficient to suggest one more instance of the world-wide effect of such purely domestic politics. In colonies a most mischievous protection is often possible, because of the fact that it does not and cannot affect the food of the people. The bounty of virgin nature is far and away sufficient for the actual necessities of the sparse population of newly inhabited countries. Thus in fertile Victoria, where a certain population was attracted by the reputed wealth of the gold-diggings, those disappointed of gold clamoured for wages, and a vigorous protection became possible, seeing that these same men happened to enjoy that predominating influence in the government of the country which is insured by manhood suffrage. In Victoria protection has already played its part in scaring capital and in disorganising labour; but it was possible, owing to the democratic political atmosphere; and to the fact that there was food enough and to spare for all, even though waste of capital and labour were proceeding in the sight of all.

In the face, then, of these actualities of the present, can we look to free-trade to remedy or prevent any of the five groups of the conditions of productive depression? Reversing our order we meet with the objection that free-trade, adopted blindly, may result in a *glut of such markets* as may be open to those who adopt it. The manufacturer of a free-trade community must exercise a self-restraint which the past tells us is seldom present with that sanguine energy which is the usual basis of successful productive exertion. Free-trade, of its very nature; of the competition it engenders; of the abundance of raw material it lands at the door of the manufactory; of the increased communication it fosters among communities of men, tends ever to accelerate and not to retard the machinery of industry. As a consequence, it has a tendency we are told to glut markets with commodities.

But previously we had found that protection has a still more powerful tendency in the same direction; and there is the redeeming feature in the present case, which does not appear in the other, that the glut springing of free-trade is the glut of rightly directed energy; the commodities are those which one country desires of another. They are right in kind. It is a mere glut of quantity. But under systems of protection there arises a glut of kind as well; a country is liable to devote its energies to the production of articles for the production of which other countries are better suited. By the very principle of free-trade the producer produces that for which he possesses national or natural advantages; and if he, of his very energy, produces too much, it is a case which time will remedy; he will have to curb his energies for a time, they have been too exuberant, but they have

T

not gone astray. There is then, as it were, a healthy glut of markets ; and it is this healthy glut which is the glut that results from free-trade.

Again, under present conditions will free-trade allay or prevent *loss of markets ?* Anomalous though it may seem the actual success of free-trade fosters protection, in the present stage of national isolation. In times of free-trade each nation will naturally see some other surpassing it in those products for which it enjoys less natural advantages. And there is an undeniable tendency in such cases to appeal to protection to counterbalance this natural inferiority. German ironmasters, seeing the English outstripping them, because of their cheaper coal and iron, at once turn to protection to remedy this inequality of nature's bounty. This unintentional result of successful free-trade thus closes markets. And again, the one-sided nature of free-trade under present conditions actually invades communities that adopt it, and curtails the market opportunities of her own producers. Thus the protected French sugar is already occupying a large space in the English home market ; and the Bristol and Glasgow sugar manufacturers complain that free-trade, as adopted in England, results not only in the exclusion of English products from foreign markets, but actually in the free flooding of English home markets with foreign products. And however beneficial this may be to a man as a consumer, yet as a producer it prevents him from making those profits which alone enable him to rank as a consumer.

In this latter case the competition is wholesome, for the home manufacturer, if he have the natural advantages, will turn to with a better will. French competition has driven English sugar manufacturers to organise and contrive better ; it has not lessened the annual output. And in regard to this fostering of protection in other communities it is evident they can only result in the economical failure of these communities. If the Germans close their market to the English, but continue to supply the English with goods, the English will cease to pay for these goods. And it is impossible for the Germans to continue giving away the products of their protected industries. At all events, the loss will be German and not English. North America supplies England with tools and food. If England is allowed to pay Canada and not to pay the United States, it is obvious that if this supply continue Canada will grow rich and the United States simply become impoverished. Free-trade in England may induce Germany and the United States to close their markets, but this loss of markets to England is only for the time, until these countries find themselves sinking for want of the aid of others, and so re-enter the productive world by reopening their markets. This evil is, in its very nature, temporary. Other nations consciously depriving themselves of a share in the productive advantages, natural or national, of the free-trade community, in the long run impair their own prosperity. The result is all evil for themselves. And if, as in the case of the United States, with her vast virgin resources, protection does seem to have created within her boundaries a profitable industrial vitality, it must be remembered that the sole earnest of a balance of profit is that the future shall see her open her country to the world. And, during the interval, if she have developed any distinct national or natural productive advantages these will be enjoyed by other nations in proportion as they open their doors freely to the importation of such products. Englishmen can profit by the ingenuity of American tools and feed on the fat of American prairie land; Austrians deprive themselves of these benefits. The tendency of protection in two communities is to shut the one out from all participation in the successes of the other; it is towards an absolute productive isolation. And free-trade, being the exact converse of this, even though it may not find a free market in a protected community, is nevertheless free to share the successes of the protected community.

Again, under present conditions, will free-trade

allay or prevent the *Failure of Natural Agencies?* Such a prospective result is the undoubted boast of a worldwide free-trade. All acknowledge the " free-trade basis of natural advantage." Yet the question has been asked—Does this fact obtain under the conditions of the present ? If one country practise free-trade and the other practise protection, can they be said to enjoy each other's natural advantages ? The answer is that even in such case free-trade insures the widest surface of supply *possible :* in other words, the great *possible* means man enjoys for the present of combating the uncertainty of the bounty of nature. Free-trade, so far as it can penetrate, so far extends the earth's surface put under contribution for supply. Free-trade brings to a community that practises it an influx of the goods of all the world, and in return free-trade opens, for the goods of that particular community, the markets of such other communities as adopt its principles. To this extent then it does succeed in levying contributions from the largest possible surface. And this surface, be it remembered, is far more extensive than that which protection allows, even though it fall far short of that which universal free-trade would insure.

This beneficial effect of free-trade is specially noticeable in times of commercial depression. It has then a most positive value in affording actual means of subsistence to large numbers, by reason of the low prices that it engenders by means of increased supply. In England commercial depressions in protectionist days involved starvation, famine, bread riots, actual absence of food. But since free-trade has been practised the surplus of good harvests, English, American, Hungarian, or Australian, has found its way to England, and starvation has not again raised her threatening head. Travellers know that ripe pine-apples, pomegranates, and bananas, are often to be purchased from the costermongers on Cornhill as cheap and as good as in Galle or Kingstown. The grapes sold in the London streets at fourpence a pound compare favourably with the same priced grapes in the capitals of wine-growing countries. Free-trade improves the general well-being, enhances the facilities of life to a degree that has great and good effect on the sustaining or recuperative energies of a community suffering from commercial depression.

It has, however, been objected, that in the case of this partial free-trade the one country will, indeed, be open to the products of nature's bounty in the other ; but at the same time, will such country not be able to exchange anything for their products, seeing that it is debarred from selling its commodities in the markets of the other country? We are told that under the conditions of free-trade, when " bad times" occur, the consumer is, indeed, supplied better than ever, yet the producer does not prosper. But this is to revive the seemingly ineradicable fallacy that one man is a producer and another a consumer. If the producer does not prosper when the consumer is better supplied than ever, and if we remember that the producer is also the consumer, we shall acknowledge the true consequent to this statement, that the producer would prosper still less were not the consumer better supplied than ever. It is because the shipowner, as a consumer, pays less for everything, that he can as a producer or distributor profitably continue to carry goods which must be conveyed at lower freights, because of their lower prices. Free-trade, by benefiting a man as a consumer, enables him the better as a producer to stand " bad times."

And for the same reasons, by benefiting him as a consumer, that is, by increasing the purchasing power of his profits, it enables the producer in a free-trade community to pay out of this extra gain the necessary tax which the folly of protectionist communities obliges him to pay for the privilege of entering their markets. It is thus the Englishman can enter and pay for what he buys, but he has a great balance in his favour in the transaction, and no unimportant portion of that balance is the fact, that as a consumer he is supplied from as wide a surface as possible ; and is thus able to make the most of nature when in her liberal moods, and so efficiently to counterbalance any evil prospects when nature is in less liberal mood.

Again, under present conditions, will this partial free-trade allay or prevent *waste of labour?* Unproductive labour, labour which fails to maintain or to increase the fund of stored work possessed by a community, is waste of labour. And it is of this bad type of labour that free-trade is the one efficient preventive. The competition it engenders may safely be trusted to stifle all unprofitable undertakings. It will insure in the end the survival of the fittest. But there is another waste of labour, more insidious, because more natural to man, which results from the non-use of labour. This is in a measure a product of dawning free-trade. When free-trade brings its fertilising presence. into a community, a first result is the improvement of the condition of all classes ; then comes about a more equable distribution of the results of work. All men come to possess more of this fund of stored work ; but all men do not come to possess a sufficiency of it. And those that do not possess this sufficiency are still the labourers, but labourers with increased power and influence in their hands. Labour thus wins more efficient advocacy ; and a great step is made in the direction of human material happiness ; for those that have find they can no longer tyrannise over those that have not. The remuneration of labour is thus more likely to attain to a true level ; a level in truer economic relation to the sacrifice made. And in such case the more the hope for the labourer ; the greater the incentive to him to resist and overcome the proverbial human aversion to exertion.

But with this increase of influence there enters the inevitable tendency to overreach which we have seen result in the phenomena of strikes. It is to free-trade we can look with most confidence to resist the waste of labour resulting from this suicidal non-use of it. Free trade implies the competition of other labour and other commodities, and thus introduces a powerful sanction against the misuse of so double-edged a weapon as strikes. Thus free-trade tends to secure a right level in the remuneration of labour which shall, on the one hand, prevent unproductive labour, and, on the other, non-use of labour ; thereby insuring, both to those that have and to those that have not, that sufficiency of " stored work," which is the due reward for any sacrifices they may make.

Briefly it may be remarked that free-trade does, under present conditions, allay and prevent waste of capital. Competition prevents its unproductive use; and in an atmosphere of the true conditions of trade speculation of the wrong type and all unwholesome manipulations of capital meet with conditions most uncongenial to their presence. Neither is capital hoarded in idleness, for the productive surface is enlarged to the greatest possible limits ; and when one investment turns out unprofitable others are accessible, and there is no necessity to shut up capital for want of better opportunities.

Thus the partial realisation of free-trade insures a proportionate amount of the benefits of an absolute realisation. Enthusiasts have hoped that the essential truths of free-trade must some day break upon all the world with the force of new and irresistible light. And they hold that for a community to struggle as the harbinger of this saving doctrine is at the least noble, even if it be not profitable. And one of the main arguments in support of this plea is the plain fact that, at all events, protection is no better preventive or remedy of productive depression. Even if it could be held that partial free-trade is no cure, yet to this contention it can be, with logical force objected, neither is protection. Thus the witnessing to this new gospel does not any the more involve martyrdom than does the upholding the old faith. But, beyond this, we have seen that though protection is not a better cure than partial free-trade, nevertheless partial free-trade is a better cure than protection. And thus that, though the upholding of the old faith involve death and destruction, the embracing the new faith secures life and preservation.

Partial ·free-trade will not absolutely prevent the recurrence of commercial depressions ; and for the main reason that it is not universal. But it is found to mitigate every one of the conditions of this evil state of things ; and to be capable of indefinite expansion in its useful influence in this beneficial direction.

CHAPTER XIII.

EFFECTUAL REMEDIES FOR COMMERCIAL DEPRESSION.

§ 1. Free-trade the right basis—§ 2. Thrift, honesty, and
knowledge the right instruments to national prosperity.

§ 1. *Free-trade the right basis.*—We have reviewed
in order the policies regulating productive energy,
including the positive pole of protection, the negative
pole of partial free-trade, and the intermediate measures falling under the term reciprocity. We have
seen how far, under the present conditions of civilisation, they succeed in the task marked out for them.
It remains, then, to consider what practicable policies
are most desirable to secure the end sought. And if
we first consider what is generally true, we shall be
the better able to exemplify such principles by the
particular case of England's prospects.

We have seen that in so far as the absolute
principles of free-trade are encroached upon, in so far
are the best conditions of productive energy hampered. And though under present conditions absolute free-trade is an impossible panacea, nevertheless
the pilot who knows the route to productive pros-

perity unhesitatingly sets down the course as free-trade. Blowing away from this haven of prosperity will be met the dangerously balmy breezes of protection. But the State which shall for a moment yield to their influence and run off its true course, will find itself rapidly losing ground in its voyage towards prosperity. Yet these headwinds are sure to be encountered, and they must often be met by the seamanlike expedient of tacking. Circumstances over which we have no control; the perverseness to reason of the average human intellect; the short-sighted selfishness of individuals and classes;—these may baffle us in our direct course ; and we may have to adopt that zigzag route which the good ship follows when beating to windward : now forced from our direct course by the obstruction of some country setting about its own destruction by the means of protection ; now forced from our direct course by the obstruction of some country lead off by the misleading pleas of reciprocity : yet each tack places us nearer to port ; we yield no unnecessary inch of our course. We have a compass that can be trusted, and in the teeth of unfavourable gales and in misleading fogs we must keep the head of our good ship ever as near as may be to our true course—free-trade.

We have grouped the conditions under which commercial depressions become fact under five heads.

And under five heads we will now pass to consider their true preventions.

§ 2. *Thrift, honesty, and knowledge the right instruments.*—As with the individual so with the community at large, it is at once producer and consumer, and the true basis of industrial success is an economy which shall be equally prominent in consumption and in production. We are always proceeding on the ground that, in the material world, man is working all the good he can out of nature. What his efforts store to his command for future use, is *capital.* And the general principles which insure a due and proper use of this stored energy, may be set out under the three terms, thrift, honesty, prudence. A community will reap the profits of capital in proportion as it enjoys these three attributes. The formation of the national or prevailing character has everything to do with this. On the one side, we have morality, and, on the other, science, on the one side we have education and culture, on the other, instruction and information; on the one side we find our aid in religion, in sentiment, in learning; on the other, in business, in technical instruction, in skilled training. To insure a due application of its capital as well as of its labour, and so to avoid their waste, a nation must rear among its citizens *perseverance*, honesty, and knowledge. Those who have command of capital must be educated to a habit of application to the pursuits of this life which shall involve as little waste as possible ; to a steadiness of purpose proof against all allurements and inclinations to stray into side paths; and to a self-restraint ready to baffle such temptations as leads to vicious speculations. These are the preventive qualities necessary. Yet no less necessary are a right enthusiasm or well-balanced spirit of adventure ; a boldness which shall at once lower all obstacles that oppose progress along the right path, and also enable those in command of capital to penetrate into fresh regions to carry on their legitimate enterprises.

A second class of attributes is equally necessary if the success of the use of capital is to be lasting. These fall under the somewhat comprehensive head of *honesty.* The man that would succeed must be true to himself and above all true to those with whom he has dealings. All sham and shoddy, however profitable until discovered, are certain, so history tells us, in the end to bring the sources of their origin into commercial contempt and so to material failure. It is to such dishonest application of capital that many manufacturers have owed their ruin.

Knowledge is, however, the one great instrument to the prevention of the waste of capital. But it is a power very difficult of acquisition. It is a knowledge which embraces the productions and the needs of other lands ; which includes that particular experience which a deep study of statistics gives ; and which embraces a perfect comprehension of the modes not only of production but also of exchange. The technical education of the manufacturer of every type of product, of the merchant or exchanger of every type, of the carrier of every type—this is the prime need of a community that would not waste its capital. And in proportion as knowledge and morality and perseverance flourish among the capitalists of a community, in similar proportion will the best use be made of its capital.

When we would insure to a community the best value of its *labour*, we must remember that labour is peculiarly an individual product—each article supplied differs from the other in kind—essentially is it heterogeneous in character. The main desideratum is that so large a proportion as possible of this supply reach to a certain standard of value-in-work. Labour is placed in the market in the individual form of the labourer; and the object to be sought is that each labourer attain to a high standard of perfection in his own calling. Again, there is pressing need of *morality*. Perhaps one of the most sure roads to discredit and consequent loss of employment is that species of scamping which is far from unknown in many centres of industry : which follows the motto that bad work means more work ; and that all things are lawful that are " good for trade." There is no worse stage possible below that where the workman endeavours by bad work to rob the commodities of qualities which imply endurance, thereby hoping for more employment in replenishing their places with new. From this lowest type work rises through many gradations of dishonesty, every one of which implies so much labour wasted, and eventually so much discredit thrown on the workman's powers. Nothing can be more baneful to the commercial success of a community. Yet almost equally vicious is another phase of immorality which assumes the form of an alluring idleness. This is a sure sign of inefficiency on the part of the workman, and usually comes prominently forward in " good times ;" a rise in wages and concomitant fall in prices give to the labourer the necessaries of life at smaller exertion. Thus there remains over a great temptation to less exertion. Because he finds himself well off as a consumer he commences to remit his exertions as a producer. And, with the short-sighted earnestness of those who themselves have not mastered the truths of political economy, Trades Unions seek not for higher wages but for shorter hours as the one desideratum. This realised power exercised awrong by the labourer, adds another element of uncertainty to that great factor of production—labour. It is one of the inherent difficulties of assured productive progress that labour is naturally uncertain in supply. The amount actually present in the local market is the actual supply available. In its very nature it is not capable of ready transferrence. And to add to this natural drawback the artificial uncertainty of a capricious idleness, is to rob the community of one of its main sinews of industrial success.

Nevertheless, the rewards of labour are low when compared in the scale of the distribution of wealth in a community. The ranks of labour become thus swelled by those who, from one cause or another, lead what is known as a " hand-to-mouth" life. There is little capacity to tide over bad times, and when good come there is less endeavour to do otherwise than enjoy to the full the passing sunshine. Thus it becomes a main duty of an industrial community to oppose this particular evil. "Abstinence" has been proved to be the one great assistant in this cause ; and it is of special value in regard to the proper management of labour. Thrift is the main instrument by which the labourer, rising above a mere hand-to-mouth life, becomes an independent worker in a community ; a worker attracted to every form of reliable steadiness by the fact of being superior to the actual wants of the moment. That Friendly Societies accomplish much good in this direction is palpably evident. Their attractiveness, in other words, the scope of their good, often depends on what the thoughtless term a waste of their funds in ceremonies and festivities ; but such expenditure is the beneficial advertisement of really good things, and it is in addition a relaxation and a cheering pleasure to a life that sadly needs such good cheer. Of a cognate type are the inducements to thrift offered by such institutions as the Penny Banks. That they are means that achieve their end is to be seen from the fact in Mr. Bartley's London Penny Bank no less a sum than £164,000 has been deposited in the three years of its existence. The institution has not yet, of course, become universally known ; yet these deposits are all in small sums, a vast proportion being of one shilling and under. This sum, then, represents an enormous leaven of thrift instilled into the labouring classes. Those who enjoy the larger prizes in the distribution of wealth can in no way better insure a due enjoyment of their winnings or their luck than by fostering such institutions by all means in their power, for they tend ultimately to enrich the community, by doing away with one great factor of productive backsliding—waste of labour.

Knowledge is necessary to the proper application of capital ; it is indispensable to the proper application of labour. National aptitude for any particular branch of productive industry is often nothing more nor less than an inherited education in its details. The technical skill of the Glasgow engineer or the

mechanical ingenuity of the American, are examples
of what education, proceeding on sound lines, may do
to educe latent qualities and capacities.　And there
are two branches of profitable effort in this direction :
the one is to give the labourer due opportunity, and
the other is to lead him of himself to make use of
due opportunity, for the acquisition of knowledge.
Waste of labour is greatly caused by want of knowledge.　And want of knowledge is readily remedied
in endless forms.　Schools for the young, classes for
the older at times convenient, exhibitions of technical
interest, are among the means to this end.　The
energetic producers of the colony of Victoria set
much store by their Juvenile Industrial Exhibitions,
in which every exhibit is the work of persons under
age.　Such exhibitions are of high use, inasmuch as
they turn the pliable mind of youth along the paths
of inquiry and emulation.　It is this increase of
technical knowledge in the labourer which must
insure a more proper application of his energies, and
by obviating waste of labour the steady profits of
productive energy are assured.　The caring for technical skill develops any latent ingenuity in the ranks
of labour, and the community which sets most store
by such action is the community which suffers least
from the waste or misapplication of the exertions of
the labourer.

Production and consumption are signally dependent on the *bounty of Nature.* We have seen that the human intellect has as yet failed so far to pierce the secret of Nature, as still perforce to suffer from what, under the cloud of such imperfect knowledge, is regarded as her capriciousness. It is the late survival of that anthropomorphic comfort of ignorance which, in a less enlightened age, set earthquakes down to the human wrath of Poseidon. We have seen that the practical alleviation of this undeniable, even though unexplained, fact is the increase, so far as possible, of the area of supply. The food that enables man to work, and the raw materials that give him the where-withal upon which to set to work ; the material and the efficient cause, Aristotle would call them ; these he derives directly from Nature. The community must then endeavour its best to extend the area of its supply. Minor means to the same end are found in the increase of a knowledge of Nature ; this enables man piecemeal to rescue to his own command successive natural domains, previously, so far as he could explain, in the hands of that capriciousness of which we have spoken. Mining, in its many branches ; the vast chemistry of agriculture ; the physiological lore, which opens out the secrets of animal and vegetable growth ; the science of meteorology, which is already rapidly determining law after law in that emblem of capriciousness, the weather ; and even the temporally despised science which treats of the physical influences that the planets of the solar system exert on the earth. These are some of the heads of knowledge, the successful pursuit of which are of invaluable aid to increasing man's knowledge of nature.

But when we say that the area of supply must be enlarged, we are at once brought face to face with the fourth group of conditions, which seek the extension of *markets.* At the market there must be exchange ; and further, there must be exchange of equivalents. In other words, for what the producer parts with in the market he will receive something of which he can make use. He will be supplied. And the wider the market for his products the more can he depend on selling, and at the same time the larger will be his area of supply. The community that would succeed in this respect must be perpetually ready to open up new markets and to keep hold of the old ones, more especially when they exist in centres of increasing populations. Luckily, the community is aided greatly by the universal human desire to admire and to purchase what is foreign and new. " Omne ignotum par magnifico." " London made" is the popular brand in country districts, and in the shops of any country in the world the most prized commodities are those of foreign origin. To open up new markets becomes a favourite pastime with the adventurous and enter-prising ; and this form of human energy is sure to appear in every community. To retain old markets needs all the skill and industry of the capitalist and the labourer of which we have spoken.

The fifth group of the conditions of productive depression, embraces that *glut* of markets which comes of over-production. The prevention of these evils is matter of much difficulty. The occurrence may be due to fault on the part of the producer or of the consumer. The producer may produce more then he can part with from sheer recklessness, or from ignorance, or from misguided reasoning ; he may speculate criminally ; he may know nothing of his markets ; he may make mistakes even with the best intentions. Provision against such errors is to be found in the morality and the knowledge we have advocated. Yet altogether beyond the control of the producer may be the action of the consumer. Earthquake, war, pestilence, famine—all these have robbed producers unexpectedly of assured markets. Nor are the causes always so glaring. Thus, for the Christmas of 1878 there was an unprecedented glut of poultry in the Leadenhall market. For some years the supply had fallen short of the demand, to the consequent benefit of the producers. But in 1878 this good news for producers had spread. The poultry breeders, both of North America and of France, determined that year on sharing in these profits. Large consignments of poultry arrived in London, both from America and from France. Two grave causes of error, however, existed. In the first place, the producers were *ignorant* of the fact that the great poultry clearance at Leadenhall took place the week before Christmas. Englishmen have a habit of sending their presents or laying in their stock the week before the busy Christmas-tide. And these new consignments all arrived during the Christmas week, when larders and hampers were all arranged for. In the second place, American and French producers had failed to grasp the effect of a widespread commercial depression in lessening the consumption. These two causes combined brought about a glut which was most unprofitable to the producers. Thus it appears that the main preventive of this group of conditions lies in the better morality, and, above all, the more perfect knowledge, of the producer. In these days, perhaps, one of the most profitable uses to which the telegraph has been put is the description of markets. Thus the producer is more able to understand the wants of the consumer. This accession to his powers he will make of profit to himself, and to all, so long as his morality and his technical knowledge are not at all at fault.

Thus, without entering into detail, with due prevention of waste of labour, waste of capital, waste of natural agencies, loss of markets, and over-production, is it necessary that a nation duly develop a character and training of all its members which shall clothe both their production and their consumption with the attributes of thrift, honesty, prudence, skill, and knowledge. Such a national character, developing in its dealings with others, in all its efforts at exchange, true free-trade principles, will possess the highest human security against the evils—in anticipation, in experience, and in effect—of commercial depressions.

PART IV.

ENGLAND AS AN EXAMPLE.

CHAPTER XIV.

ENGLAND IN GENERAL.

§ 1. The good of Bad Times—§ 2. England must depend on Free-
trade and her own special superiorities—§ 3. True Economy, both
in production and consumption, is the secret of Prosperity.

WE have set down waste of labour, waste of
capital, failure of natural agencies, loss of markets,
glut of markets, as the five heads under which the
conditions making up commercial depressions may
be grouped. On the occurrence of one or more of
these five groups of conditions, there is immediate
risk of " bad times." It is then of general value to
emphasise, by a particular example, the actual efforts
needed to mitigate or obviate the possibilities of such
conditions. And if we adopt as our particular example the England of 1879, we shall have a community engaged in the exercise of productive energy,
whose course has, over and above its general value to
the on-looker and the theorist, a very particular value
to the statesman and the practical man at the present
conjuncture of affairs.

§ 1. *The good of Bad Times.*—The one great economical benefit of commercial depressions is their monitory power. " Bad times" break through the crust with which prosperity always veneers the subtle processes of social energy. Bad times set men a-thinking. The tendency of the human mind, in practice, even if it accord not with some theories, is to work *by* conclusions instead of working *to* conclusions. Individual minds have an undoubted tendency to leave all they can to other minds ; to adopt principles, not to create them ; to borrow, not to make. No doubt in this there is a considerable saving of labour ; but there is a concomitant drawback in the resulting danger of the adoption of wrong principles. In the bad times of 1878 there was brought to light a plentiful crop of the logical fallacies which are the bases of protectionism. These fallacies were put forward with much noise and pretension ; and it became matter of surprise that the public mind should so glibly and readily listen to these once-discarded fallacies. Correct principles were lying silent the while ; and it may well be conjectured that had not bad times laid bare the whole matter, the insidious leaven of protectionism would have permeated the national mind to a far greater degree.

Among other monitory benefits conferred by bad

times, is the showing up of faults in a national system of production. They lead producers to reflection. When things go wrong men blame, not themselves, but one another. They search for some scapegoat; and in the search they turn over all causes, real and unreal, actual and supposed, true and asserted. Vexed with bad times, the man will lay out for inspection the errors and faults of the master, and the master will deal similarly by the man. Each will abuse the other; but out from under the veil of this promiscuous abuse will shine forth the countenance of truth. And both man and master, each by the teaching of the other, may recognise, if they will, where they themselves may amend their ways. International exhibitions forward the same ends by laying bare the facts of rivalry and competition. The prejudices and misleading contentment which is bred of isolation fails to maintain itself in the face of open intercommunication. These lessons are indeed thus offered to the world, but they are only forced on the world by bad times. On the compulsion of bad times, a nation will take to heart these lessons, and, by the exercise once more of due thought, entirely avert the evil and even disastrous consequences previously imminent.

And in no less degree do bad times show up faults in a national system of consumption. We may instance the phenomena connected with prices which so intimately affect the nation in its capacity as a consumer. Adam Smith has handed down to us the enunciation of the fundamental law of prices. It survives through all mutations of supply and demand, and he words it as "the gravitation of market towards natural prices." These normal or natural prices are those "which suffice, and no more, to yield to producers the average and usual remuneration for their sacrifices." And it is towards this that fluctuations of price should always tend in a healthy state of things. But the severe pressure of bad times often reveals an unhealthy state of things. In a complex civilisation, in which exchange of products proceeds, as it should, with a vigour commensurate with the prosperity enjoyed, middle-men appear as the direct agents of this exchange. They are a necessary, and in every right way a beneficial, feature. But there is a tendency, natural with human nature, of which selfishness is a leading ingredient, to exceed and depart from a legitimate position. From a variety of actual causes the London coal-merchant could not profitably sell his coal under 60s. a ton in the year 1873. In 1878 he could sell it at a profit at 20s. a ton. In the interval, while the price of coal at the pit's mouth was rapidly falling, there was a great temptation for him to abide, so long as he could, by the previous high prices. Bad times, leading men to consider and inquire into their expenditure, usually discover instances of this tendency of the middle-man to absorb most of the advantages of a fluctuation in price. In bad times there is often an outcry from the farmers, that though the prices of the carcasses have fallen greatly, butchers still charge the same to their customers for joints. In England this tendency has been so marked, that many an innocent middle-man has now been brought to suffer for the sins of his overreaching fellow-tradesman. Co-operative stores have risen as a protest on the part of consumption, and an apparently enduring protest, against this illegitimate overdoing of a legitimate source of profit : and the small retail tradesman will have to yield his position to those larger concerns which must be regulated by the principles of true political economy, and in which private selfishness and petty ambition have no place. These large concerns may fall to the direct charge of the consumers themselves ; or of that growing class of middle-men who are claiming the title of " Universal Providers." But in either case the consumer will enjoy some security that the market prices are charged, and that the middle-man is not absorbing profits out of all proportion to the sacrifice he makes.

Bad times also effect much good by putting an effectual drag on the personal extravagance of a people, and so at once preventing much waste of capital. This was very evident in the immediate effect of the commercial crisis in the United States in 1873. A large and widespread renunciation of luxury and extravagance ensued among all classes. At the time the United States were largely indebted to the rest of the world. Between 1869 and 1873 the excess of imports over exports was valued at 100 millions sterling. But in five short years this state of things was reversed, a result in great measure due to the salutary, if severe, lesson taught by the bad times of 1873. The bad times of 1879 may be looked to to teach England many valuable lessons. They will induce reflection and self-examination; lead to the firmer adoption of true principles, and to the acknowledgment of the weak points in the national systems of production and consumption.

§ 2. *England must depend on Free-trade and her own natural superiorities.*—There must ensue a firmer adoption of the principles of free-trade. This alone is the true line of procedure. But in order to be able duly to profit by such procedure it must be remembered that, on the one hand, universal free-trade is not a fact, and indeed perhaps not possible, at all events for the present. On the other hand, due regard must be given to what are England's national or natural superiorities of productive capacity.

That free-trade is not universal is a fact, and the only alternative for England is to attempt in every way to extend an approach to this desired universality. Paradoxical as it may seem, one great obstacle in England's path is her native superiority in many branches of production. Many communities resort to protection at the present day for the avowed reason that otherwise they could never compete with England. This gives to certain foreign vested interests great profit, and this high-pressure creation of industry only results in increased waste in production. The sugar bounties of America and France, the more they succeed the more do they raise the price of sugar—in other words, the more do they curtail their own market. Thus do these protectionist nations invade the English home market, raise prices, and eventually deprive English native producers of a portion of their legitimate remuneration. But it is greatly to the profit of those individual foreigners immediately concerned, even though, in the end, it inevitably impoverishes producers and consumers generally. Thus there is a strong party in each foreign community eager to press on its own present productive energy. And the more it is made evident that any particular community falls behind England in productive capacity the greater the effort to do away with the natural inequality, even at the price of inevitable future ruin.

It cannot be denied that this foreign opinion, which seeks to hedge itself round with bounties and tariffs, is right in its opinion of England's productive superiority. Thus, in supplying coal England has a natural mine of wealth not yet fully developed. Statistics prove that English coalminers produce far more coal per man than foreign miners. Again, the carriage of coal for long distances is far cheaper by sea than by land. Holland takes four times the amount of coal from West Germany that she takes from England; but England supplies to Russia six times as much coal as Germany supplies. England possesses a decided national and natural superiority in the supply of coal to the whole world. Again English sugar refiners have successfully competed with French refiners, though the latter enjoy all the material advantage of a bounty of 30*s.* to 60*s.* per ton. And if we look for signs we find that in the face of all this protective energy and in view of the *whole* of productive success, England has advanced further and faster than any other community. And there stands out the fact that liberal tariffs aid the other parties to them just as much as they do England.　Norway, Sweden, Denmark, and Belgium grant liberal tariffs : with these countries, during the last twenty years, our trade has increased 300 per cent.　But with Germany, Austria, and Italy, with their far more restrictive tariffs, 100 per cent. is the amount of the increase for the same period.　That all this is advantageous for England there is of course no doubt.　The completely free ports of the Channel Islands give us a trade of £20 per head of their population ; the liberal tariffed Belgium yields us £7 per head ; but the more protective States only £2.　Again, from the subjective point of view in the strictly protectionist days preceding 1846, England exported no more than £2 per head of population of her own products.　Free-trade came in 1846—in the succeeding decade this value rose to £3 10*s.* per head.　Between 1858 and 1864 it increased to £4 15*s.* And in 1873 it nearly quadrupled the protective results and reached the high figure of £7 15*s.*　Free-trade has, as a fact, given for each Englishman four times the amount of wealth that protection gave.

Her free-trade and her characteristics give England a national productive superiority which serves greatly to enhance her natural superiorities.　There is every reason, then, for Englishmen to pursue the even tenour of their ways and to stand to their free-trade colours. But, as we have seen, their very success engenders a spirit of jealous opposition in others, which results often in the adoption of a suicidal protectionism. English producers have their part to play ; they can trust implicity to the survival of the fittest : the efforts of other nations towards their own productive destruction will of course affect English industry in their course, but national and natural superiorities will outlive all this ; and nations which shall have humbled themselves by the misguided attempts of a selfish but fallacious protectionism, will, in the end, see their only chance of resuscitation in following, far astern indeed, in the wake of England's free-trade course.

Englishmen may then trust firmly in two principles —free-trade and productive superiority. There are commodities which English environments, in their totality produce with less expenditure of labour than other lands—these form England's wealth. So are there other commodities which would with the presence of freedom fulfil the same functions for other lands. The wealth of all will attain the highest value when free exchange of such commodities is established. In the meantime, those nations which advance nearest to free exchange will insure the greatest attainable value to the " stock they win from nature," and the greatest available opportunities for winning such stock.

x 2

§ 3. *True economy, both in Production and in Consumption, is the secret of Prosperity.*—To secure to productive energy its best success, we must secure to it its right opportunities *and* its right rewards. Right economy in production and right economy in consumption are the inseparable pillars of productive success. The right ordering of supply and demand is the one necessary condition of this. As a producer the nation needs a due supply of material. Whether all things are ultimately reducible to one element ; whether all matter is merely differing forms of one " Vril;" man has, nevertheless, to deal with its complex forms, and not its fundamental unity. In his hands he holds the power to combine and disintegrate these forms, and the exercise of this power is Productive Energy. But these forms must be placed in his hands, or he cannot exercise this power upon them. The material may be the chemically impregnated soil, plus the latent germinancy of the wheat seed, plus the hoarded results of labour represented in a plough—or his materials may be the cotton fibre from India, plus the machinery and plant from Sheffield ; or his materials may be gold thread, plus flowered silk, plus jewellery. He may be far from or close to " nature." Equally he will need materials to enable his productive δυναμεις to put on a due ἐνέργεια. He may produce sacks of wheat or cotton cloth, or elaborate cloaks—in each case he will need materials—in each case he will need supply.

And again, as a consumer, the nation needs a due supply—but in this instance, it is supply of materials which may be described as the facilities of life. The producer exists as a consumer ; and the greater the ease of this existence, the greater his capacity for actual production. The "facilities of life" include food, furniture, clothing—all and everything that is an aid to enabling the producer to set about his work in life. And times of distress are often largely relieved (though this may escape passing notice), by the fact that when the producer suffers the consumer often gains.

It is then necessary for Englishmen to remember that economy in production and economy in consumption are the two inseparable ends of true national endeavour, if economical success is to be attained. And as supply is necessary to each, so is demand necessary to each. The consumer is the possibility of the producer, and the producer the possibility of the consumer. It may be held that A, B, C, &c. produce a, b, c, &c. commodities ; but they can only continue so to do provided A consumes b, c, &c. and B a, c, &c. and C a, b, &c. commodities. There must be a right ordering of demand as well as supply. Every member of a community is a consumer ; and this fact largely

explains the popular fallacy that all members are not
producers.   It is no new thing to speak of the
classes, " Nati consumeri fruges." But the most literal
and bare explanation of such a class is that they
"live on their own means." It cannot be denied that
these " means" are simply stored capital, or, in other
words, the results of productive energy ; and these
means are not consumed, they are expended in consumption. In other words, these profits of production
are exerted to maintain the demand which alone
enables the continuance of production. Such expenditure seems to be in truth a new channel of exchange ;
such a class is like the hand that is dipped into the
seed-bag to scatter seed. The product of past labour
is by this means distributed for further productive
use. Thus the true economy of consumption is no
less a necessary consideration than the true economy
of production.

CHAPTER XV.

ENGLAND IN PARTICULAR.

§ 1. Economy in Production ; Prudence—§ 2. Morality in Production—§ 3. Skill in Production—§ 4. Economy in Consumption.

ECONOMY in production and economy in consumption either and both urgently call for the exercise of qualities which may be discerned under the heads prudence, morality, skill. Cavillers, it is true, at one time were loud in their ridicule of political economy as a science because, as they asserted, there was no place allowed in it to the human personality as an element in production. It was maintained that this science treated alone of the hard and fast rules of wealth; and disdained to notice the inevitable complications involved by the presence of the human mind, and individual human natures in all human efforts. And that is to take an erroneous and misleading view of the true scope of a science which seeks to explain the actual. Nowhere is this more palpably evident than in the examination of true economy in production and consumption.

§ 1. *Economy in Production: Prudence.—Prudence* is a first necessity. Without prudence the producer

is fated to go astray. Without prudence the consumer is fated to go astray. The one will waste his
energies; the other will waste his winnings. The
labour in either case will be in vain. The one will
exert himself on unprofitable work; the other will
dissipate the gains of even profitable work. This is
a false economy. The producer, labourer as well
as employer, often shows sad lack of prudence. In
most cases is this the result of *thoughtless ignorance.*
There is a glut in the market; employers say we
must lower wages and increase hours—labourers
say no, lessen the hours, lessen the "output." The
labourer, in the selfish blindness of non-ownership,
forgets that unproductive plant is the equivalent of
the proverbial stabled horse. He forgets that the
corn thus uselessly devoured is the fund from which
his own wages are supplied. The labourer, with a
selfishness which is the leading characteristic of the
higher forms of animals, regards alone his own immediate benefit. Selfishness proceeds blindfold, in
no case does it regard consequences, in every case
does it invite future disaster. The labourer, shut
within the horizon of the short-sighted, will hold
that fewer hours and less work means more men
required for the work. His arithmetic is correct;
but logic he wots not of. He knows not that his true
success rests on the fact of work done; that the more

profitable work done the more there will be to do. Profit is the fountain-head of wages. The more the capitalist gains, the more capital he can set into profitable motion; the more he will be desirous of advancing as wages.

In all productive industries some capital is necessary. This capital is capable of yielding profit in whatever way applied, provided it be set in motion. It is, say, invested in the plant and "fixed charges" necessary to the maintenance of some manufactory. The interest on this sum is £50 a week. In other words, when invested elsewhere or used for other purposes, it would yield the manufacturer this sum. Set down the wages at the manufactory per week of fifty hours, at £50. Say that one week's work of fifty hours produces some certain commodity. If this be sold for anything over £100 the business pays. But if the labourer have his way and work only twenty-five hours a week, there will be two weeks' interest on the capital to be refunded, and unless the manufacturer can get for the commodity the raised price of £150 the business will not pay, and the labourer will no longer get wages. Such thoughtless ignorance in the labourer must be cured; habits of industry must, in these days of schooling, be based upon a knowledge of such broad facts of political economy. And it is in England that we may most hopefully

look for this great base of productive security—where
the people are not led, but suffered to lead themselves.
It is not only to the profit but is the duty of employers to endeavour to disseminate such truths
amongst all classes—and the associations of labourers
—the great Trades' unions—could find no more really
profitable use of their energies and their funds than
in availing themselves of the best opinions of thoughtful minds, and impressing their opinions on their
fellows in labour. Trades' unions, mechanics' institutes,
labourers' clubs, popular lectures, and the countless
modes in which employers of labour have of late years
striven to raise the tone of those they employ, can
have no higher or more profitable aim than in dis-
sipating this thoughtless ignorance.

And another effect will follow. It may be asserted
the best prosperity is in proportion to the equality of
the distribution of wealth in a community. Each
member must have his *fair* share. Now there is a
thoughtless ignorance, that is not even intentional, far
less criminal, that is sometimes shown by employers
as well as by labourers. And it is this which often
impedes a due distribution of profits : and it is the
vague and undefined knowledge of its presence which
on occasion begets mistrust, discontent, and suspicion between labourer and employer. At once
the harmony of common effort is upset, and its pro-

fitable issue gravely imperilled. Instances of this frequently occur. The exports of some trade fall in nominal value; the unthinking look for a reduction in wages; yet there prevails a dim consciousness that the profits of the trade are nevertheless on the increase: this may result, for instance, from a fall in the price of the raw material: and if this fall be not attended to by the employers in their relations with their labourers, sooner or later the fact will protrude itself and confidence be upset.

But an enemy to prudence, even more hurtful than thoughtless ignorance, is the want of *thrift*. People are even more prone to waste their winnings than their energies. And yet to waste winnings is to lessen their value. Professor Leone Levi, in the *Times*, thus words the conclusion to which his extensive knowledge has brought him: " In no other country are wages more liberal, but in no other country are they more wastefully used than in the United Kingdom." The coalminer indeed will do all in his power to raise wages, but when he spends half of his week's earnings in champagne he will never own that he is himself lowering his wages by onehalf. There are distinct means already in existence working to this desirable end. Mr. Bartley's Penny Banks and the Post Office Saving Banks endeavour to prove, by the solid accumulations of small increments, the benefits of thrift. Such institutions as the Parochial Mission Women's Association seeks to collect savings locally by inviting the poor to trust their pennies in safe-keeping. In twenty years by this particular agency, no less a sum has been rescued from indiscriminate waste than £150,000. And this, coming from the poorest of the poor, represents a large amount of the wages of labour rescued from annihilation. Friendly societies and all such clubs are likewise of great material aid in staying this waste. Above all, these and all kindred institutions are invaluable by the aid of the examples they afford. Every movement in this direction is of the highest national benefit. The wealthy, more especially those whose profits are derived directly from employment of labour, have no more profitable call on the charitable side of their duties than the furtherance of all measures which shall instil and foster a national thrift.

Yet another form of prudence is that which seeks to engender the *confidence of knowledge.* Both to employer and labourer is this of the highest imporance. Trust in the future is the one guarantee of calmness in the hour of danger or distress. Knowledge of the future is the one guarantee of following the right course through bad as well as through good times.

All men can prepare only too well for an extension

of activity; few can seriously set about meeting shrinkage. This latter destiny is most often faced simply as a disaster, and with the callous yielding of despair. Yet the signs of coming shrinkage are even more palpable than those of inflation. The cotton-trade in 1878 is a most instructive case in point. A knowledge of facts reveals that in that industry in England shrinkage rather than increase is the probable future prospect. In 1850 there were twenty million spindles profitably employed in England. Ten years ran this total to the great height of thirty millions. The next twenty years had added only another nine millions; and good authorities agree that 25 or even 30 per cent. of this machinery was, in 1878, not in profitable employment. It is known that since 1860 very little increase has taken place in the amount of cotton-cloth disposed of. It is true there are markets still open, and there are markets in prospect, but there is the converse fact that Englishmen are no longer the sole pur-veyors. England, in the first half of this century, practically supplied the world with cotton goods. The United States, indeed, put in an early appear-ance in competition; but her "Great War" put her out of the field once more for some time; and it is only of late years that she has again come near to her former position. She has advanced to some effect : and chiefly for the reason that, while forced to abstain from competing with us as a producer, she, in addition, became a great consumer. For this she must needs pay by some day turning producer. And accordingly in 1878, the United States takes only one-quarter of what she took twenty years ago, and there is prospect of this particular market still further failing English producers. Again, the continent of Europe is commencing to make appreciable efforts towards supplying itself; and the same is the case with India.

Now a knowledge of these facts is necessary to prevent further waste of productive power. Instead of steering the vessel with the eye steadily fixed on the successes of the past, the producer, facing the present and the future, will see he must transfer his redundant energies and powers to other fields of production, rather than sink them in the thankless and unprofitable task of hopeless competition. Such transference of effort is a mode of true economy in production, and it arises in confidence begot of knowledge. This will cheer and not depress; this will brace and not palsy the productive energies.

This confidence begot of knowledge is most valuable when loss of markets has to be faced. The Germans close their markets to the entrance of the rest of the world. Knowledge tells us that the very first and immediate effect of this is an enhanced price in Germany on all ironwork of no less than 15 per cent., imposed by the "protected" ironmasters of Germany. This rise in price at once enables foreign competition in some measure to enter the market. The German nation, taxing itself in order to keep out foreign competition, gives higher prices for its commodities than foreigners obtain elsewhere; and out of this enhanced price foreigners can pay the duty or price of entrance through the barriers of protection. Whether all this benefits the German or the foreigner is no very obscure problem.

Another example of the use of this knowledge is seen in the recognition of the fact, that the greatest economy in manufacture is to work machinery to its fullest powers; for this involves the obvious draw-back of the consequent risk of a surplus of commo-dities. These commodities, if they are sold in the "natural" market, must be sold at less than cost price. Knowledge reveals two profitable methods of such forced sale. In the first place, by the kind aid of protection in other lands, these commodities, even after paying high import duty, can be sold at a price that can successfully compete with the prices in the protected market. And, in the second place, it often "pays" to sell such surplus "at a sacrifice," by way of advertisement. This becomes, under certain conditions, a legitimate method of opening up new markets. American meat and American tools, the surplus of a glut in the home market, advertise themselves in the English market, chiefly by means of their abnormally low prices. But, when once established in that market, the ensuing regular demand makes them no longer surplus products, and their prices inevitably rise ; yet they have won for themselves recognition in a new market by making due use of an otherwise useless surplus.

Perhaps the most notable instance of the use of this confidence begot of knowledge is in the case of agricultural depression. Land-owning in England, in 1879, is not a profitable industry ; and land-tilling is in no better way. Free-trade has flooded England with wheat, and is largely supplementing her home-grown supplies of all other foods. The direct products of the soil are falling in price ; consequently they must be produced saleable at low prices if the industry is to continue. England possesses, without doubt, all the natural qualities for agricultural success, even in greater degree than other lands ; and these have a " natural protection," in the fact that other lands have to add cost of carriage to cost of production. And free-trade England has the further advantage that, in the failure of the assistance of nature in any one branch, at once from abroad there comes a supply to remedy the deficiencies of that particular commodity. Again, good agricultural land is probably cheaper in England than in any other fully populated country. Thus, in England, there is every condition of success so far as Nature is concerned.

The fault lies with man. The question of the possibility of cheapening agricultural products seems very much to depend on the fact that the system of labour still in vogue is that of olden times, when conditions were altogether different; when the population summed up barely one-third of its present total; and when rigid protection still deprived the population of the benefits of the bounty of Nature in other parts of the world. In England land becomes owned by those who from sentimental and traditional reasons desire to become landowners. The first object of every Englishman who has made a way for himself in the world has always been to follow in the steps of previous successful Englishmen, and become a landowner. Thus the land comes to be owned by men who have no direct desire or intention to make the most of it. This fact of ownership, it must not be forgotten, is one of the most beneficial features in the national life; this class of landowners forms the backbone and sinew of the staid " solidarity" of English history. And although the landowners do not make direct use of the soil they own, they do hand it over to others to utilise for their own purposes, demanding a rent which is far below the profits of the same capital if invested in other undertakings. This system of landowning on a residential, rather than on an industrial basis, is at present further burdened with certain evils incident to that life-ownership of tenantry-in-tail which forces men to live on land they have not the wealth properly to develop, or the liberty to part with to others.

The production of agricultural commodities is in the hands of the tenant-farmers ; and they in their turn employ agricultural labourers to aid them. Both these latter classes have worked on the ground of mere subsistence at the least possible sacrifice; though the term "mere subsistence" implies, in the one case, a pony-chaise and luxuries of education, whereas, in the other, its connotation is little else than the staving off of hunger and weather. The tenant-farmer trusts to good seasons for the profits which shall carry him through bad. He will also adopt the rough-and-ready method of a variety of crops as some insurance against the uncertainty of the seasons ; and if rain destroy his wheat he will know that it is fatting his swedes; and if the latter lack moisture he will rejoice that his wheat is ripening well. And, on the whole, he will take things easily. If he have ambition, it will expend itself on extending his holding as much as possible, so as to increase this comfortable variety of supply. This is personal, not scientific, farming; and it is not making the most of the bounty of Nature. It is a course that insures a rough independence to the farmer and his family, and it insures to him personally a life of superintendence ; a life specially inviting to all men. But he will prefer grass to plough ; ease to toilsome enterprise. And the agricultural labourer of the present day merely seeks to do as little work as possible, and get as much as possible for so doing. He has no interest or share in the profitableness of his work ; no anxiety or responsibility for the failure of its results. His application of labour is purely personal, and by no means scientific.

But there are remedies for these things. The labour, both of brain and muscle, given to the soil, must be incited to the best exercise of its abilities. It is acknowledged that, theoretically speaking, large farms and the consequent scientific agriculture must give the best economic results ; but it is none the less true that most excellent actual results follow the labour of the proprietor in his own soil. The fact is, science is of little profit without the willing and intelligent co-operation of man. The keen spur of competition is driving the agricultural industry in England to reform itself according to the needs and lights of the day. Landowners will be led to increase the productiveness of their land; they may seek this end by giving greater encouragement to their tenants; by instituting conditions of tenure more favourable to the encouragement of high-class agriculture; by agreements and leases which shall encourage and not hamper improvements and outlay; and there are remedies for the evils of the entail system: or they may devote more personal and direct influence to the work, and in greater measure associate themselves with the actual working of their own land. Farmers, for their own benefit, must give up seeking to tide over the uncertainties of Nature, and the troubles of labour by extended "earth-scratching;" and set themselves resolutely, by concentrating their energies on lesser and more manageable areas, to win the higher profits of a more economic system of agriculture. They must also set about the better supply of such commodities as eggs and the rest of the good things that in recent days have become so much cheaper when brought all the way from France than when produced on English farms.

But, above all, the labour question must be dealt with. The agricultural labourer must be raised out of his present position. He must be given some impulse to more sustained and intelligent work. In many cases this end may be attained by means of a modified form of co-operation which shall, by offering facilities for the investment of his savings, give to the labourer a share in the profits of his labour. But in the main he must be treated by means of wages. The wage-earner is, and always must be, by virtue of his associations and by character, less advanced in knowledge than is desirable; and though he would eagerly share the profits accruing, he would never be brought to acknowledge his share in the losses. Wages themselves are, in short, a sign of this. In return for receiving them, a large portion of mankind is content to leave all risk, enterprise, profit, and failure to the rest of mankind; and deems it sufficient for itself to receive a certain present profit of hard cash, the sum of which it allows is most properly not so great a meed for its exertions as if it included the uncertainties of the future. Piece-work and a more vivid and exacting discrimination in the adjustment of remuneration, between good and bad work, between energy and sloth, between skill and ignorance, are practical means of forcing on the labourer the fact that the value of his labour to the employer is not merely so much time, but so much result.

Agriculture, thus proceeding on a truer economy,

with the ensuing cheapness of agricultural products, will be enabled successfully to compete with the imported food supplies which are now driving it to a renewed life of more durable and scientific vitality.

§ 2. *Morality in Production.*—Morality plays an important part in the true economy of production and consumption. Immorality and commercial depressions are joined to one another in a circle. On the one hand, immorality in production brings about some of the conditions of commercial depression, and these in their turn induce immorality in production. When we are told on high authority " unfortunately the English stamp is no longer the sign of the genuine article ;" when we hear of merchants who, from an excess of the speculative or ambitious spirit, are finally forced to a desperate mode of business, and even induce manufacturers to supply them with fictitious commodities ; we see at once a blow irredeemably dealt to one outlet at least of the products of national industry.

Again, in the very presence of severe depression, those who have profited most are generally only too eager to alleviate the distress of those by whose aid they have themselves been elevated. Those most charitably disposed are those most susceptible, and most liable to allow their goodness of heart to get the better of their judgment. And, oftentimes, instead of relieving distress, their efforts result in becoming mere premiums on idleness, mere reimbursements on reckless expenditure. These good men invite wage-earners to enjoy to the full the squandering of wages while wages are being earned by holding up the certain inducement of gratuitous help when wages cease to flow. There can be no more sure and certain road to the utter demoralisation of a class such as that of the wage-earners, which, by its ignorance and comparatively low intelligence, is specially obnoxious to such plausible influences.

The English poor-law system has, indeed, been described as a unique national institution for the discouragement of thrift in that very section of the community in which thrift is least likely to appear of itself. It is true the English labourer has a most proper contempt for the "workhouse;" a contempt which, on the introduction of a similar system into Malta, the Maltese labourer was not found to have for the "Ospizio;" but the English labourer, the more he looks forward, the more he reflects—the more, that is, he comes under the influence of the conditions in which thrift is possible and probable—the more does he recognise the fact that, after all, the only sure and unfailing prospect for him or his family is the workhouse. He may starve on his wages ; he may starve on his savings; but he cannot starve in the workhouse. In many instances, in spite of the wholesome and widespread national feeling of independence, there must present itself the question, Why save, why work? And this question must press itself with special force in those "bad times" when, with work in full swing, the labourer finds himself no better off materially than were he in the workhouse. The hypothetical suppression of workhouses has been put forward with some pertinence. In such case, it is asked, would not the labourer be forced to greater exertion of production and of abstinence; his desire for wealth would be stimulated at the expense of his evil love of ease; in position and in character he would improve vastly: he would become a propertied, a respectable, and in every respect a more efficient member of society. The city of Lisbon, at no very remote date, was known as the city of beggars: all its .passages and places were thronged by the able-bodied as well as the maimed, basking in the sun and deriving precarious sustenance from the charity or convenience of passers-by. An astute minister, however, presently devised an institution known as the "Asylo." Whoever asked alms in public was, *ipso facto*, condemned to the "Asylo," and there had to work for his living for a period. The consequences were immediate; and the idling noisy beggars of the market-place transformed themselves forthwith into porters and labourers and boatmen. A similar effect, a similar development of energy, it is said, would follow the abolition of the promiscuous alms-giving of the workhouse.

Any system of State poor-relief· has to struggle against rewarding sloth and vice with that generous aid they are only too ready eagerly to usurp, but which is in truth the highest moral due of misfortune and sickness. It seems only too true that any system of poor-relief which insures *future* benefits is bad in principle, if we regard its actual effects ; for it can but induce a vicious trust in eventual aid. The honest and the industrious will shrink from even momentary thought of the workhouse ; but the prospect of this sure haven is the entirely vicious support of immorality and idleness. Yet so hard is it to discriminate, at the time, among antecedents, that the very fact of its being good in the one case almost renders it a necessary evil in the other. The great remedy for this at the present is the multiplication of substitutes ; such are Friendly Societies and all such organisations that lead men, while in working order, to prepare for the eventualities of a less lucky future ; but to found their preparations on their own exertions. It may be suggested that were a portion of the poor-rates actually granted as State subsidies to the various Friendly Societies, the balance of good effect would be great. At the present day, at all events, the unsatisfactory condition of labour is very largely due to the premium set on sloth and "unthrift" by the open doors of the workhouse.

When we find immorality and commercial depressions thus proceeding hand-in-hand, we also discover the favourable part of the concomitant existence of monitory conditions of peculiar force. For instance, in times of depression, the baffled spirit of honest enterprise can *with effect* declaim against the immorality which has brought distress on all. The reckless speculator, the dishonest trader, the demoralised workman, can no longer afford to smile at the denunciations of the righteous; for the community, brought to its senses by distress and anxiety, is in no humour to pass over faults and sins. Thus times of depression come to exert a wholesome influence in yielding from time to time opportunities for the checking of immorality. They may thus be made good use of to destroy gradually one of the conditions of their appearance.

And of the means to this end there is, perhaps, none of greater power than the influence possessed by the clergy. We have here a body of men in the aggregate boasting better trained intelligence than any other body in the community; possessed, too, of proper enthusiasm in their work; and enjoying a professional position which makes them the recognised and trusted advisers of every class of society. The clergy form, as it were, an independent chain, extending through the whole of society and forming oftentimes the only recognised link between some of its grades. They are known to be students of the best thoughts and ideas, and exponents of the highest principles and deepest learning of the day. Workmen see in them the personal advisers of the capitalist and the landowner ; and yet the rich know them to be intimate friends of the working-man and the poor. They thus have it in their power to oil the wheels of society ; and so to add vastly to the efficiency of the whole machinery of national production. They can preach morality and kindliness and the pursuit of knowledge to the rich and the employers of labour. They can preach thrift and self-help to the labourer. They can set to work in their parish, with the rich and with the poor, to secure the active existence of local branches of such valuable institutions as that new, but none the less eminently useful, National Thrift Society. In endless ways the clergy may prove of the very highest economic use, and go far to increasing the material well-being of their parishioners. And this must needs prove the most powerful and practical foundation on which readily and easily to build up the moral well-being of their cures.

The labourers, too, amongst themselves, by combining, seek to improve their condition.   But in the late history of these efforts there is lamentably evident the lack of knowledge and of a properly intelligent spirit. Trades Unions seem to have devoted the greater proportion of their energies to exactly the wrong purposes.   In many ways they have succeeded in impairing the efficiency of labour ; that is, in other words, they have succeeded in curtailing the profits of labour. They have opposed piece-work ; but piece-work is the real base of the only sound theory of wages ; which makes them depend on the quantity and quality of the work done ; and thus incidentally induces that intelligent interest in his work which not only cheers the labourer in his labour, but adds vastly to the value of the product.   Their tendency has been to reduce all emulation, and so to bring about one dead-level of work.   Better heads seek, by educational and other means, to raise work to as high a level as possible ; but Trades Unions, by stifling emulation, force the skilled workman to fall back to the lower and far less profitable level of the stupid workman. And yet it is competition and emulation which are known so largely to improve capacity, and moreover to give intelligence and ability their due reward, and so to encourage and cheer labour with the bright example of labourers risen to affluence by the exercise of their own good qualities. Trades Unions have a vastly profitable field for their exertion in increasing the efficiency of labour and in giving full scope and opportunity to all energy and talent. The freedom of his labour, all men agree, is the actual and inalienable right of man. But Trades Unions prostitute their energies to stamp this freedom under foot. They will, for instance, force labourers, like so many slaves, to sit by idle and abstain from work with as much hopeless loss of liberty as though they were chained down in the hold of a slaver. But this is the tyranny of ignorance, against which education will some day rebel with effect. It has often been shown that the true way to secure for labour a proper meed of reward is the periodical publication of authoritative prices of staple materials and products. The sanction of all public opinion would then side with labour, and the appeal to the honesty, to say nothing of the liberality, of employers would never be in vain. In these days, Trades Unions, if they have the welfare of the labourer at heart, must increase and not decrease his power of effort and the efficiency of his work.

§ 3. *Skill in Production.*—Skill is perhaps the main element in the true economy of production. Production may be described as the exertion of the human mind on the materials around it, in order to benefit itself. And this exertion, from the very first, is skill. To improve a process of manufacture, is to lower the cost of production. The Australian black, who uses a knife given him by a settler to fashion his boomerang in the place of the old-fashioned shell-scraping, has so much the more leisure to hunt his opossums and kangaroos. The vaunted " scientific appliances" of the present century are the latest development of this skill in production. But as the human mind in general advances in this skill so does it become increasingly important that each particular human mind be educated up to the standard of the age. A main lever to the manufacturing success of the citizens of the United States has been the remarkable affluence of mechanical invention. Ingenuity in productive works has there been largely stimulated chiefly by means of the easy conditions for taking out patents. Labour and power-saving appliances are continually making their appearance ; and though much time and labour and thought are no doubt spent on futile and useless endeavours, still a balance of good appears to result. This balance is indeed often hard to appreciate ; and much, it seems, may be said in favour of the opposite system of patent law prevailing in England. At the present the somewhat partisan statement of the case has been to the effect that " for a payment of six pounds or eight pounds an American inventor receives absolute protection for his invention.   In England an inventor pays two hundred pounds." It is true that, although this high English tariff may prevent much misapplication of energy, it does nevertheless materially stifle the aspirations of inventive genius.   And we may thus welcome that recent reconsideration of our patent laws, in view of the extensive ramifications of " scientific" appliances, which had indeed become imperative on any government which has at heart the productive success of England.

This skill and ingenuity has no greater stimulant and preservative than the dissemination of knowledge.   England is an old country, in many ways linked to a past when books were rarities, and when science and knowledge were the exclusive possession of a somewhat despised class.   Our descendants in the United States and our brethren in our various colonies seem, however, to have been born to life with books in their hands.   To the traveller from Europe, one of the most striking features of our colonial cities, as of those of the United States, is the inevitable and prominent presence of public and lending libraries.   Already, however, in the old country has a movement been started, which bids fair shortly to bless England with those opportunities of knowledge which have become an indispensable portion of the life of to-day. Those who feel in heart or in pocket the success or failure of home productive energy have no higher task than aiding in thus placing knowledge at every man's door. In Massachusetts the public libraries circulate annually an average of five volumes per head of population. The statistics of a Scotch manufacturing town give a similar average of only one per head. It is to be hoped that this average will rise rapidly in England.

Technical education is another means to the same end. The State is doing excellent duty in this direction, and this again would be a far more profitable expenditure of the funds of the great Trades Unions than the supporting their members in idleness in fighting with the hand that feeds them.

§ 4. *Economy in Consumption.*—There is skill, too, in consumption ; and skill that is to be acquired by much the same means as the skill in production. It is far more in accordance with the dictates of true science—if not, indeed, of common sense as well—for the wage-earner to secure the due value of his wages in their expenditure than to spend his energies in attempting, too often vainly, to increase their nominal amount. So, too, for the capitalist is it more necessary to obtain the full value for what he spends than to struggle on perpetually to obtain more to spend.

One of the main pillars of national prosperity is the existence of a truly national economy in expenditure. For the various stations in life there are the various modes of this economy. Primarily it lies with parent, secondarily with the various more public forms of private endeavour, and in the last instance with Government, as the supervisor of these two, to promote national economy in consumption. Allowance has no doubt to be made for the vast variety of individual character and circumstance ; but the object to be attained is more or less clear and distinct—and this is to maintain in a community as high an average as possible of this economy in consumption.

It may be well to instance as provinces in this field the saving of food, the preservation of health, the management of clothing. For both high and low the procuring and the cooking of food is a most important art—over and over has it been shown that in this department of consumption there is a sad tendency to ruinous waste. Prejudice, both in the kind and manner of feeding, deprives endless households of many benefits of food. Ignorance cuts down their list still further. The remedy lies in the wider distribution of knowledge. Science has for some time been making clear the relative advantages of food ; commerce has been popularising new types and sources ; again, in the preparation of food England has been busy with cooking schools and cookery in general. The good old " final cause " of woman is to preside over the household, and whether she combine all its services in her own actual hands, or simply superintend a vast staff of handmaidens, equally will her knowledge of cookery as of other household matters prevent waste of materials and of energy. This knowledge of serving food is capable of much complexity. There is, for instance, the valuable historical view. The sedge-grown fish-stews of the country side in England bear witness to a time when carp and tench occupied the place on the table which increased facilities of communication have usurped for turbot and soles. One hundred years ago tea was only to be had at prohibitive prices. Now it has in great measure superseded the mead of our more remote ancestors. There are old foods, there are strange foods, there are new foods—to all of which the economical consumer by study may devote his energies. The wife of the labourer can make his wages " go twice as far;" the wife of the doctor will make his home twice as comfortable ; the wife of the millionaire will be able to make twice the show ; if wives be educated according to their various prospects to a due knowledge of scientific feeding. Poor and rich, humble and noble, all should be brought to a desire for this knowledge ; and so far as in them lies, all true citizens will do their best towards the spread of this knowledge.

And the same is true of the knowledge which leads to a preservation of health. Doctors can give advice, but they cannot make people follow it ; otherwise it needs no prophet to assert that there would be far less ill-health than there is. But the dissemination of hygienic knowledge is the doctors' great hope. The human frame is subtle and tender in its susceptibilities—at the same time, when once out of order it can no longer work. Dyspepsia may ruin the success of a newspaper through the stomach of its editor. Typhoid may throw the labourer and all his household on the parish. England has been doing much towards the improvement of national hygiene ; these efforts are deserving of the very best support of all true citizens. They enable a right economy in consumption by indicating one great cause of waste of energy. They add vastly to the facilities of living : they neutralise the evil effects of ignorance or folly. The more material of these hygienic efforts are in the hands of the rich so far as organisation goes. The erection of more healthy dwellings, both in cities and villages ; the most efficient organisation of water supplies and drainage ; these are the leading questions for those with leisure and with wealth. But the effects of such activity bring home to the poorer classes the lessons of hygienic science in a way that is at once practical and irresistible. Here, then, is more scope for those who are wisely bent on developing a national economy in consumption.

As an adjunct to these economies in consumption the art of clothing may be noted. It is in this province that luxury is first to show herself. The first earnings of the servant-maid disappear in ribbons; the first profits of the speculator find their way to the fashionable tailor. These are the outcomes of two human elements, vanity and selfishness, scarcely distinguishable as the two are at periods of existence from desire and ambition. These qualities being fundamental characteristics of human nature must be allowed for; and a true economy will only seek to set bonds to their transgressing the limits of use and entering the illimitable expanse of luxury. Care and thought in the management of clothing are far easier instilled in youth than taste and judgment in the obtaining of clothing. But all these talents should be sought for in order that some may be obtained. Of two girls of precisely similar position and prospects, one will dress well on £50 per annum, and another only badly on £150. Here, then, is a palpable saving in consumption which means the increase, by no less than two-thirds, of an income. There are many persons possessed of the true qualities of good management, and it should be their object to extend as far as possible the benefits of their influence. The dissemination of homely precepts affects some; example affects others; sober reasoning yet others; actual control yet more. And this question of clothing is here introduced to show that even to the smallest details economy in consumption is invaluable to a nation. For the increment of these small details sums up to a total of a national economy in consumption which will go a long way towards insuring a national prosperity, which will do nearly half the work of guaranteeing to men the due profit of their best exertions. Thus, from the very fact that economy in consumption is largely concerned with details which are liable, of their very minuteness, to be relegated to the unheeded limbo of the insignificant—this important basis of national prosperity often escapes the care and the notice of the scientific and the thoughtful. Economy in consumption, no less than economy in production, becomes thus one of the two ends to be sought by those who would secure true prosperity to their country.

CHAPTER XVI.

ENGLAND IN HER EMPIRE.

§ 1. England and others—§ 2. Foreign States; Reciprocity by Treaty—§ 3. The Semi-civilised; Opening-up Markets—§ 4. England's Colonies.

§ 1. *England and others.*—We have seen that England has certain national and natural superiorities in production; and that to give full scope to her profitable privileges of free-production she requires little else than the security of free-exchange. We have reviewed the national or local conditions of these right opportunities and right rewards of productive energy. We now turn to the wider area of conditions which exist beyond the actual limits of the British Isles. And if these may be termed international, they must be held to include the strictly "international" which exist between Englishmen and all foreigners, as well as the "intranational" which subsist between the various British communities which hold so many points of varied productive vantage ground over the face of the earth. Thus are we led to acknowledge the

political as well as the economical element of the
subject.

There was an old toast of the Pitt Club, " Ships,
Colonies, and Commerce." Its accepted signification
was "to conquer and occupy fertile spots of the earth,
and bind them up in one close trade with England."
There is now a larger signification for this toast which
the new spirit of free-trade would suggest ; and this
may be worded "people and cultivate the earth's surface, and let those who are best able exchange from
land to land the best products of each ; and let their
wages be the profits due to him who supplies the
wants of his fellows." England's mission, beyond her
own shores, so far as economical progress or prosperity
is concerned, is to secure free assured trade over as
large a surface as possible. But the surface of the
earth is held by communities other than that governed
directly by the St. Stephen's Parliament ; and thus
this surface is not everywhere under the rule of free-
trade. We find it presided over by four classes of
communities: we have a large class of foreign civilised
countries ; we have foreign countries semi-civilised,
according to Western ideas, such as China and Japan ;
we have uncivilised tribes, to be found in the interior
of Africa or of Borneo ; and lastly we have the civilised
Colonies of the English race. In inverse order are
these communities amenable to English political in-

fluence : in inverse order are the prospects of free-trade promising between them and England.

§ 2. *Foreign States ; Reciprocity by Treaty.*—In the present political atmosphere it is matter of considerable difficulty for one independent State to secure unrestricted intercourse with another.   And England has encountered special difficulties in this direction.   The example of her industrial success, by the means of free-trade, seems to have aroused jealous opposition rather than wise imitation.   Nor are the diplomatic resources of reciprocity or treaty any more efficacious for the purpose, if we are to judge by results. This should not be matter for marvel if we bear in mind the fact that independence necessarily proceeds out of diversity of conditions ; that thus ideas and interests that rule in one State do not rule in another ; and policies, issuing from such differing bases, cannot but differ in themselves.

England, ruling her own commercial policy on the basis of free-trade, is asked to conduct her commercial relations with foreign States on one of two courses, the one positive, and the other negative. On the one course she may attempt by reciprocity to win, and by retaliation to force, other nations to free intercourse.   On the other course she may attempt to coerce others by denying them all intercourse that is not free.   But to refuse all trade with nations that will not have free-trade is to adopt a panacea that is an impossibility. Were England, by thus allowing the abstract statement of a principle to blind her to her real duty in its furtherance, thus to cut herself off from markets for her energy, she would do herself irreparable injury. We are told that for England to open her market to States that maintain a close guard on their own, is sure to lead to her ruin ; and England is asked to close her markets against all that will not admit England to theirs. But in the long run, unless there are buyers in the English market, it will not pay sellers to appear there ; and buyers supply sellers with something they desire. So long as business goes on in a market both buyers and sellers profit ; and the more business done the greater their profits. If all the countries of the world shut themselves up in themselves, there must be less business done ; so less profits made ; and consequently less industrial prosperity.

Of the positive courses which seek to win by reciprocity, and to force by means of retaliation, it must now be maintained that they have no more succeeded in prevailing on others than has the bare example of the successes of free-trade. At the same time, this class of measures has a very baneful effect on the communities that adopt them. Reciprocity is a policy which often finds itself advocated on the specious plea of self-preservation, as well as of beneficial influence on others. But this plea is to mistake the part for the whole. Men would argue that England, being a factor in the world for good, has her first duty in self-preservation : and with the cloak of this duty they cover a multitude of questionable principles for action. Reciprocity and fair-trade are the terms readily adopted by individual selfishness to hide its identity in the mask and trappings of national "self-preservation." In these policies there are, it cannot be denied, germs of self-preservation. Reciprocity may retain life in certain definite industries. If we say to a State, We will not buy your wine unless you buy our cloth; and if we persuade successfully, we benefit one particular industry. But with the same stroke we injure others. Reciprocity has been aptly termed "two-sided protection," and it doubles the evil results. It is, as it were, a gun, which may indeed send its bullet with destructive aim, but the inevitable recoil brings destruction to the shooter with even greater certainty and force. He may hit what he aims at, but himself is destroyed in the undertaking. It becomes evident, once the sum total of effects is taken into consideration, that reciprocity and retaliation, even though we acknowledge them to be *per se* useful as temporary or limited stimulants, are stimulants of that unwholesome and poisonous order which leave, in after effects, a legacy of greater disease and inevitable decay. They may prop and energise one or two national organisms for the moment, but in so doing they impair and injure all others, and subsequently vitiate the whole system. Thus this class of policies does not in the long run even bring about self-preservation, although, at the first blush, this plea is set forward in support of them.

Such measures, for instance, involve as their instruments commercial treaties of a peculiarly complicated type : and here the whole question is seen to bristle with insuperable difficulties. Technical knowledge of vast variety and detail has to be supplied in the arrangement of such treaties, and still more is such application essential to their practical working. An enormous expenditure of brain-work is thus entailed, which will not gain any compensating reward in the possible good results of the measure. Such treaties are specially open to all the future uncertainties of the actual politics of each State. The fall of a ministry, the necessities of a prince, may alter the whole prospect and complexion of a treaty ; and so upset the immediate future of widely ramifying industries. Again, the necessary sanction to their effective working is that "most-favoured-nation" reservation so common in modern treaties. This clause is a necessary evil, and the frequent cause of much commercial perplexity and loss. When, in 1879, the Franco-Austrian treaty of commerce came to its end by the entirely private action of those two countries, England, Italy, and Germany suddenly found all their products taxed at the very high rates that had prevailed before France gave them lower rates in accordance with the "most favoured nation" clause. In many cases these old duties reimposed proved actually prohibitive : and yet no one of these countries had any say in the prolongation of the Treaty. Industry and commerce are thus brought under the arbitrary control of interests that have little or no connection with them.

Italy has adopted a most vigorous policy of reci-procity. She has set up a high general tariff with a view to entice other nations to enter upon special treaty tariffs. She seeks to force other nations to "fair trade" by a system of exceptionally high tariffs for all who have not special treaties, and treaties she only makes with those who will make concessions in exchange. This is undoubtedly better for Italy than following the demands of her protectionists, who are loud in maintaining "we cannot attract capital; we are too heavily taxed with the view of starting our new United Italy; and so we cannot compete with others ; let us protect ourselves." These men would coop Italians up in Italy, and jealously deny them all the benefits of the facilities of production enjoyed by countries where capital is plentiful and taxation lighter; and so would they rob Italy of all aid and assistance in her journey towards prosperity. But Italy by this policy deprives herself of all supplies from countries that do not respond to her invitation. She curtails for herself her area of supply, and discourages that increase of intercommunication which ever tends to unite nations with one another industrially and commercially; or, in other words, to create markets and to introduce demand as well as supply.

The system of commercial treaties is founded on the watchword " mutual concession." England and France have discovered the vast mutual advantages of free intercourse. The results of this—the substantial prosperity of France which so surprised Europe after the German war, and the well-known material prosperity of England—these results are the guarantees that both England and France will maintain and increase their free-trade connections. But so long as England remains a European State she must perforce have dealings with other Continental States not enjoying the enlightened statesmanship of France. If these other States determine to protect themselves to their own ruin England can do little to stay their course, however much she may regret the evils thereby accruing to the best conditions of supply. and demand. Many Continental States are liable at any moment to suffer relapse to an enervating protectionism. Germany is liable under the lead of Bismarck by this means to retire from any leading position among productive States to which the energies of her people might otherwise entitle her. And this ruinous tendency appears to be ever present in all communities that are not ruled by a wide-based public opinion. In the face of such a state of things England must keep herself as free as possible from the complex uncertainties of other independent communities ; and this is to be accomplished only by keeping her own market absolutely open to them, and pushing into theirs when and how she can, without closing her own. Italy, in the intermediate stage of reciprocity, will thus be invited to make her utmost concessions ; for England will not object to absolute free-trade with her by treaty. This freedom of intercourse can but invigorate States ; and these States thus invigorated will in no long time become the cherished support of those States which suffer a relapse to restriction and protection. In the interval harm will be done to the general cause of production ; in the end the free-trade States will more than ever enjoy the rewards, so forced on them, of a monopoly of productive energy.

There remains, however, one important class of

objections that England has to consider. Unhampered production is no less a necessity than unhampered exchange; and her own production is hampered by the "private" action of foreign nations in certain cases. And the question remains, what measures can or should be taken by England to obviate the evils of this indirect interference of outsiders with her own productive liberty. The great point to be borne in mind, and a point that is usually altogether ignored, is that this indirect interference is temporary in its nature. This it may be well to explain by means of two instances. The United States, closed against English goods, nevertheless throw into the English market a variety of cheap articles. This cheapness is in the main an advertisement. A certain amount of present profit is purposely sacrificed to afford the opportunities of greater profit in the future. It is certain that if protection continue to rule in the United States, cost of production must remain higher there than in England; and, ultimately, the higher normal prices of the articles, advertised at the first by means of fictitiously low prices, will drive them from the English market. Should protection in the United States disappear, English competition in the markets of the States will wage an equitable and satisfactory war with American competition in the English market.

Another instance is that of the competition of the French "bounty fed" sugar industry, which is held to interfere seriously with the sugar industries of England. Facts teach us that, in spite of this competition, the annual output of the English industry has not decreased ; and the only reasonable complaint is based on the fact that the sugar industry has not increased. Even so, Englishmen have some remedy in their own hands in the intelligent and active introduction of the French system of beet growing, a system well worthy the attention of landlords and farmers in the face of the low prices of wheat and the falling prices of meat and other "farm produce." It is said that in the last ten years more sugar has been produced from beetroot than for the last thirty years from cane. The English sugar industry must face this fact ; compete with the French in their own field ; and leave French tax payers to continue to support the low price of sugar in England.

In reality these interferences with the liberty of native production are nothing more nor less than bracing competition. The sugar industry itself has already taken the lesson to heart; and sought greater efficiency by the substitution of a few large and well-organised works for the many smaller concerns which previously struggled on against the drawbacks of faulty management and lack of skill and power. And if now the English farmer learn to produce beet the whole English community will have been found to have derived far more economical benefit from this French interference than the mere cheapening of the price of sugar with which the French taxpayer has kindly enriched England.

§ 3. *The Semi-civilised; Opening-up Markets.*—Foreign semi-civilised and uncivilised States are far more amenable to free-trade policies than the more civilised States. They become great purveyors of raw material, but only in less measure the consumers of manufactured products. For England to open up trade with China, Japan, the States bordering on India, and the nations of Africa, is one of her most profitable enterprises. Chiefly is it so in drawing from these lands raw material invaluable to her own manufacturers and merchants, but of little applied use or value in the land of its origin. Nevertheless, in proportion as these countries are opened up as sources of supply, so they develop a demand for many of the manufactured products of England. To preserve and extend her trade with these countries is a prime duty for all that have at heart the national prosperity. Her area of supply is thus extended; the demand for her products is thereby increased. This task may safely be left in the main in the hands of private enterprise and individual self-aggrandisement.   Treaties, conciliation, and even war, are the State means to obtaining a footing in such countries. When it is asserted to be for the material benefit of the native races to keep their markets open to products of the English, it is to assert, what the whole history of man bears witness to, that those who win most from Nature have what may be termed a natural supremacy over those that obtain less ; and that they ever exert this supremacy for the purpose of winning more.   The Englishman of the present day is, for these reasons, annexing Fiji and quenching the wasteful barbarism of the Zulus.

§ 4. *England's Colonies.*—It is, however, when we turn to the civilised colonies of the English race that we find the most urgent need of the inauguration of free intercourse.   At the present moment there is probably no single product of the earth which is not the native product of some portion of the British Empire.   Within its borders exists every known variety of soil, climate, and environment.   This assertion has never before been possible of any other single nation.   And when we are called upon to adopt as the imperial motto " Esto Perpetua," we see reason to hold that history has never yet shown the impossibility of this in regard to such a structure as the present British Empire bids fair now to become. But that this vast area of supply may be made the most of, may become self-supporting and autonomously prosperous, it must come under the beneficial influence of assured free-trade. Its commodities must be freely interchangeable and freely producible without the lets and hindrances of local or personal selfishness or ambition. Industry and commerce must be entirely freed from the arbitrary control of political and other interests that have little or no actual connection with them.

Manufacturers and merchants, and indeed all, for all are concerned, might with profit study the recorded growth of the trade of this English empire; there will they find unimpeachable evidence of the fact that while foreign trade has suffered a steady decline in value, colonial trade has made a comparatively equivalent steady rise. Foreign trade reached, in 1873, a culminating total of £530,000,000. It has since declined to £480,000,000 in 1877; a *decline* of 10 per cent. Trade with the colonies rising in 1873 to £150,000,000, has since continued to rise, till in 1877 it had reached a total of £165,000,000 ; a *rise* of 12 per cent. At the present, her outlying provinces absorb about one-fourth of England's trade; and these provinces are destined to a rapid proximate growth, whereas " foreign countries" have no immediate prospect of rapid growth, while any increase in trade with them is entirely problematical. It seems, then, certain that this trade within the empire is a most important feature in the prosperity of England; and this trade is entirely in the hands of Englishmen; can they not insure its freedom for themselves?

Both of food and of raw material, the British Empire offers an inexhaustible and cosmopolitan supply—and a supply which shall not only suffice for its own wants, but serve with its surplus the wants of other nations. As an instance, we may take wool. Australia and New Zealand have, in a brief half-century, largely monopolised the supply of wool to Europe. At present there are annually sold in the English market something like 800,000 bales of Colonial wool, and only 80,000 bales of European. Nearly one-half of the wool imported is taken up by foreign buyers. England, by means of her empire, thus enjoys all the advantages of being the world's wool-market. The winnings of the carrier and the middle-man and distributor are thus handed over to England. And this is very much to the benefit of all concerned. The market being large is steady. The competition of manufacturers yields true prices. The competition of growers yields true prices and enhances quality. And the consumer enjoys the cheaper price or better quality of the manufactured article. Practical proof of all this is to be seen in the present satisfactory prices of "woollens." We find, too, that the Australian squatter has quite eclipsed the merino breeders of Germany and Spain. In 1878 the extraordinary price of 5s. per pound was paid for some Australian merino wool. And the " cross-breds" in New Zealand are equally superior to their relatives in Europe. Such is an instance of the wealth of supply of the British Empire. Thus England, by becoming the central mart of the empire, is vastly benefited herself, and in no less degree vastly benefits her distant provinces, by affording them a steady assured market, where demand, if there be any in the world, is sure to congregate. England rises in her empire like the town of earlier stages of civilisation. Thither men bring what surplus they have to dispose of—and as matters grow the town is enabled to help them much—to secure their access to her markets—and to attract buyers from a distance. But there must be freedom of access : and this is nothing more than *free-trade within the empire.*

And there are other productive advantages in a firmly knit empire, such as that of England. Her various provinces enjoy defined and constituted laws. The spirit of the united empire scares the very thoughts of revolution and civil strife. The genius of Parliamentary Government has, Englishmen are proud to see, reappeared in every corner of the globe where Englishmen congregate ; and, with the appearance of this innate genius, peace and good government are assured. This fact, no less than the known wealth of the mother-country, gives to all members of the empire a legitimate credit which finds its profit, for instance, in the comparative cheapness of capital that they may borrow. This attribute of security is, moreover, not the only recommendation of these Colonial loans, these Colonial public debts ; they are in addition known to be expended on strictly productive or remunerative works. Other nations invest what capital they can borrow in the unproductive or rather self-destructive expenditures of wars and mis-government. Russia is offering any price for money to pay for her wars and her conquests. Turkey makes violent efforts to pay enormous interest for the money she squanders in mis-government. The nations of Continental Europe pay high for the privilege of wasting their productive energies in watching each other's ambitions. The disunited offshoots of Spanish and Portuguese nationality in South and Central America, with their wars and their chronic condition of revolution and general instability, are insatiable gulfs for the investments of the confiding and the speculative. It is, indeed, worthy of remark that, while in all these States one of the main reasons for keeping the peace with one another is the difficulty of obtaining the use of other people's money, for the various provinces of the British Empire, on the contrary, because of the fact that peace is in perpetual reign, the use of other people's money is readily to be obtained. It becomes, then, a first duty of this empire to sustain this beneficial credit and this profitable order in the conviction that most capital and the best human enterprise will ever seek so secure a field in preference to any other.

This investment of English capital in the development of the productive powers of our colonies has, of late, assumed considerable proportions. And this fact in great measure explains the nominal falling off in England's foreign export trade. More attention seems daily to be given to the productive advantages of our colonies; experience proves that within the empire is the best field for the use of capital; and this affects the amount and value of the actual products of industry within the British Isles. As a fact, British energy and British capital are spreading themselves fast from England as a centre over the British Empire. The profits of this wider application of national wealth are already greater, even though they detract from what has heretofore been regarded as the sign of the nation's productive progress —the nominal total of foreign exports. These growing profits are nevertheless spreading over the whole empire a network of mutual interests. And if this, as some would have it, is no security for the perpetuity of political connection, it is nevertheless the visible and practical outcome of harmonious union; it will survive so long as this lasts; and it will vanish only when this commercial union disappears. And it matters little whether political or national be the special epithet which fastidious reasoners see fit to apply to it. It is a reliable network of mutual interests, holding communities together in profitable union, and to the material advantage of each.

There are a few politicians who yet hold to the theory that as England survived the " terrible dismemberment of 1783," so she would survive any others ;* " that the entire fabric of the British Empire was reared and consolidated by the energies of a people ; and that if by some vast convulsion our transmarine possessions should be all submerged, the very same energies of that very same people would either discover other inhabited or inhabitable spaces of the globe on which to repeat its work, or would without them in other modes assert its undiminished greatness. Of all the opinions disparaging to England there is not one which can lower her like that

---

* Mr. Gladstone in *Nineteenth Century* for September, 1878.

which teaches that the source of strength for this almost measureless body lies in its extremities, and not in the heart which has so long propelled the blood through all its regions, and in the brain which has bound and binds them into one." The fact is, these very same energies of this very same people are, at the present day, spreading themselves over a vaster area than ever : and whether these energies are exercised in "free congenital communities," or as pertaining to "masters and foreigners presiding over lands that possess indelibly some other ethnical character of their own"—these energies are exercising themselves to the full and profitably over these same transmarine possessions. It is because the " measureless body" has extremities, and because and so long as these extremities are duly energised that the heart and the brain and the blood have the opportunity for active and healthy action and influence. Lop a limb, and by so much is the opportunity for action and influence curtailed; by so much is the field energised by a healthy vitality lessened. These energies have spread to-day in a measure that was impossible, nay inconceivable, without those aids of science which have dissipated the darkness of past generations.

And when we speak of energy and capital spreading themselves out over the empire we must re-

member that energy implies men. Much of energy
has to be applied locally and in the flesh. Capital is
readily transferable, with little regard to space or
even to political connections ; but the brain that
directs and the hand that toils are intimately affected
by these two conditions. Productive prosperity,
also, is marked by increase of this energy ; by multiplication of brains and hands. Lord Derby, speaking during the depression of 1878, said : " I think it
is a very fair question whether in this little island of
ours we are not getting packed too closely, and
whether we have not suffered from the comparative
stoppage of emigration in the last few years." With
prosperity brains and hands accumulate out of all
proportion to the local demands or needs. It is in
the absorption of such redundant British energy that
the wide-lying transmarine provinces of England are
simply invaluable.

Emigration is a subject of more importance than
appears on the surface. Useful lessons may be learned
of commercial depressions ; none more useful than
the fact that for national energy some outlet is necessary. Emigration is for Englishmen no mere safety-
valve : it is increased application of national force.
When the high pressure energy is developed in too
great force for the actual needs of the local work, it
is not dissipated and set free uselessly to the labour

in hand, but conducted along safe courses to energise and develop similar labours. The surplus of brain-power holds India for us and for what is best in civilisation ; and taps the trade of the East, of China, of Tropical Africa. The surplus of muscle-power wins the vast wilds of Canada, Australasia, and the Cape to the control of the producer. These are profitable outlets for the surplus energy of a nation ; but they must be retained as such, or this surplus energy will be annihilated in vain dissipation ; or, finding no due outlet, will itself destroy with direful destruction the engine it has so long energised.

The depression of 1878 has proved that there is a large margin of unemployable labour in England. Rapid improvements in machinery, in chemistry, in " applied science" generally, improve the efficiency of, but do not increase the demands for, manual labour. Yet the concomitant increase in prosperity is increasing the supply of labour. Emigration has practically ceased to the United States. The arrivals thence now equal the departures thither. At the same time Canada, and especially Australasia, are rapidly rising in the estimation of the emigrant classes. The colonies themselves, with a wisdom that marks their inheritance of the political sagacity of their ancestry, vigorously support this movement. The Home authorities have no less cause to support it. It is

certain that much of the decrease in English pauper-
ism is due to this movement. There is no want of
bread in new lands. The pauper in the new colony
becomes so from crime or vice or absolute misfortune ;
never in spite of himself. The rapid settlement of
waste lands ensuing benefits every citizen of the
empire ; the labourers are all of them enabled to
find work ; and the capitalist secures the labour so
necessary for the due employment of his capital.

Moreover, Englishmen have secured to their own
eminently successful ideas of rule and management
the waste spaces of the earth. As a consequence,
when a citizen of any nation would emigrate he forthwith becomes an English citizen. Thus the British
Empire is fed by a most important stream of energy
and capital flowing out of foreign States. In every
way the basis is laid of productive success on a large
and lasting scale. But the structure to be raised
upon this must be built on the sound plans of secured
and free access to markets for each man with that
commodity he can best produce. The rest of the
world may hold haughtily aloof, busied in its own
ambitions : but this structure will, at all events,
insure to its inmates the best prosperity possible
under present human conditions.

It is, however, matter of notoriety that many of
our colonies at the present do impose duties for

avowedly protective purposes. The Colony of Victoria is a notable instance, more especially as she holds to her position in spite of the tendencies of the surrounding colonies towards free-trade. But the instance of Victoria is hopeful for those who acknowledge the true course to be free-trade. Australians themselves already agree that Victoria is in danger of occupying the unenviable position of the "horrid example." The inebriate sot is placed on the platform as a warning to the intemperate. Victoria is passing rapidly to the tenacious grasp of the vested interests generated of protection. Already South Australia and New South Wales are joining hands behind her back, across the interior of Australia ; and there is the certain prospect that their liberal tariffs will now sap the whole fertile tract of back country, which is barred from its natural outlet, through Melbourne, by the barrier of the frontier line of protectionist Victoria. That such an example should set such a lesson in peace and quiet is one of the beneficent possibilities of a united empire. And no doubt the very violence of protection in Victoria will simply impel the neighbouring colonies all the faster along a free-trade course. They are already fast outrunning Victoria in the race of prosperity. Victoria, owing to the capital and population that her goldmines introduced into the country, rapidly rose to take the first place among the Australian colonies. Of late years she has remained even stationary as compared with the neighbouring colonies. And with the baneful assistance of a rigid protectionism she is allowing them to close fast upon her in the race for the premiership among Australian colonies, in which she obtained so eminently favourable a start.

Again, in the case of Canada many men have justified protection. Sir J. Macdonald, one of her best statesmen, declares, "If the Americans raise up a Chinese wall by which not a single article Canadians produce can go in untaxed, we will raise up a similar wall." Here we find local politics set up to justify policies of retaliation which involve protective policies. Canada strives thus to coerce the United States into reciprocity, at all events, even if not mutual free-trade. Are these local necessities to be allowed for one moment to endanger the continuity of a persistent and inviolable free-trade between Canada and England?

All men acknowledge that free-trade is good, provided there be two sides to it; free-trade, indeed, is held to be impossible without the two parties necessary to all contracts. In the mother-country and the colonies we have the two parties, and when free-trade comes to reign definitely and for ever between them, prosperity must needs be assured to all concerned.

It may well be asked, why have any of the provinces of the British Empire the right, how have they the license, to adopt other than free-trade principles ? And the answer is to be found in the examination of the peculiar constitutional arrangements that have come of the grant of self-government. When British communities, as the empire developed, found themselves growing to prosperous strength in distant parts of the earth, it was only natural that they, with the full concurrence of the Home authorities, should take upon themselves the task of managing their own affairs. And with the grant of self-government came the undeniable duty of contributing towards the management of their corporate concerns ; and, with this duty, the right to a voice in the amount and kind of sacrifice necessary for the due performance of this function. When the Imperial Parliament delegated some of its powers to distant communities of Englishmen—because of the fact that their corporate concerns could best be managed on the spot—it delegated among other powers that of taxation for the purposes of carrying on the corporate duties of the community.

This fiscal liberty has now, in some cases, become the cloak of commercial license. So long as a province taxes itself for itself by measures that do not affect or injure other provinces, all is well.

But once it passes beyond this, and taxes itself for purposes over and above those of revenue, or, in other words, the support of its corporate action; and above all when, by so doing, it affects and injures other provinces; at once the interests and rights of other members of the empire become involved, and the case passes from the care of that particular community to that of the national authority which presides over the interests of all the various communities or provinces which constitute the empire. In a word, by the imposition of duties for purposes other than those of revenue, a province of the empire at once invades the domain of Imperial interests; at once challenges the control of the Imperial authorities.

The Imperial Parliament, before this latter-day development of self-governing provinces of great power and influence, never had its authority questioned or even appealed to in regard to the general commercial policy of the empire. Now the case is altered: and it is evident the Imperial authorities must resume this forgotten duty. But they must resume it, bearing in mind the fact that, in the interval vested or prescriptive rights have come into being; various of these prosperous provinces have now an equitable right to a voice in the matter. In order to institute free-trade in perpetuity for the British Empire, its various self-governing communities must be brought to mutual and, in a measure, spontaneous agreement. The development of self-government has brought into existence the necessity, on grounds, both of equity and of expedience, for an appeal based on the principles of voluntary union. The Imperial Parliament can indeed, and should, remain the constitutional guardian of some such new charter of union, once such a charter be instituted by mutual agreement. And under the strict terms of this charter will fall any future delegations of self-government or of fiscal or other powers to separate communities of Englishmen that may, in the future, develop the acquisition of self-government.

Such are the rational means to this desirable end. That they are eminently feasible at the present conjuncture of affairs is not to be doubted. They will derive great countenance and assistance from the silent but powerful influence of English opinion on the whole empire. English statesmen are the pick of a large and well-qualified field; and it is no wonder that their utterances are treasured up and valued most highly by the statesmen of the Colonies. There is much indirect influence at work, both in the counsels of government and in private authority, towards insuring a true concordance of colonial with home opinion ; and to this we may confidently trust to aid in the great work of eventually doing away with protectionism throughout the empire.

Some would seek to hasten this by a course of differential tariffs and other measures which should seek to encourage the provinces of the empire to consolidated action ; but which should take no notice of the existing fiscal policies of any particular colony; which should draw no line but that between all provinces of the empire and free-trade foreign States on the one hand, and, on the other, as beyond the sphere of such commercial charity, all foreign protectionist States.   But there seems to be little need for such directly precipitate measures. There are but two or three colonies, out of the total number of fifty, that avowedly put in practice protective principles, or that impose duties on imports for the purpose of protecting their industries.   All others are ready in principle to join in such union; and there is nothing impracticable in the prospect of the various provinces of the British Empire banding themselves together, in their various degrees of constitutional spontaneity ; and jealously maintaining as secured freedom of intercourse among themselves, as close a commercial union as that rigorously maintained by the citizens of the United States.

Yet, whether by direct political action, or by these many means of indirect influences, certainly one of the gravest and most profitable tasks of English statesmanship, both of that which exercises itself in the crowded arena of the mother-country, and that which rises to a vigorous life in her many provinces, is to aim at the consolidation of the empire in regard to the exchange of its products ; the inauguration of a true free-trade era ; the commercial unification of the empire.

The value to the theorist of the example of England is obvious ; and in examining that example there are brought to light many necessary suggestions, many distinct proposals, many clear and undeniable claims on the statesmanship of the present. We have seen that in the world of production England can only hope for a leading position in virtue of her national and natural superiorities in certain branches of human endeavour. This claim of hers is, however, greatly enhanced by the determined protectionism of other States. They seek to cut themselves off from benefiting by that highest form of the " division of labour" which allots to each State the duty of supplying others with what it can produce with greater facility than them. England, perhaps, cannot help this ; cannot wean them from this their folly. Indeed, the more she herself succeeds the more do these other States draw themselves back from the race ; the more do they allow their statesmen to "pull" them ; and they fall hopelessly into the ruck. English common sense, however, will recognise the true principles of success, and strive, wheresoever it may be thriving in the empire, to institute the absolute blessing of free-trade. Englishmen, standing to the colours of their great prosperity, will push free-trade so far in every direction as they can. This will help them to stem "bad times" as it has helped them before. This will in their case, in the case alone of those who adopt free-trade, form an atmosphere uncongenial to the existence or appearance of commercial depression ; and it will in time so weaken and paralyse the circumstances in which the conditions of depression are engendered, that "bad times" will come to be regarded among Englishmen as the curiosities of the past or the results of the unaccountable follies of foreigners.

INDEX.

THE END.